LOST IN CHRISTIANITY
Dare Ask Why

LOST IN CHRISTIANITY

Dare Ask Why

(A "LAYMANS" PERSPECTIVE)
By:
Bobby W. Ramsey

XULON PRESS

Xulon Press
2301 Lucien Way #415
Maitland, FL 32751
407.339.4217
www.xulonpress.com

Printed in the United States of America.

Paperback ISBN-13: 978-1-6322-1154-5
eBook ISBN-13: 978-1-6322-1155-2

THE AUTHOR

*"When they saw the courage of Peter and John and real-
ized that they were unschooled, ordinary men, they
were astonished, and they took note that these men
had been with Jesus" – Acts 4:13. NIV[1]*

I am not a pastor and have never attended seminary or Bible college.
I consider myself a "preacher"–not in the sense that most view –
one who stands behind a pulpit sermonizing for twenty minutes to an
hour on Sunday mornings and occasionally Sunday evenings, but a New
Testament "preacher"–a "kerusso"[2]– a messenger and proclaimer – an
instrument of the Holy Spirit. Through that same Spirit, I have come to
realize my mission lies outside religion's four walls.

I was born on December 25, 1952, in Greenville, South Carolina,
and received a Bachelor of Arts Degree in Economics from Clemson
University in 1974. Upon entering the business world, I assumed an
order entry position at a metals company and would later become
President and CEO of a partnership involving metal fabrication. I retired
in 2017. I am presently married to my wife Barbara, soon to be forty-six
years and am the proud father of two children – Erica and Elizabeth,
and son-in-law Don. Erica has special needs, suffering from the effects
of a traumatic brain injury as the result of an automobile accident at
the age of five years. She is a walking miracle and testimony of God's
grace and the power of prayer. We presently reside in the Upstate of
South Carolina .

Being raised by Godly parents and reared in a traditional Protestant
church, I have served in practically every church office afforded to a

"layman" (a non-Scriptural word) – deacon, trustee, Sunday School Teacher, Associational Leader, etc. I am presently involved in the start-up of a Hispanic fellowship, which not only has been instrumental in reaching out and ministering to Hispanics, but also to young people and children of other ethnic backgrounds. I remain a part of my child-hood fellowship and have been a member of The Gideons International since the late 1970's.

This book is the product of the Holy Spirit. It was written because of my concern for the traditional "church" and how it has evolved or dissolved since *Acts 2:42-47*. Is it the church of Jesus Christ – OR – is it man's church built on his tradition, ritual, formality and doctrine? I cannot help but ask myself as I have many times—has my spiritual sojourn been in service to religion through "church," or in service to Jesus Christ through His *"ekklesia"*? That is the question that haunts me and my purpose for writing this book.

TABLE OF CONTENTS

FOREWORD

"There is no avoiding war. It can only be postponed to the advantage of one's enemy" – Machiavelli

As one peruses the pages of this book, it is the prayerful desire of the author, he/she does not see a vindictive spirit, conjecture or opinion, but rather share in a culmination of life-long questions, convictions, and heartfelt concerns over the "church" established by Jesus Christ and implemented by His Apostles, and the *"subtlety"* to which it has evolved into what we serve today. *"Subtlety"* is defined as, "making use of clever and indirect methods to achieve something, so delicate or precise as to be difficult to analyze."[3] *"Now the serpent was more 'SUBTLE' than any beast of the field which the Lord God had made. And the serpent said to the woman, 'Ye shall not surely die: For God doth know that in the day ye eat thereof, then your eyes shall be opened, and ye shall be as gods, knowing good and evil.' And when the woman saw that the tree was good for food, and that it was pleasant to the eyes, and the tree to be desired to make one wise, she took the fruit thereof and did eat and gave also unto her husband with her and he did eat"–Genesis 3:1,5-6. "But there were also false prophets among the people, just as there will be false teachers among you. They will secretly ('SUBTLETY') introduce destructive heresies, even denying the sovereign Lord who bought them – bringing swift destruction on themselves. Many will follow their depraved conduct and will bring the way of truth into disrepute"–2 Peter 2:1-2.*

An anti-war movement is defined as "a social movement, usually in opposition to a particular nation's decision to start or carry on an armed conflict, unconditional of an existing just cause; pacifism."[4] We are a war. Most professed believers do not care or are intentionally oblivious and carry on life as usual. Even during His earthly ministry, Jesus experienced the same nonchalant, uncaring and uncompassionate sentiment, even among His closest followers – *"Jesus went through all the towns and villages, teaching in their synagogues, proclaiming the good news of the kingdom and healing every disease and sickness. When He saw the crowds, He had compassion on them, because they were harassed and helpless, like sheep without a shepherd. Then He said to His disciples, 'The harvest is plentiful, but the workers are few. Ask the Lord of the harvest, therefore, to send out workers into His harvest field'"* – Matthew 9:35-38. Even though our war is spiritual, the collateral is eternally more serious – the human soul itself.

Paul, in writing to the church at Ephesus, noted–*"For our struggle is not against flesh and blood, but against the rulers, against the authorities, against the powers of this dark world and against the spiritual forces of evil in the heavenly realms"* – Ephesians 6:12. Our enemy is a well-oiled and organized machine. In the verses to follow he details the armor we are to wear in preparation for battle. The "church" of today is indeed at war – but not for souls – for members – affluent ones. Rather than enlist and train soldiers for spiritual battle, today's church is fostering and supporting anti-war pacifism. Our strategy is defensive – hunker down within our four walls, advertise to a degree, market our product and open our doors to those who might by chance venture our way, but heaven forbid we take up the mantle of evangelism commanded by Christ Himself and take to the unharvested fields.

I am concerned today's church has become the insatiable product of a religious system established and based upon human authority and it must be fed. Its existence and survival depend upon it. To supplement such requires finances beyond belief, placing financial burdens upon its members and making it necessary to be selective in searching for additional folk financially able to assist in its maintenance. Two issues result – first, membership is restricted; one must be a card-carrying, financially affluent contributor to participate, thus taking the focus away from the masses to the elite few -*"Suppose a man comes into your meeting wearing a gold ring and fine clothes, and a poor man in filthy old clothes also comes in. If you show special attention to the man wearing fine clothes and say, 'Here's a good seat for you,' but say to the poor man, 'You stand there or sit on the floor by my feet,' have you not discriminated among yourselves and become judges with evil thoughts?"- James 2:2-4.* Secondly, competition between the entities erupts – not for souls but for affluent members. One must be prepared to "keep up with the Jones'" – bigger buildings, bigger staff, taller steeples, bigger gymnasiums, bigger coffee kiosks, bigger, bigger, bigger! Suddenly our focus is turned to entertaining the "99," making the "1" completely insignificant *(Luke 15:3-7).*

Some, including myself, have spent virtually our entire spiritual lives viewing service to the Lord as the number of light bulbs we have replaced in the receptacles of the church building. What we have failed to realize is the service God honors is our witness to those blind and lost receptacles of the world, devoid and starving for the Light of the World– Jesus Christ. This is the true service Jesus expects from His followers but unfortunately the traditional "church" of today has closed its eyes, choosing rather to serve and service itself – *"...and if you spend yourselves in behalf of the hungry and satisfy the needs of the oppressed, then your light will rise in the darkness, and your night will become like the noonday" – Isaiah 58:10.*

At first glance, this book may appear to be a diatribe against the "church." It is! Not against the church of Jesus Christ – "the *ekklesia*"– but against the "church of man." There is a distinct difference. When Jesus came the first time, He was rejected by the religious elite and those that supported that system. To make sure that system survived, they fought Him tooth and nail, and when that did not work, they took His life. He came to destroy 2000 years of religion – formality, tradition, rites, ritual, etc. When He comes again, He will come as a conquering King and for the final time, will destroy at least 2000 more years of the same and take *"the few" (Matthew 7:14)*–who truly see through this façade–home to be with Him. Many believe they are Heaven bound simply because they have supported and been a card-carrying member of man's "church." Unfortunately, this will not be the case – *"But small is the gate and narrow the road that leads to life and only a few find it" – Matthew 7:14.*

PREFACE

The "church" we serve today has rendered its members helpless, to the point of accepting the fact, "the Word of God is classified (and dangerous) material that only card-carrying experts can handle. Our right to function as a full member of Christ's body has been stolen. It has rendered us a mute spectator who is proficient at taking sermon notes and passing an offering plate. It has overthrown the main thrust of the letter to the Hebrews – the ending of the old priesthood. It has made ineffectual the teaching of *1 Corinthians 12-14*, that every member has both the right and the privilege to minister in a church meeting. It has voided the message of *1 Peter 2*, that every brother and sister is a functioning priest. We can all be certain that God does not endorse any church practice that violates New Testament principles. Today's church has hindered spiritual transformation because it encourages passivity, limits functioning, and implies that putting in one hour per week is the key to the victorious Christian life. We grow by functioning, not by passively watching and listening."[5]

Never in my wildest dreams would I have ever imagined myself compiling a book. The young high school and college student who loathed literature and the accompanying grammatical baggage that came with it – unbelievable! But here I am – in the palms of the Holy Spirit – sharing my heart and my deep desire that God would wake up the "church" and mold it as the potter molds the clay – into the *"ekklesia,"* or body of believers He called us to be. The question that needs to be considered–and will be in this book – is today's "church" salvageable in the eyes of God?

I wish to thank my family, especially my dear wife and children who were patient with me spending countless hours on the computer – their prayers, love and support I could never repay. Then to my beloved parents, who raised me in a Christian home where prayer, the Word and fellowship with God's people dominated – thank you! Someday soon I look forward to that grand reunion in that place you so often told me about.

I especially thank my father who was my best friend. My mother was raised in a Christian home where fellowshipping with the people of God was dominant. My grandfather, her father, was probably the most dedicated follower of Jesus Christ I ever met. As a child, I never recall any word spoken or any negative connotation against any individual uttered by my Grandfather. He was never a flashy person or an out-spoken church leader. In fact, the only position I knew him to possess in the church was passing out bulletins on Sunday morning. He took the job seriously and his smile and dedication as a greeter touched many lives. He lived his faith and my mom was a blessed result.

My father was different, not being raised in a Christian home. With the assistance of Uncle Sam, he migrated southward from rural south-eastern Ohio, where he met my mom and through her efforts and others, met the Lord Jesus Christ. He too was dedicated to his church, serving in every leadership capacity afforded, to the point I could not help but wonder if he might be considering a potential call to ministry. He was my mentor, my friend, and my idol. I saw in him what I desired for myself – a self-made hard worker and a dedicated man to both his family, his God and His people. He was not perfect – none of us are – but he taught me to love the Lord and His church and to be faithful to both. I broke his heart on many occasions, but my prayer is that he saw in me at least some of what he taught and lived come to fruition. He passed in 2006. Dad, I love you, and even though "thank you" seems too trivial – "thank you!"

I cannot help but love the "*ekklesia*" – God's people – they being bred into my being. My hope as one reads this book, they will see it as a dia-tribe against what man's "church" has become, and in most instances, what positional, titled, compensated and lackadaisical leadership has produced – a passive group of *professed* believers who honestly believe church attendance, membership, alms giving and an inconsistent prayer life, coupled with a total ignorance of God's Word, will produce an eternity with Jesus Christ. I once again am reminded of Jesus' words in *Matthew 7:21-23* – *"Not everyone who says to me, 'Lord, Lord,' will enter the kingdom of heaven, but only he who does the will of my Father who is in heaven. Many will say to Me on that day, 'Lord, Lord, did we not prophesy in your name, and in your name drive out demons and perform many miracles'? Then I will tell them plainly, 'I never knew you. Away from me, you evildoers'!"* You will note these verses, along with others, repetitively utilized throughout this book. They are repetitive for a reason.

INTRODUCTION

The word "deceit" and its derivatives are found over sixty-five times in thirty of the sixty-six books of the Bible. Scripture's first mention of "deception" is found in *Genesis 3:1* where the writer warns us, the *"serpent"* (Satan) was *"craftier"* (*"arum"* – sly, cunning) than any entity created by God. He is the father of deception. My worst fear and a driving force for compiling this book – "what if I am one of those who have been unknowingly deceived?" Not intentionally, but *subtle* like Eve succumbed – "deception" of falling for a "religion" that addresses my wants and comforts but excuses my neglect of those outside its borders. Is this what I serve?

No one has interest in what I believe. Truth be known, I do not care what they believe. People want truth, not what someone believes is truth. Man has been searching for it since the Garden of Eden. Some believe it is found in philosophy; some believe it is found in New Age Principles; some believe it is found in nature; and some believe it is found in man himself. Truth will not be found in the pages of this book. Truth is found only in Jesus Christ and the pages of His Book – the Holy Bible. What you will find in this book are more questions than answers–questions that have plagued me my entire life regarding the religious system I serve – the "traditional church" – the "church of man." My desires and hopes are that this book will encourage and challenge you – not to think like me – but rather think with me and dare to ask *"why."*

Jeff Foxworthy is a witty comedian with a knack for clean humor. His jokes are usually tailored to family situations and sometimes begin with the phrase, "Ever wonder why...?" To ask *"why"* as a child is sometimes taboo and as I recall was the same for me. I say this not as a negative connotation to my upbringing, but simply to state a fact most parents and children alike can relate. A young three-year-old is told to do something and the common reply is, "*why*?" After a half-hearted explanation from the parent, the same question ensues – "*why*?" This dialogue usually goes on until the parent finally stops the questioning with the abrupt answer – "because I said so."

As a young Christian maturing from the milk onto the meat of the Word, I often wanted to ask "*why*" many times in my life, especially when it came to matters of the "church." These were questions I felt required answers for me to maintain my spiritual development. I was taught by parents, grandparents and church leaders alike – "it is not for us to question God." My reply was and is today – "*why not*?" Unanswered questions led me as a child to mistakenly see God as a wrathful, vengeful Deity, who sat on a throne all day with a "divine paddle" in His hands waiting to pounce on me because I wanted to ask a simple question – "*why*?"

It is my contention unanswered questions from the traditional church of today is one of the reasons she is losing ground with youth and young adults—they are asking the "*why*" questions and the church responds – "because we say so." "*Why*," is not a bad word and it does not necessarily bring God's wrath. Job questioned and he received answers. They may not have been the answers he sought or expected, but nonetheless, God addressed his questions. The traditional church of today is in crisis mode and one of the reasons is, the "*why*" questions are not being addressed, or when they have, it's usually with – "because we've always done it this way and it's not for you to question – just do it." We continue to spoon feed those seeking answers with creeds, rituals, rules, traditions, formalities, obligations and regulations that have become accepted as "gospel" but are nowhere close to the truth we half-heartedly attempt to proclaim, eerily similar to the Pharisaic system Jesus destroyed 2000 years ago. Again, this book poses more questions than it provides answers but at the very least it gives me the opportunity to finally ask—"*why*?"

Chapter 1

WHY CHURCH?

"It is always easy to let ritual take the place of love. It is always easy to let worship become a matter of the building instead of life outside it. The priest and Levite could pass by the wounded traveler because they were eager to get on with the ritual of the temple. This scribe had risen beyond his contemporaries" – William Barclay.

"And we urge you, brothers and sisters, warn those who are idle..." – (The Apostle Paul)–1 Thessalonians 5:14.

Ask anyone to define in five words or less – "church"–and the most likely response will be – "a place of worship." There are two fallacies with this definition. We will discuss the first here and the second in a later chapter. The New Testament "church" was not a place. It was people – believers – referred to in the Greek as the *"ekklesia."* Based on *Acts 2:42-47*, the *"ekklesia"* grew spiritually by celebrating the sacraments, study of the apostle's teachings, fellowship, prayer, meeting needs and outreach. The place of meeting was never important – no buildings, no campuses, no edifices – just pure spiritual growth accomplished through small groups meeting in homes. And oh how God did bless – *"And the Lord added to their numbers daily those who were being saved"* – *Acts 2:47*!

Today's "church" tends to garner headlines, but for all the wrong reasons. According to a recent television news report, a large non-denominational megachurch meeting in an abandoned building in Greenville, South Carolina, had been served an eviction notice from the building's owner, believed to be a former pastor. According to the report, staff members met with the current pastor to discuss. According to one staff member, when the pastor was confronted, "the room shifted. It shifted tremendously, to a sense where I no longer felt I was at church. I was concerned about some of the leaders that jumped up and rushed me and the security that verbally assaulted me." It was confirmed in the report police were called and a complaint filed.[6]

Is this "church?" If so, whose "church?" When the love of money and the desire for it infiltrates a body of "professed" believers to the point their misguided faith and trust is placed in human beings serving in positions of Pharisaic leadership, nowhere mandated in Scripture or envisioned by the apostles, this is the result. There appears not one shred of evidence linking man's "church" of today to the *"ekklesia"* of *Acts 2*. Religious deception is real, contagious and epidemic! Be warned and beware! *"Evildoers and impostors will go from bad to worse, deceiving and being deceived" – 2 Timothy 3:13.*

There is nothing more exciting than a family trip, especially one to an exotic place where the family has never ventured. I recall as a kid my dad retrieving the old "Esso" road map from the desk drawer – the one ripped in the seams and the one I never learned how to re-fold. Depending on the destination, he would literally sit for hours calculating the most direct route to get from "here to there," and I might add, one where directions from an outsider would never be necessary – it was more manly to remain lost than seek directions. Today the fun has been removed since all we need do is punch a button on our GPS and it is done for us–in only a few seconds – detailed directions on getting from "here to there."

The "traditional church" – the "church of man" – has been on a journey. It began in *Acts 2* with the New Testament Church of the Apostles, built on the foundation of Jesus Christ. Analyzing this journey, the question arises, how did we get from "there to here?" What route or routes did we follow? Whose road map did we utilize – one authored by human hands or the one inspired by Jesus Christ–the Holy Bible? Whose advice did we seek – human intuition from men assuming man-made positions (paid ones at that) – or the Master Planner Himself? It appears in getting from "there to here," we may have been misguided, digressing to the point of "wandering the wilderness." Will we ever waken, come to our spiritual senses and seek direction from the One – the only One – capable of putting us back onto the right road? Or – have we passed the point of no return–our Kadesh Barnea (*Numbers 10:11–14:45*)? Have we been abandoned to wander the "wilderness," which we seem happy doing? *"The Lord says: 'These people come near to Me with their mouth and honor me with their lips, but their hearts are far from Me. Their worship of Me is based on merely human rules they have been taught'" – Isaiah 29:13.*

Satan is never happy when God's people are at work. He is elated today. He attacked the early New Testament church with a vengeance from the outside (*Acts 8:1 – "On that day a great persecution broke out against the church at Jerusalem, and all except the apostles were scattered throughout Judea and Samaria."*). When that plan backfired *(Acts 8:4 – "Those who had been scattered preached the Word wherever they went."*), he was forced to attack from within, using *subtle*, less dramatic means to influence those claiming to be of God that a workless service to each other, along with the worship of money and lip service religion is okay; one does not need to worry about those outside the four walls of the edifice–just stay busy doing what we are doing on the inside and we will be fine (*"They keep saying to those who despise Me, 'The Lord says: You will have peace.' And to all who follow the stubbornness of their hearts they say, 'No harm will come to you'." "I did not send these prophets, yet they have run with their message; I did not speak to them, yet they have prophesied" – Jeremiah 23:17,21*). Those that adhere to that message have been deceived; those "preaching" it are deceivers (*"Watch out for false prophets. They come to you in sheep's clothing, but inwardly they are ferocious wolves" – Matthew 7:15; "But there were also false prophets among the people, just as there will be false teachers among you. They will secretly introduce destructive heresies, even denying the sovereign Lord"–2 Peter 2:1; "For such people are false apostles, deceitful workers, masquerading as apostles of Christ. And no wonder, for Satan himself masquerades as an angel of light. It is not surprising, then, if his servants also masquerade as servants of righteousness. Their end will be what their actions deserve" – 2 Corinthians 11:13-15*). If this service to each other comes at the expense of a lost soul and this is the assurance one is basing his/her eternal destiny – we may be in for a rude, eternal awakening and unfortunately, most are falling for its deceiving message (*"Many will follow their depraved conduct and will bring the way of truth into disrepute. In their greed, these teachers will exploit you with fabricated stories" – 2 Peter 2:2-3*).

Several years ago, I was invited to do a three-day Bible study in Myrtle Beach, South Carolina, for a gathering of senior citizens representing numerous denominations from multiple churches across the Southeast. It was a fun time of gospel music, preaching, eating, and fellowship, attended by almost 700 people. I based my lectures on the "The Fall of The Church of Man." I shared pictures of traditional churches, both from within and without my own denomination, that had closed or were in the process of closing – empty buildings, razed ones, and those with "For Sale" signs posted on the front lawn. These pictures included large, ornate complexes being sold or razed to make room for condominiums, parking garages, or just "out-of-business." Their property value had far exceeded their spiritual value.

During one of the sessions I made the statement, "The traditional church – the one you and I were raised – is dying. It is dying right before our eyes and much quicker than any of us could have imagined. The sad thing, based on what the church has become, I'm not sure God really cares."

A dear elderly lady approached me after one of my sessions and asked to speak with me in private. "Oh boy," I thought, "here it comes." She let me know up-front she was 92 years old. "How," I could not help but wonder, "do you reply to a 92-year-old lady, other than, 'yes ma'am'?" She began to weep profusely, to the point of concern on my part for her physical well-being. She began to share she was a charter member of a large Protestant church in Greenville, South Carolina (I was familiar with this church since it was located in my hometown; each July 4, they decorated the campus with hundreds of American flags; at one time probably over 1000 attendees), and she informed me the upcoming Sunday a vote was being taken to sell the campus or disband. A mega-church from a nearby community had approached them about pur-chasing the complex and allowing the few remaining members to continue worshipping on-site, in-turn allowing the mega-church to conduct funerals and weddings as needed. The church was to vote the upcoming Sunday – sell or close the doors. As you might have guessed, attendance had dropped to less than fifty members and her reply said it all–"we cannot pay the bills." This is a typical scenario nationally.

According to George Barna, founder of "The Barna Group," a market research firm specializing in studying the religious beliefs and behavior of Americans,[7] "there is an ongoing silent migration away from the church of an estimated 3,500 individuals every day. Several factors are contributing to this trend, but most individuals who are leaving the church report that they no longer feel connected. This movement away from the church has been ongoing for several decades. The number of churches that are closing their doors every year is leading to an overall decline in church attendance."[8] Per Dr. Richard Krejcir -pastor, teacher and author–we are already seeing this happen.[9] Based on United States census bureau statistics:

a. "Every year more than 4000 churches close their doors."
b. "Every year, 2.7 million church members fall into inactivity. People are leaving the 'church of man;' reasons provided – hurt, wounded, victims of some type of abuse, disillusionment, emphasis on money, or neglect."
c. "At the turn of the 19th century, there was a ratio of twenty-seven churches per 10,000 people; there are now eleven churches per 10,000 people."
d. "The US now ranks third, following China and India, in the number of people who are not professing Christians; we are becoming an ever-increasing 'un-reached people' group."
e. "20.5% Americans 'frequently' attended church in 1995; 19% in 1999; 18% in 2002; by extrapolating the data, we can estimate the number of frequent church attendees will be under 15% by 2025."

I recently contacted my denominational state office[10] and was supplied a professional survey utilized by the convention providing pertinent mission data[11] compiled from local as well as national sources and based in-part on state and federal census information. Reports are available based on choosing a focal- point and extending outward for a pre-determined distance. I requested a report, using my church as the focal point and extending outward for five miles:[12]

   a.   Total population 19,481.
   b.   Not active in a religious community – 11,124 (57.1%).
   c.   Of those not active, percentages and reasons provided for inactivity:
       1.   44.3%–Faith not relevant
       2.   66%–Religious people too judgmental
       3.   65.4%–Religious people too focused on money
       4.   61.2%–Do not trust religious leaders
       5.   19.9%–Never been invited; *and oh, by the way, there are 55 churches within a five-mile radius of my church, including 27 of my own denomination.*

The church of the Lord Jesus Christ, the *"ekklesia,"* is not a cathedral or a financial institution that guarantees windfall paybacks depending on what the investor is willing to invest. His *"ekklesia"* are the people of God–believers. There is a distinct difference between the *"ekklesia"* and the traditional church of today. For the most part, today's "church" has been turned into a confused mass of passive, inactive pew-warmers, who honestly believe attending a service, tithing, listening to a sermon, singing a few hymns, and being entertained, believing all along they are doing it in His name, is Biblical. Most of this system appears based on tradition and man's intuition which leads one to seriously question its Biblical foundation. Dare we ask *"why"* has this happened?

Whether you are a Christian (a "fruit-bearer" – *Matthew 7:16-20*), a "professed" Christian–one who thinks, claims or even believes he/she is a Christian but is not (a non-fruit bearer)–or one who is lost (bad fruit) and considering becoming a part of a fellowship, you may be asking yourself, "Do I Need The 'Church'?" The answer is both "yes" and "no." As noted, there are two types of "church" – the "church of man", which we regularly reference when we speak of "going to church," and the church of Jesus Christ – the *"ekklesia"* – the body of believers that make up the kingdom of God. The "church of man" typically meets in lavish, ornate structures, which offer the attendee comfort, entertainment, music to suit their tastes and most of the time, a pat on the back – "good job and keep up the good work." It is led by titled and paid profes-sionals and consists of programs, rules, rituals and traditions, set up for you to consider spiritual success as sporadic attendance to its "worship services," and designed to make you feel good about your non-existent efforts outside its four walls. Perhaps the greatest fallacy of today's "church" is summarized by Paul in *2 Timothy 2:8-9 – "Remember Jesus Christ, raised from the dead, descended from David. This is my gospel, for which I am suffering even to the point of being chained like a criminal. But God's word is not chained."* One need only review the number of salvations and baptisms in the vast majority of today's traditional churches to affirm the Gospel has indeed been *"chained."*

To the Church of Laodicea–*Revelation 3:14-18–"These are the words of the Amen, the faithful and true witness, the ruler of God's creation. I know your deeds, that you are neither cold nor hot. I wish you were either one or the other! So, because you are lukewarm – neither hot nor cold – I am about to spit you out of My mouth. You say, 'I am rich; I have acquired wealth and do not need a thing.' But you do not realize that you are wretched, pitiful, poor, blind and naked. I counsel you to buy from Me gold refined in the fire, so you can become rich; and white clothes to wear, so you can cover your shameful nakedness; and salve to put on your eyes, so you can see."* According to some theologians, the seven churches in *Revelation 2-3* are indeed churches, but also represent periods of church history. If accurate, these same theologians believe the church of today is presently in its final period, or the Laodicean Age. Jesus details two problems with this church – no spiritual outreach or concern for souls – *"lukewarm"*–running wide open as an engine in neutral – spiritually unmoving. This group has busied itself with programs, committees, meetings, and monetary obligations to the point nothing outside its realm of inward influence is a concern. The needs of a lost and dying world are unaffordable – both spiritually and fiscally.

The second problem with this church, it is interested in only one thing – your pocketbook – *"You say, 'I am rich; I have acquired wealth and do not need a thing'."* Money and the desire for it is its god. It must eat and since it has a hearty appetite, must keep its members happy by appealing to their wants and comforts and provide them with acceptable entertainment to make sure they keep the cash coming. This church attempts to serve both God and money – *Luke 16:13 – "No one can serve two masters. Either you will hate the one and love the other, or you will be devoted to the one and despise the other. You cannot serve both God and money."* This is the "church" of the "end-times" – today's "church of man."

International Christian author Andrew Strom makes some very blunt and poignant statements regarding his experience with "church:" "As I have seen again and again, for year after year after year – church leads absolutely nowhere and is likely never to lead anywhere as it is conducted today. The church is supposed to be about brokenness, testing and preparation. God has led many of us there for that exact purpose. Yet why is it that so few seem to allow themselves to be truly broken? Why are they still so willing to judge by "form and structure" instead of the "heart?" If this thing is about "preparation," then why are so few prepared? Why do most of them never do anything? "Church" is diametrically opposed to the very pattern of God."[13]

After my freshman year of college, in the summer of 1971, I decided to enroll in a summer school class in hopes of getting ahead and remaining on what I hoped (along with my parents) was the "four-year plan." I was fortunate to graduate "on plan," but looking back, a couple of more years would not have been so bad, even though my parents would have vehemently disagreed. My summer school class was in U.S. History. The professor was young, well-versed and obviously well educated, but possessed extreme liberally biased views. If I were to rate my college professors by their liberality, this one would have taken the cake. He tended to "crucify" those who disagreed with his opines.

The early 1970's was a time of major turmoil and upheaval in this country. The Viet Nam War was in full swing with soldiers in body bags plastered on the evening news. It even wielded its influence upon religion as some sought refuge in the ministry as a means to escape the draft. There was an upcoming election involving a liberal from the Midwest by the name of George McGovern. I recall his anti-war platform thus appealing to young people and war-weary parents. Being raised in a poor conservative Midwestern home, my dad was nowhere near the McGovern bandwagon. At the time, politics was of little or no interest to me, so if asked, I typically rolled with the flow – the flow being what my parents believed. Looking back however, one cannot help but surmise what possible benefit did that war accomplish and for what purpose did 58,220 of my peers sacrifice their lives?[14]

My dad was not prejudiced in any way, but his candidate of choice was a rather outspoken bigamist from Alabama. The candidate's name was George Wallace. During the first week of our class, the professor decided to take a straw poll in the form of a "secret ballot" involving all 35 class members to gauge the candidate of choice. Not being the least bit politically motivated, I cast my ballot for Mr. Wallace. I had no reason for doing so, other than I knew he was the candidate of choice of my parents and that was good enough for me. I had heard enough one-sided dialogue around the dinner table to believe he might make a good President. When the votes were counted, the class was somewhat evenly divided among other candidates, but to my embarrassment, there was only one vote for Governor Wallace. Who was the oddball that cast that ballot?

Even though this was to have been a secret ballot, the professor addressed the class with an inquisitive look and bluntly asked, "who cast the Wallace ballot?" After a few agonizing seconds of deciding if I wanted to be a political martyr, I raised my hand. Never have I been so embarrassed in my life. For the entire semester I was literally castigated by that professor. During the morning roll calls, each student was called by their last name until he came to my name and sarcastically called out, "Mr. Ramsey – our token Wallace supporter – is he present?" I was but wished I were not.

Nevertheless, I ended up with a "C" in the course, which based on my four-year effort was not all bad. I did however garner one important charge from this class. After our final exam, the professor made an impassioned statement that caught my attention. His most important take-away for us from this class was to "question the norm" – not to blindly accept it – not be afraid to ask, "why." His intent was not to necessarily encourage us to question our political and social beliefs – whether liberal or conservative – but to make sure our beliefs were based on truth, and not tradition alone; not to blindly accept a belief because mama, daddy, grandma or grandpa said so, but because it is truth based on fact. That same premise works in the spiritual world. The intentions of family may be sincere; in fact, the intentions of the Sunday School teacher or even the pastor may be sincere, but it is *our* salvation that is at stake. As Paul says to the believers at Philippi – *"... continue to work out YOUR salvation with fear and trembling, for it is God who works in you to will and to act in order to fulfill His good purpose"–Philippians 2:12-13.*

Why do we believe what we believe? Are our beliefs based on truth or are they based on the blind acceptance of religion, tradition or what we have been taught and accepted as truth? I recall asking my Sunday morning Bible Study class the question – "Why are you a Southern Baptist?" The common reply was, "because I was raised a Southern Baptist." Most answered they were Southern Baptists because Southern Baptist beliefs were in symphony with what they believed. So, I ventured to ask the next question – "What do Southern Baptists believe?" Surprisingly, the vast majority did not have a clue what Southern Baptists professed to believe! Amazingly we are willing to risk eternity on denominational precepts we assume to be Biblical and factual without *"testing the spirits to see whether they are from God" – 1 John 4:1.*

Tradition is defined as "the transmission of knowledge, opinions, doctrines, customs, practices, etc., from generation to generation."[15] Tradition is not necessarily bad, unless it is not truth-based. "Truth" is Jesus Christ and His Word, the Holy Bible. Many of the attributes of present-day Christianity are based on sacred texts, rituals, ceremonies, and man generated beliefs or traditions. "Consequently, the living and dynamic characteristic of rituals and ceremonies, which are practiced within the church, serve as an integral part of a believer's life, in molding their action and most fundamentally, their worldview of life's enduring questions. Tenets, dogmas, doctrines and values contain crucial ideas or beliefs that are then considered genuine and highlight the self-understanding of a tradition for the believer as fact."[16] In other words, how much of what we consider Biblical-based spiritual legacy in today's church is based strictly on tradition alone and has nothing to do with Biblical precepts?

To accept tradition as gospel without verification is dangerous, regardless where it might have originated – family, denomination, religious icons, etc. For example, the evangelist D.L. Moody (1837-1899) is credited with the instituting of the solo hymn following the pastor's sermon, the "decision card,"[17] and "in addition, was the first to ask those who wanted to be saved to stand up from their seats and be led in a "sinner's prayer."[18] There may be nothing inherently wrong with these formalities, but to blindly assume, as many do, the Protestant order of worship is Biblically-based and descended from the Apostolic worship in

Acts 2:42-47, is not necessarily true. In fact, many of today's "church's" formalities are heavily influenced by tradition.

To mistake tradition as truth is eternally dangerous when it comes to things of the spirit. All of us – every single one of us – will stand before the Almighty to be judged – either for our works' rewards (if we are saved), or for eternal damnation (if we die without Jesus Christ). For some reason, using the excuses–"but my pastor told me," or "my Sunday School teacher mentioned," or "Grandma always said"–may not cut it. We should not base our salvation on tradition or what we have been told, even from a pulpit! *1 John 4:1-3 – "Dear friends* (fellow Christians), *do not believe every spirit, but test the spirits to see whether they are from God, because many false prophets have gone out into the world. This is how you can recognize the Spirit of God: Every spirit that acknowledges that Jesus Christ has come in the flesh is from God, but every spirit that does not acknowledge Jesus is not from God. This is the spirit of the antichrist, which you have heard is coming and even now is already in the world."*

We possess His "Handbook of Truth" – His Holy Word–and contrary to what tradition has taught us, its truths are not reserved for a select elite few. Be sure of your salvation! Dare to ask *"why!"* Are you finding those answers in today's traditional "church of man?" If so, you are indeed blessed, since statistics show most are not. "Satan doesn't come into the church to cover people with open sores or explode their skulls like in the movies. He comes to deceive them. He does not need to convince us that evil is good to achieve victory; all he needs to do is move the church somewhat off the center of God's revealed counsel. In subtle deception, Satan does not need to persuade believers to deny central teachings, such as Christ's atoning death, His resurrection, or even Biblical authority. Instead, he seeks to shift the emphasis from the important to the unimportant and misleads people on more peripheral issues. The resulting group may bear little resemblance to the church described in the New testament."[19]

Jesus says, *"And on this rock I will build my church, and the gates of Hades will not overcome it"–Matthew 16:18.* There is translational debate here, as some believe Jesus is referencing the modern day church; others believe, since this is addressed directly to Peter ("*petros*" or "rock"), it is a charge to him and his ministry to the Jews; and still others believe it is directed to the other Apostles and their ministry to the Gentiles. There is also another possible translation that few ever mention. When Jesus uses the word–"*gates*" – what exactly does this mean? A "*gate*" is something that guards the entrance to or exit from a place. In the context used here, the place is hell. Jesus may be referencing the fact–His church–the "*ekklesia*"–recognizes its mission and by carrying the Gospel into the world, are literally attacking the "*gates of hell*" and the one who controls that dreaded place. Satan, nor hell itself, can withstand His power working through His people. The difference in the "church of man" and the "*ekklesia*" of Jesus Christ is the recognition and application of His command – "*doers of the Word and not hearers only*" (*James 1:22*).

Another key word in this verse (*Matthew 16:18*) is "*church,*" which in the Gospels is only used three times–here and twice in *Matthew 18:17*. In the Septuagint (the pre-Christian Greek translation of the Old Testament), "*church*" is used for the congregation of Israel; in the ministry of the New Testament Apostles, it references a "body of believers," or the "*ekklesia,*" as we have already introduced. In other words, any New Testament believer who believes and confesses (mind and heart) the life-saving blood of Jesus Christ, is considered a fully vested member of the body of Christ and a member of His "*ekklesia.*"

We will discuss salvation in depth in a later chapter, but it is important to note Paul's explanation to the believers in Corinth in *1 Corinthians 15:1*. Not only has His "*ekklesia*" "*received it*" – the Gospel–they "*stand upon it*"–meaning it begins in the mind, goes to the heart and moves to the mouth. Paul confirms in *Romans 10:9-10* – "*If you declare with your mouth, 'Jesus is Lord,' and believe in your heart that God raised Him from the dead, you will be saved. For it is with your heart that you believe and are justified, and it is with your mouth that you profess your faith and are saved.*" One can possess a "head knowledge," but without standing upon it – living it and confessing it to others, one proves his/her belief is not genuine – of the heart. And if it is not of both mind and heart, he/she is not saved, regardless what religious doctrine might mandate.

Genuine belief always results in confession – which Jesus likens to "bearing fruit" – *Matthew 7:17-20; 13:23; Luke 6:43-45.* James expounds on this in *James 2:24* – "*You see that a person is considered righteous* (declared not guilty) *by what they do and not by faith alone."* If our church–traditional, contemporary, steepled, mini, mega – whatever – is not leading and training us for service outside its doors, we need to re-evaluate where we are serving or considering serving. "Ingrown churches don't reach meaningful numbers of people for Christ and instead merely compete to attract one another's members."[20]

As noted, I am a senior citizen over sixty years of age with no pastoral background. I am a layman (even though that word is not found in the New Testament). I count it a true blessing that in God's sovereign plan, He made a place for ALL brothers and sisters in Christ to participate in the sharing of His Word – the Gospel. Seminary experience is not required nor mandated. One of my favorite verses in Scripture is *Acts 4:13.* Peter and John had healed a man who was crippled from birth. They were seized and brought before the Sanhedrin, the Jewish supreme court because, they were not only healing the sick, they were proclaiming the resurrection of the dead and the saving grace of Jesus Christ. *Acts 4:4* states people were responding – *"the number of men who believed grew to about five thousand."*

The rulers, elders and teachers of the law – the religious elite–were not happy because these proclaimers of the Gospel were challenging their religious system with its obligations and traditions. As Peter and John were pulled from a jail cell where they had been housed overnight, they were brought before Annas, the high priest, Caiaphas, John, Alexander and other men of the high priest's family – titled and compensated men of man-made religious "position." The message they were sharing is found in *Acts 4:12* – *"Salvation is found in no one else, for there is no other name under heaven given to mankind by which we must be saved."* But notice *Verse 13* – *"When they* (the court judges) *saw the courage of Peter and John and realized that they were unschooled, ordinary men, they were astonished, and they took note that these men had been with Jesus."*

What a blessed message for the ones today's church calls "laymen!" God can take ordinary men and women and use them in the most important ministry of life! A ministry that has eternal ramifications! That means you and me! There may be a laic/clergy distinction in the "church of man," but none to be found in the Scriptures! Are we growing in the Spirit and being taught to exercise the expression of the Holy

Spirit in our daily walk and witness on behalf of the Gospel? Can that happen in the "traditional church of man?" Yes, it can – but it is rare.

"Per one denominational expert in church planting, nationwide church growth averages 3% growth by conversion. The rest is all transfer or biological growth (members having children)."[21] Perhaps it is to these 97 percenters, Jesus was referencing when He quoted the prophet Isaiah – *"These people honor Me with their lips, but their hearts are far from Me. They worship Me in vain; their teachings are merely human rules"* – *Matthew 15:8-9*. Once more, if religion has taught us service to each other is more important than service without, we are in the wrong place and need to immediately rethink our position. Such teaching is not of God.

As noted, Christian parents raised me in the nurture of a Christian home and made sure I was an integral part of a corporate body of like-minded believers to help me grow in the knowledge of my Lord. I will be eternally grateful to them for the love and sacrifice they showed me by making sure I was involved from an early age – Sunday mornings, Sunday nights, Wednesday nights and literally any other times the church doors were opened. My Father became a Christian around the time of my birth when a gentleman he was working for as a brick-mason shared the Gospel and encouraged him to seek the Truth, especially with a newborn on the way. Thankfully, he listened, and God moved. This was my life and I am thankful for it. I have met many Godly people through the traditional church who have shaped my life and helped me to grow from the milk onto the meat of the Word as commanded by Paul.

At the age of twenty-one, I began to follow in my Father's footsteps, participating in church leadership. I became a first grade Bible Study teacher and in subsequent years taught third grade, fourth grade and eventually an adult couple's Bible study group. I shared numerous times with my adult Bible study members, leading them was a breeze compared to children. Children tend to ask the *"why"* questions, expecting answers. Adults, for the most part, just take what they are told and either accept it for what it is, ignore it, do not care, or purposely forget.

At the age of twenty-five, I became a deacon in my church like my Father before me and so began my tenure in serving in about every leadership capacity offered in the traditional church. It was at this time I began to question the true intent of my service to "church." "Church" to me was a necessary part of my spiritual life and the adherence to its rules, obligations and regulations were a necessary part of spiritual growth. The ultimate question that began to haunt me—had I immersed myself in "church" and turned a blind eye to the mission Jesus had called me to perform? The performance of "church service" was assuring and comfortable, but the challenges of outreach were untimely and seemingly unimportant. The realization began to sink in—If this is the plight of today's "church"—then I am the problem.

My job required travel and a lot of it. Traveling can be boring, but I found "talk radio" to be addictive. Unfortunately, most of the conversation deals with politics, of which I have limited interest. I caught myself listening to a local AM station originating from a small town in the Southeast. The host shared a personal testimony from Rob Wilkerson, pastor and blog writer, regarding what he called, "Churchianity vs Christianity." The radio host shared an introductory paragraph from one of his blogs stating, "I've had a love/hate relationship with 'Christianity' for many years; since, eleven years old, as a matter of fact. Here is the part I have loved: the Jesus I see in Scripture. Here is the part I have hated: conformity to a system or structure that I could not see in Scripture. So, I have come to call the thing I've loved, 'Christianity,' and the thing I've hated, 'churchianity'."

The radio debate centered on his characterization of the condition of the modern-day Christian church and how different its teachings are from the original message of Jesus Christ. His introductory comments stirred up the listening audience, but his closing comments of the blog pushed them over the edge – "I am a former pastor, but I no longer 'go to church,' but rather am journeying down a path of deconstructing and Biblically re-defining church, detoxing from 'churchianity,' and seeking the new creation and new life of the new covenant wherever Jesus leads me through the Holy Spirit. Perhaps now is the time for you to say, 'no more' to 'churchianity' and 'yes' to Jesus and Christianity. If so, take that step, whatever Jesus is telling you to do next. Then sit back and watch what God is about to do next!"[22] Hark! He just summarized in one paragraph the questions that have troubled me for a lifetime.

The audience was stirred, but not in the way you might think. Most agreed with his analogies and admitted to possessing the same guilt feelings, but afraid to ask "*why.*" Christian Identity minister, author and talk show host Eli James notes—"Today's church has developed into a social club, stressing adapting to the modern world instead of purging the evils out of this world. Instead of being driven by the ideas of exposing and opposing sin, today's church strives to make the pew occupants feel good about themselves while society self-destructs. It has abandoned the Ten Commandments in favor of promoting Self-Help, amplified with Bible verses. The *Book of Revelation* actually predicted this development, calling it the church of lukewarm people."[23] Reverend David Platt, pastor and President of the International Mission Board of Southern Baptists adds—"Jesus actually spurned the things that my church culture said were most important. I am convinced that we, as Christ followers in American churches, have embraced values and ideas, that are not only unbiblical, but contradict the gospel we claim to believe. This is where I am most convicted as a pastor of a church in the USA. I am part of a system that has created a whole host of means and methods, plans, and strategies for doing church that require little if any power from God."[24]

It is entirely possible for one to find peace, comfort, serenity, fellowship and even salvation and certain levels of spiritual growth in today's traditional "church." But in the "Laodicean Church" of the end-times, Jesus says peace, comfort, and serenity will be its predominant characteristics; concern for those without will be "*lukewarm*" or nonexistent. True believers understand once we have received His gift of salvation, our lives are all about "works" – service on His behalf. Paul notes in *Ephesians 6:12* – "*For our struggle is not against flesh and blood, but against the rulers, against the authorities, against the powers of this dark world and against the spiritual forces of evil in the heavenly realms.*" Our enemy is organized, powerful and battletested. Are we? Is our fellowship or the one we might be considering training us accordingly? I have personally come to realize, serving each other through committees and positions in "church" defines "*lukewarm*" and seldom ever results in attainment of the spiritual maturity required to serve Him.

Can the "church of man" grow you spiritually and train you properly to serve in the army of God? Yes, it can – in some cases. However – it is rare; statistics already shared bear witness, in addition to Jesus

Himself stating as much – "*The harvest is plentiful, but the workers are few*"–*Matthew 9:37*. A quick review of the salvations and/or baptisms of your fellowship or the one you might be considering are an accurate measuring stick in assessing a fertile training ground for battle. "*Lukewarm*" churches have no concern for lost people and are easily identifiable–"*you can recognize them by their fruit.*" The church of Jesus Christ, the "*ekklesia*," prepares its peoples for work outside its four walls. In addition:

a. It is an everlasting, unfailing believer's body, because it is built on the precepts, teaching and directives of Jesus Christ – "*And on this rock I will build my church, and the gates of Hades will not overcome it*" – *Matthew 16:18*.

b. It is "organic." Webster defines "organic," as "having the characteristics of a living organism"[25] – it is alive! All participate! You are not relegated to a pew and trained in passivity; the Corinthian church, although misguided in many of its precepts, sought to be that type of church – "*What then shall we say, brothers? When you come together, each of you has a hymn, or a word of instruction, a revelation, a tongue, or an interpretation. Everything must be done so that the church may be built up*" – *1 Corinthians 14:26*.

I recently attended a college booster luncheon and football scrimmage for my college football team. After the scrimmage and lunch, one of the coaches was coming to discuss the team and prospects for the upcoming season. Gates opened at 10:00 am, with lunch at 12:15 pm and the coach's speech at 1:00 pm. When I arrived at 9:45 am, every single table at the front of the room was taken, with pocketbooks and coats placed neatly to reserve seats closest to the podium; I was relegated to the rear of the room and watched much of the speech on closed circuit TV. This has never happened to me in a traditional church service. In fact, if one does not arrive early, he/she are relegated to the front/middle pews; to secure a rear pew requires extensive effort and early arrival. What is the difference?

It is much easier to slip in the rear of the traditional church, pick up a back pew, sit passively, leave unnoticed, go home and say

– "I've done my church obligation for the week; I'm good to go." In an organic fellowship where all participate, that would not be possible. Notice from *Acts 2:42-47* the inclusive pronouns – *"they", "themselves", "everyone", "all the believers", "together", "their possessions", "they gave", "they continued", "they broke bread", "their homes", "all the people", "and God added to THEIR number."* In the New Testament church of the apostles, based on Jesus Christ as its Head – *we* are the *"ekklesia"* – an integral part of a working fellowship of active, fruit-bearing believers.

c. It is patterned after the churches of the New Testament. No paid professionals or budgets – therefore, they were afforded the blessing of being able to *"devote themselves to the apostle's teaching, to the fellowship, to the breaking of bread* (communion) *and to prayer"* – *Acts 2:42*.

d. It does not have money as its God – *"They sold property and possessions to give to anyone who had need"* – *Acts 2:45*. They gave, and they gave cheerfully – but not out of obligation. Their giving was need-based – not "want" based – and gave attention to those both inside and outside the fellowship.

e. It believes and acts on the Great Commission – *Matthew 28:19-20* – each member acting and serving based on his/her spiritual gift or gifts – *"Now to each one the manifestation of the Spirit is given for the common good"* –1 Corinthians 12:7.

f. It has as its foundation the infallible, inerrant, Holy, divinely inspired Word of God–*"Above all, you must understand that no prophecy of Scripture came about by the prophet's own interpretation of things. For prophecy never had its origin in the human will, but prophets, though human, spoke from God as they were carried along by the Holy Spirit"*–2 Peter 1:20-21. If "church" – any "church"–is not based on the Word of God, it is doomed to failure. In the New Testament church, they knew nothing of the Bible being a poison that needed to be handled only by "paid professionals."

g. It recognizes its mandate to reach outside the four walls of the "house" in which it worships, not burying itself in programs and entertainment designed to "throw open the doors and announce to the world – 'here we are – come on in'." Some will respond to that type invitation, but most do not, and those that do, typically represent a selective group. The mission field lies outside the four walls and so is our mandate – *Matthew 28:19 – "GO"*; *Mark 6:7 – "Calling the Twelve to Him, He began to SEND THEM OUT..."* The church of Jesus Christ – the *"ekklesia"* – sees the mission field as *"white unto harvest,"* and recognizes the *"field"* is not inside a building.

h. It teaches you to take ownership of your salvation. Salvation is not based on tradition or ritual, as religion tends to promote. *"Ekklesia"* helps one understand true salvation through Biblical truth, encouragement and exhortation from true believers – both mind and heart committed – recognizable by the fruit they bear. *"Examine yourselves to see whether you are in the faith; test yourselves. Do you not realize that Christ Jesus is in you – unless, of course, you fail the test?"–2 Corinthians 13:5*; *"Therefore, my brothers and sisters, make every effort to confirm your calling and election. For if you do these things, you will never stumble, and you will receive a rich welcome into the eternal kingdom of our Lord and Savior Jesus Christ"–2 Peter 1:10-11.*

i. It affords you intimacy – not only with Christ, but with your brothers and sisters in Christ. Most find this type intimacy is near impossible in a "traditional church" setting – *"For where two or three gather in My name, there am I with them" – Matthew 18:20.*

j. It affords you individualized spiritual growth; salvation is an on-going process. Nowhere does Scripture say to walk an aisle, get saved, stay glued to a pew and live happily ever after – *"Anyone who lives on milk, being still an infant, is not acquainted with the teaching about righteousness. But solid food is for the mature, who by constant use have trained themselves to distinguish good from evil"–Hebrews 5:13-14.*

k. It provides you with encouragement and exhortation, so easily lost in a large body. Miss a few worship events in a large body and see how many may notice; miss one event in an organic body and see how many become concerned. Christians need encouragement, due to the calling that has been mandated to us to take the Gospel to the world; the world is not always receptive—"*And let us consider how we may spur one another on toward love and good deeds, not giving up meeting together, as some are in the habit of doing, but encouraging one another – and all the more as you see the Day approaching"*– Hebrews 10:24-25.

l. It is a template for spiritual success in outreach—"*And the Lord added to their number daily those who were being saved"*– Acts 2:47. It fosters natural growth, especially among those who most likely would never enter a building with a steeple on its roof.

No "church"—traditional, contemporary, house, charismatic, cell-based, emergent, seeker-sensitive, etc.—is perfect. Where man is involved, there is no perfection. Do we need "church?" No, we do not need "church." What we need is "*ekklesia.*" There is a marked difference. The "*ekklesia*" – the church of the New Testament—worked 2000 years ago – and God blessed it. It still works today.

> "*They devoted themselves to the apostles' teaching and to fellowship, to the breaking of bread and to prayer. Everyone was filled with awe at the many wonders and signs performed by the apostles. All the believers were together and had everything in common. They sold property and possessions to give to anyone who had need. Every day they continued to meet in the temple courts. They broke bread in their homes and ate together with glad and sincere hearts, praising God and enjoying the favor of all the people. And the Lord added to their number daily those who were being saved"* – Acts 2:42-47.

Chapter 2

WHY A BUSINESS?

"It is the whole business of the whole church to preach the whole gospel to the whole world" – Charles Spurgeon.

"Whether pastors want to admit it or not, they are the leaders of a religious charitable organization. As such, it must be created with articles of incorporation, and eventually a constitution and bylaws. This means there is a hierarchy. After all, somebody must determine who gets paid and how much they get paid. And if it is not one man, it is usually less than a handful of men. Like it or not, this necessarily makes a local church an organization which reports to the government. And just because it's tax exempt doesn't really make it any less what it essentially becomes: *a business.*"[26]

A "business" is defined as – "an organization where people work together on a regular basis to produce and sell goods and/or services to earn a profit for the services it offers."[27] Based on that criteria, should we consider today's "church" a business? Without question– *yes!* In *Luke 19:45-46 ("When Jesus entered the temple courts, He began to drive out those who were selling. 'It is written,' He said to them, 'My house will be a house of prayer; but you have made it 'a den of robbers'.")* on a visit to the temple courtyards, Jesus began driving out moneychangers who were buying, selling and exchanging money denominations for foreigners to pay the temple tax in the name of a "tithe." He accuses them of making God's house a *"den of robbers."* One wonders what would happen if Christ came back today and sat through a typical "church" business meeting?

I have served in the business arena for over forty years in both management and ownership capacities. Business has been my life. Serving in various decision-making roles in a Protestant church, I have been respectfully confronted and reprimanded by sincere brothers in Christ, "the church is not a business and as a result, should not be treated as such;" or, "it may be a business, but it's the most important business because it's God's business." My reply to such reasoning has always been–unapologetically, but respectfully – *"YES* – it is a business! It's a business because man has made it a business! And no, I'm not so sure in the eyes of God, He would classify it as 'His business.' I do not believe the God who created the universe cares I sit on a padded pew that costs six digits or more annually, but rather is more concerned what I do to address the numbers of lost and needy outside the front doors of the church building where I comfortably reside."

A real awakening for me came at the age of twenty-eight when I was recommended by my Pastor to serve as part of a wonderful Christian business-men's association, called the Gideons.[28] The sole purpose of this organization is to win men, women, boys and girls to the Lord Jesus Christ by personal witnessing and personal testimony, and by planting "spiritual seeds," or copies of God's Word, into the hands of lost souls. Gideons are international in scope and serve as an evangelistic arm of the local church. Financial support for this ministry comes from the Gideon's themselves (membership dues cover all administrative expenses), and from the churches who choose to support. 100% of all monies received from the churches go to purchase Scriptures, which are then placed at the expense of the members themselves. A wonderful ministry I am so thankful to have been a part.

Annually Gideons' go into local churches as allowed by the pastor and report what God has done in the ministry during that particular year. I have always laughed and compared Gideons to Marines in the fact we continually have to "improvise." Pastors are typically reluctant to give up their pulpits; some may yield the entire service to a visiting Gideon – maybe thirty minutes; some may only give five minutes or anything in between. Preparing for a thirty-minute service, only to arrive at the church and find out for whatever reason, you need to reduce your time to five or ten minutes, forces you to "improvise" on the spot. This was indeed an experience I encountered on one of my earliest church reports.

Supporting churches range in size from just a few attendees to mega numbers. The church I was assigned was a large church with some 1000 plus in attendance. In addition, once I arrived, I found out it was televised. This was exciting but concerning, as I never envisioned myself as a television speaker.

As I met to pray with the Pastor and prepare for the service, he shared with me an unscheduled business meeting was necessary and I may need to pare down my report. I agreed to accommodate to whatever time was afforded. After the welcome, a couple of songs and prayer, the Pastor called the church into conference. The conference was to present to the church the recommendation to purchase a new Grand Piano. The cost of the piano (back in the early 1980's) was in excess of $50,000. There was limited discussion, a motion and second, a vote, and the church bought a new piano.

As the conference ended, I took a bulletin and a pen from my coat pocket and began to calculate–$50,000 divided by $1.50 (the cost at that time for a Gideon New Testament with Psalms and Proverbs) and came up with the astounding figure of 33,333. Wow!!! For that amount of money, the Gideons could have placed at no charge to that fellowship, a copy of God's Word in the hands of every man, woman and child in a town of 30,000 plus people! My heart was pierced. Reality hit home as I recognized our expenditures really do define our mission – *"For where your treasure is, there your heart will be also" – Matthew 6:21.* Is God pleased with this type of "worship," if we can even call it that? How could an investment like this do anything to further the cause of Christ and bring that lost, homeless drunk in the gutter outside the church to a saving knowledge of Jesus Christ? "Forgive us God!!! Big government, big business, big oil, big tobacco, and big church. The church has become part of the problem. We are not living like Christ. Of course, they think we are hypocrites – because we ARE! Forgive us God!"[29]

Is the church indeed a business? Let us compare. A church operates on "faith;" a business does also – it's called "risk." A business operates

23

to make a profit; so does a church – how else can it meet its budget and pay its bills? A business has staff to run the day to day activities; a church has staff also and for the same reason. A business has contracts; so does a church – landscaping, custodial, office equipment, etc. A business makes capital investments; so does a church – buildings, furnishings, property – so much so, it could qualify as a medium to large size corporation in economic terms. A business makes capital improvements; a church does likewise – new facilities, upgrading current facilities, etc. A business has maintenance responsibilities as does the church. A business has a CEO (Chief Executive Officer); so does a church – usually the Pastor. A business has a board of directors; so does a church – usually a group of individuals charged to make decisions under the direction of the Pastor – deacons, elders, trustees, stewardship committees, etc. A business has employees; so does a church. A business has salaries to pay for its employees; so does a church. A business has an income flow to maintain the solvency of the operation; a church has an income flow called "tithes," without which it could not survive. A business has a budget which details projected income and expenditures; a church does likewise. A business has accounting procedures – checks and balances, audits; so does a church. A business maintains inventory which needs to be monitored; so does a church – vehicles, literature, furnishings, office equipment, musical instruments and supplies, libraries, etc. A business has compensation packages for its staff; so does a church. A business is required to have insurance for its capital investments and its employees; so, does a church. A business is in competition with other businesses to survive; so does a church (wrestling professed believers and the income that hopefully comes with them from sister churches). A business is required to pay taxes and participate in government programs such as social security and workman's comp; although a church is tax exempt for now, it still has governmental obligations on behalf of its staff and employees (church taxation will be discussed in detail in a future chapter). A business renders community and charitable support – United Way, food banks, etc.; so does a church – typically. A business has stockholders; so does a church – members which have a vested interest. And finally – failure to succeed in a business results in bankruptcy; failure to financially succeed in a church, results in bankruptcy also. With the "church" it is usually the spiritual awakening of its investors that result in its financial bankruptcy and vice versa. As the saying goes, "if it looks like a skunk, acts like a skunk and smells like a skunk, then chances are, it's a skunk."

If the church "looks, smells, and acts like a business," it must be considered a business, so why not treat it like one?

So, is the church indeed a business? I will let you be the judge, although be warned—God may already have. And speaking of bankruptcy, any business where 15% of its workers perform 100% of its work and less than 30% of its employees even show up for work, that entity is doomed to failure before it even begins. The "church of man" is no different.

Consider the following:

1. "US Christians control trillions in assets while at any given time 200,000,000 brothers and sisters starve."[30]
2. "95% of all church budgets in the US are spent on our own comforts and programs. Less than 1% is spent on evangelism."[31]
3. "One padded chair in my Bible Study class costs $35. This would feed an entire family in Liberia for an entire month; the podium in my class costs $150 – this would feed an entire family in Burundi for two months."[32]
4. "Churches in America spend 82% of the average church budget on personnel, buildings, and administration. In comparison – for the same items – Red Cross 8%; World Vision 14%; Compassion International 16%. It's made worse by how funds are allocated – 3% children, 2% adults, and 1% benevolence."[33]
5. "Churches in America spend and invest $3.6 trillion each year."[34]
6. "Religious groups in American own $630 billion in property, and this is low since it does not count other property in addition to church buildings."[35]
7. "The estimated annual spend of the Catholic church in the US alone is in excess of $171.6 billion."[36]
8. "Every year in the US we spend more than $10 billion on church buildings. In America alone, the amount of real estate owned by institutional churches is worth over $230 billion."[37]
9. "The Catholic church is the biggest financial power on earth. Wealth and investment of the Vatican, which in the US alone, is greater than that of the five wealthiest corporate giants in America. When added to that all the real estate, property, stocks and shares abroad, then the staggering accumulation of wealth becomes so formidable as to defy any rational assessment."[38]

10. "Annual church embezzlements by top monetary custodians exceed the entire cost of all foreign missions worldwide. Emboldened by lax procedures, trusted church treasurers are embezzling from the church $5,500,000 PER DAY. That is $16 billion per year. For reference, total spending on foreign missions is only $15 billion."[39]

11. "Of every dollar given to a Protestant church, the average amount that goes to overseas missions is two cents. And what do churches do with their money? In 1920, the percentage of giving to missions from the total offering was 10.09%, just over a dime out of every dollar. In 2003, evangelical and conservative denominations gave 2.6% or about three cents out of every dollar. The combined average for overseas work is about two pennies per dollar. Where is the money going? The sprawling church campuses that have become the norm today are expensive to operate. The number of staff members and the amount of salaries have risen. The numbers completely demonstrate an increased emphasis on internal operations over the broader mission of the church."[40]

12. "Nearly 50 percent of large churches (1000 members or more) spend between 39% and 52% of their annual budget on staffing costs, translating to 1 full-time paid staff for every 51 to 90 attendees."[41]

Darren Shearer, the host of the "Theology of Business Podcast" and the director of the "Theology of Business Institute," notes in a recent blog, "religion in the United States is a $1.2 trillion dollar industry." Based on his analogy, there are approximately 300,000 Protestant churches in the United States with an average of 162 weekly attendees. Annual collections for the average size Protestant church is $217,170, which means Protestant churches in the U.S. collect approximately $39.9 billion in revenue annually. According to Shearer, this is $10 billion more than the entire health club industry in the U.S. which is estimated at $30 billion. His comments are noteworthy – "As a business owner, I happen to believe business is an ideal place for Christian ministry. However, I do believe it is disingenuous to operate a business and attempt to convince its stakeholders that it is something somehow more noble and spiritual than a business."[42]

Author and Church Consultant Tony Morgan posed an interesting question in a recent article – "Would Jesus Want Your Church to Be Run Like a Business?" Based on the words of Christ Himself during His earthly ministry, Morgan provides several reasons he believes the answer to his question is indeed – *"yes"* – "He does want our churches to be run more like good businesses:"

A. Businesses stay focused on reaching new markets. *"I must proclaim the good news of the kingdom of God to the other towns also, because that is why I was sent" – Luke 4:43*. His ministry began in the synagogues from His headquarters in Capernaum. He was not afraid to change His strategy to further His outreach – moving from town to town and ministering in the highways of life.

B. Businesses hold employees accountable. *"The servant who knows the master's will and does not get ready or does not do what the master wants will be beaten with many blows" – Luke 12:47*. Businesses are not hesitant to fire employees for lack of productivity; nor should churches.

C. Businesses make plans before committing to projects. *"Suppose one of you wants to build a tower. Won't you first sit down and estimate the cost to see if you have enough money to complete it?"- Luke 14:28*. Churches are too quick to approve ideas without fully considering the ramifications.

D. Businesses stop things that are not yielding results. *"He cuts off every branch in Me that bears no fruit..."- John 15:2*. Churches spend too much time and effort on nonperforming programs.

E. Businesses are responsible for demonstrating a return to their investors. *"From everyone who has been given much, much will be demanded; and from the one who has been entrusted with much, much more will be asked" – Luke 12:48*. Churches teach stewardship better than they practice it.[43]

Believe it or not, with decreasing financial support from its members, the new trend for today's church is business investment. The premise being, since the church is indeed a business and requires finances to maintain its existence, utilize the governmental advantages afforded and invest in separate business ventures to help fund the ministry. According to "Outreach Magazine," "investing in a business creates a source of revenue that is entirely independent from tithes and offerings.

This additional income gives pastors freedom to do what God has called them to do, without having to worry about lack of resources or numbers of members. As the business makes money, it pays the ministry in the form of dividends. The dividends are 100% tax-free to the church, and the church or ministry can then use those funds however it wishes. "Legit" businesses suggested for consideration: coffee shop, landscaping, bookstore, brewery, restaurant, bed and breakfast, media production, recording studio, T-shirt company, conference, design firm, real estate, magazines and newspapers, software repair, retail and clothing line."[44]

Is today's "church" a business? Absolutely! Is it the most important business since it is considered "God's business?" I think not since today's "church" has adopted the same strategy as industry establishing money as its god, which should not come as a surprise since Jesus prophesied it in *Revelation 3:17-18*—*"You say, 'I am rich; I have acquired wealth and do not need a thing.' But you do not realize that you are wretched, pitiful, poor, blind and naked. I counsel you to buy from Me gold refined in the fire, so you can become rich; and white clothes to wear, so you can cover your shameful nakedness; and salve to put on your eyes, so you can see."*

> *"Sometimes people don't want to hear the truth because they don't want their illusions destroyed" – Friedrich Nietzsche. "To those who sold doves He said, 'Get these out of here! Stop turning my Father's house into a market'!" (John 2:16) – Jesus Christ.*

Chapter 3

WHY THE TITHE?

> *"All through scripture, we read that God wants to bless us. And not only does He want to bless us, He has a way to bless us. He has a system set in place so that when we do things His way, we get His results! Remember you cannot out give God and when you become a giver and a tither, you can wake up every morning and say, 'I am positioned for a blessing!' Give freely and become wealthier; be stingy and lose everything"* – Victoria Osteen (wife of Evangelist Joel Osteen).[45]

Attempting analysis rather than critique, the business of *"peddling the gospel"* is lucrative to say the least. Obviously, there are those serving the pastorate who are literally living off the "widow's mite," but some fare well in the business of religion – very well. Even those who are on the payroll of the "widow's mite," must acknowledge the "widow" supplying the "mite." According to "Online Magazine," the net worth of the top wealthiest men of the cloth are: 1. Ken Copeland–$760 million; 2. T.D. Jakes–$150 million; 3. David Oyedepo–$150 million; 4. Pat Robertson–$100 million; 5. Joel Osteen–$60 million; 6. Benny Hinn–$42 million; 7. Jesse Duplantis–$50 million; 8. Creflo Dollar–$27 million; 9. Rick Warren–$25 million; 10. Joyce Meyer – $25 million; 11. Jamal Bryant–$20 million; 12. John Hagee–$5 million; 13. Paula White–$5 million; 14. Noel Jones–$5 million; 15. Louis Farrakhan–$3 million.[46] No doubt many of these have earned a great deal of their fortune through television, book sales, prayer cloths, etc. However this does not take away from the lucrativeness of their endeavors in the name of the gospel, much of which no doubt comes from the wallets and pocket-books of individual tithers and contributors.

One of the evolutions of the traditional church that has caught my atten-tion over my lifetime is the adopted requirement of paying everyone for everything they do for the body of Christ. In other words, we now pay someone to preach to us, sing to us, play our instruments, take care of our teenagers, babysit our kids, answer our phones, type the pastor's sermon notes, keep the pastor's appointment book, take care of our money, vacuum our floors, cut our grass, set up and take down our gymnasiums, work our coffee kiosks, etc. – all at the expense of the tither. In addition, comes funding the complex – again at the expense of the tither – which is not new.

As a business, the "church" requires cash, so it mandates an obligation called the "tithe" which is imposed on its members with the premise, "the more you give, the more you will be blessed in return." Some see this return as blessings of health or prosperity, but some modern-day evangelists, such as Joel Osteen, believe it is monetary blessings. Who can argue as he comfortably resides in his 17,000 square foot home with an estimated value of $10.5 million.[47] The tithe (or the tither) has certainly worked for him. I also recall one evangelist from years back, Reverend Ike (Frederick J. Eikerenkoetter II), who blatantly advertised – "the more you give the more you will receive, so just give it to me." He boasted of a large line of high dollar vehicles, proving how this scheme worked for him. His slogan, "You can't lose with the stuff I use," certainly fit his calling.[48] But what about the person who has always heeded man's call, tithed to the church his "fair share," but has not garnered these "so-called" blessings that have been promised – *"His disciples asked Him, "Rabbi, who sinned, this man or his parents, that he was born blind?" – John 9:2*? Where did he/she go wrong? If all this be true, it tops the best of any Wall Street opportunities on the market.

The power of taxation has never been reserved for government. Religion has historically wielded its influence, beginning with the Jews. Herod the Great undertook one of the largest construction campaigns in the first century A.D. The Jewish historian Josephus noted his main interest was to leave lasting memorials to his name through massive building projects, including the temple. He also provided detailed descriptions of its ornateness, including the inner and outer facades, which he notes were of marvel beyond compare. He describes the outer façade to be so impressive, one could see the glittering sunlight beaming off the gold colonnades from miles away. He was also quick to note these projects, especially the temple, were paid by heavy taxation upon the masses in the name of a tithe .[49]

Church extravagance and its accompanying financial burdens are not new, nor relegated to first century Herodians. The concern is what do they take away from its mission to the world outside? The Temple tax of a half-shekel (about two days wages for a common laborer) was paid by the Israelites and Levites for the upkeep of the Temple. Some believe this tax was collected through a census, but it was likely paid annually during the festivals – Passover, Pentecost, or Tabernacles.[50] Jews believed the basis for such a tax was found in *Exodus30:13*. Every Jewish male over the age of twenty was required to pay the temple tax. It is also referenced in the New Testament when Peter was cornered by the Temple tax collectors and questioned if he, along with his leader – Jesus Christ – intended to pay the tax (*Matthew 17:24-27*). Pagans and heathens did not pay the tax, along with high ranking Jewish priests who exempted themselves. Why pay when the money was just being funneled back to them anyway? Despite this, Jesus decided to pay the tax in order not to cause offense.[51]

Interestingly with the end of the Old Covenant through the coming of Jesus Christ and the destruction of the Temple in 70 A.D. by the Romans, the requirement for such a tax became unnecessary. Stephen, responding before the Sanhedrin to those Jews who refused to relinquish their Old Covenant ways in holding on to their religion and the worship of its temple, affirmed the day had arrived when God was no longer housed in a building, but rather through His Holy Spirit would reside in the hearts of true believers–"*The Most High does not live in houses made by human hands. As the prophet says: 'Heaven is my throne, and the earth is my footstool. What kind of house will you build for me, says the Lord? Or where will my resting place be? Has not my hands made all these things?' You stiff-necked people! Your hearts and ears are still uncircumcised. You are just like your ancestors: You always resist the Holy Spirit!*"–Acts 7:48-51. Paul echoes in *1 Corinthians 3:16* – "*Don't you know that you yourselves are God's temple and that God's Spirit dwells in your midst?*"–and in *2 Corinthians 6:16* – "*For we are the temple of the living God. As God has said: 'I will live with them and walk among them, and I will be their God, and they will be my people'."* The Romans, however, saw profitability in the Temple tax for their pagan temples and continued to collect the tax by force further humiliating the Jews.[52]

An interesting point to ponder is, "should what the traditional church of today calls the tithe be considered a tax?" Although the tithe is not a tax from an official standpoint, there are similarities:

a. Taxes are required to support government and its functions. Tithes are required to support today's "temples" and their operations (personnel, buildings, admin) which as previously shown, consumes an average of 82% of the "tithe."[53]

b. The U.S. government, through the Internal Revenue Service, sets tax brackets and rates for each bracket based on income and whether one files individually, or, if married, jointly. Federal income tax rates are progressive, and increase based on income. They are arranged in brackets ranging from 10% to 37%. The "tithe rate" has been set at 10%, and according to Ken Copeland Ministries, "is based on one's gross income before taxes as mandated in *Proverbs 3:9*."[54] If this be true, one could assume those tithers who are retired and drawing from social security and pre-taxed investments, are exempt from the tithe since during their working tenure, they tithed off their gross.

c. Avoiding paying taxes is illegal and punishable by law. Avoiding the tithe, according to those whose salary is dependent upon it, is amoral, unbiblical, and punishable by God's denial of blessing.

d. One literally has little influence on where his tax dollars are spent, other than the power of the ballot box. One also has little influence over where the tithe is spent other than his support or non-support of his church budget.

e. The tax is compulsory; the tithe is considered voluntary but most religious leaders preach a compulsory tithe, the refusal of which will result in Godly retribution. All seems to be lost in the fact churches are spending an overwhelming majority of the tithe on their own extravagance which includes the exorbitant salaries of those demanding it – a real "Catch 22."

Consider the following from "Health Research Funding" (HRF):

1. Only 3-5% of Americans who give to their local church do so through regular tithing.
2. In 2000, American evangelicals collectively made $2.66 trillion in income.
3. Total "Christian" income in the U.S. is $5.2 trillion annually, nearly half the world's total.
4. When surveyed, 17% of Americans state they regularly tithe.
5. For Christian families making less than $20k per year, 8% gave at least 10% in tithes; $75k and more, 1%.
6. 3 out of 4 people who do not attend church make donations to nonprofit organizations.
7. The average donation by adults attending U.S. Protestant churches is about $17/week.
8. 37% Evangelicals attending church weekly do not give any money to their church.
9. 35% of those who tithe have a net worth that is valued at more than $500k.
10. Tithers are three times more likely to support their church's building program than they are to support children and orphan causes.

When "non-tithing church attendees" were confronted with the statement – "tithing could bring about greater success for the American church" – the overwhelming response was – "so could better financial stewardship and a focus on Biblical priorities."[55]

First Church, Anytown, USA, has an annual budget of $750,000. Forty percent of the overall budget goes to pay staff and services rendered (custodial, financial, grounds upkeep, etc.); 12% goes to debt retirement for a new expansion. First Church averaged 270 in formal worship attendance last year. Considering formal worship includes first time visitors and those attending only on special occasions – holidays, Mother's Day, Father's Day, special events, etc., we will estimate average supporting attendance to be 260. Estimating the average family size in First Church as 3.5 members, this would equate to 74 families. Obviously in any church, not all "tithe" or contribute. Let us make a safe guess that First Church is above the average and 80% of its attendees contribute to some degree (208 contributors or 60 families) to the budget needs. All things equal, each contributing family (regardless of size) must then contribute $12,500 annually to meet the budget. Even though the 10%

"tithe" died with the Old Covenant, First Church continues to obligate its members accordingly from the pulpit. Based on First Church's annual budget and the 10% tithing mandate, each contributing family, regardless of size, would need to gross an annual salary of $125,000 to meet the church budget.

Using the same metrics, evenly dividing First Church's budget by the number of estimated contributors (208) – every man, woman, boy and girl would need to contribute $3605 to meet the budget. This means a family of one (widow, widower, etc.), typically on a fixed income, would be obligated to $3605 annually; a family of three to $10,815; a family of four to $14,420; a family of five to $18,025; etc. These metrics are based on participants contributing their "fair share." In the event one individual or family falters, another would need to pick up the slack. Based on the 10% "preacher's" mandate, a family of five will need to have a gross annual income in excess of $180,000 to pay their "fair share."

Older members of First Church complain they are on fixed incomes and cannot tithe this amount of money and as a result, the younger families in the church will need to "step up to the plate" and bear more of the burden. Some folks have even voiced orally in business meetings, "the younger families are not "tithing" and need to be taught the principles of the obligation." Quite frankly, as a lifetime vested member of the traditional church, I am not sure I fully understand the logic.

Bottom line – is this fair? A more important question – is it Biblical? How many families, other than maybe the senior pastor, gross this kind of income and can afford this kind of debt? Does God care I sit in a fancy building being entertained by a staff of paid professionals and the bulk of His "tithe" going to pay for that luxury? Is this mandate from the pulpit to "tithe" my fair share of 10% in line with Paul's message to the Corinthians that giving should be free from obligation and from the heart? It may just be First Church's young families are smarter than the senior citizens are giving them credit – they do not live extravagantly and obligate themselves to such debt at home – why should they here? From a financial accountability standpoint, First Church without question is living beyond its means. Sadly, they are not alone.

Your financial advisor rings your cell phone. "My brother," he implores, "I have a wonderful investment opportunity for you." "Great", you reply, "give me some information so I can make a rational decision." "Absolutely", he replies, "ask me what you will." "Tell me something about the opportunity you are offering me", you inquire. "Well", he answers, "The company has 1000 employees." "Wow, that's a large company." "Yes, it is", he states, "but there is a downside. Out of the 1000 workers on the employment roll, only 300 or so show up for work. We are truly not sure where the other 700 or so are and the company is bound and cannot drop them from the employment roll. On top of that, out of the 300 that show up on a sporadic basis, only about 35-40 do all the work. The other 250 or so show up when they like, but rarely lift a finger to do anything to contribute to the well-being of the whole." "What about the financial side of things?", you ask. "Well," he replies somberly, "over 85% of the budgeted income goes to cover administrative, maintenance and overhead costs. Less than 2% of budgeted monies, on the average, actually go to fulfill the vision or the mission of the company."

Considering your financial advisor's offer, would you consider this company a wise financial investment? If you are a smart businessman (or lady), the overriding answer is, "No", and you would probably hire another financial advisor. The bottom line, the "company" described above is the church of today – the "church of man"–and millions of young millennials are beginning to see through this façade and thus its impending financial collapse. Young couples struggling from paycheck to paycheck and living off budgets, are beginning to see the fruitlessness of investing in a man-made financial obligation to meet man-made debts beyond financial prudence. They may have a legitimate point.

Per "nonprofit source.com.," "tithers make up 10-25% of the average Protestant congregation and contribute an average of 2.5% of their gross income. According to "Lifeway Research," "based on a sampling of over 1000 churchgoers, 32% confessed they do not believe tithing is a New Testament mandate."[56] This number is growing as church contributions in all instances researched are dwindling. "Barna Research" notes, "while theologians' debate whether or not the practice of tithing – donating 10% or more of one's income to churches – is Biblical, Americans have pretty much made up their minds on the subject. Their views are discernible through their behavior. If this transition in the perceptions and giving behavior continues to accelerate, the service functions of conventional churches will be redefined within the next eight to ten years, and conventional churches will have to adopt new ways of assisting people in need."[57]

Looking at the largest Protestant denomination in America—Southern Baptists – an article in the October 2, 2019, "Baptist Courier" by Rudy Gray, states, "in 2013, Southern Baptists averaged giving 2.3 percent of their annual income to the local church." He references a 2015 article ("Why Southern Baptists Are Not Tithing") by Joe McKeever—cartoonist, retired pastor and Director of Missions – stating, "Southern Baptists do not tithe because we do not teach tithing, even though pastors may occasionally preach on the subject." His answer to the problem was for churches to systematically teach what the Bible says about giving and tithing. His point seems to be lost in the fact "giving" in the New Testament was need-based; "tithing" as so defined by the modern church, is "want" based; there is a huge difference. There is also a reference to Bryan Holley, Chief Financial Officer for the South Carolina Baptist Convention, who stated that his perspective on giving is that "people don't understand that everything belongs to God, and they don't trust Him to take care of them, so they are afraid to give anything away. We should teach people that what we do with the amount we keep also matters. That is where stewardship comes in."[58] Once again – does this include "tithing" to a "religious entity" spending 85-95% of its contributions on itself?

Jayson D. Bradley, writing for "Pushpay," an organization that offers fundraising help, stated: "Tithers make up no more than 25 percent of any congregation."[59] So, why aren't Southern Baptists giving more? Or why aren't more Southern Baptists giving? While several factors can be cited, the obvious determinant is that we choose not to tithe because we do not want to tithe, or we do not believe in tithing. When Christians say they cannot afford to tithe, preachers usually answer with something like, "You cannot afford not to tithe." While some Southern Baptists give beyond 10 percent of their income, many do not give anything. Former Lifeway President Thom Rainer wrote, "our giving is decreasing because of lower church attendance, generational shifts, giving to purposes rather than organizations, little teaching on tithing and not as much discretionary income among churchgoers."[60]

I personally recall sitting through sermons regarding *Mark 12:41-44* and the "widow's mite." Jesus, along with His disciples, were watching temple attendees placing their "tithes" into the temple treasury when a poor widow lady placed two mites – the lowest denomination of Roman currency – into the alms plate. Most "preachers" expound on these verses referencing the widow as exemplary of true sacrificial giving and stewardship since she gave all she had. Dr. John MacArthur in his "Commentary on The Gospel of Mark," takes a differing view on this passage – "Typically, these passages are used to show how stewardship is measured, not the amount given, but the percentage of one's resources offered. However, since Jesus made no point about giving by either the widow or the rich, it would be difficult to interpret as any type of lesson regarding stewardship and taken in context with the previous verses, it appears the widow is not the hero of the story as most attribute, rather, she is the victim. In context, she was duped by religious leaders into giving all she had by the false promise of Jewish legalism and subsequent promised blessings. She is an example of corrupt religion at its worst and how widows were being *'devoured.'*"[61]

2 Corinthians 2:17 – "Unlike so many, we do not peddle the Word of God for profit." We have all heard from the pulpit, "Tithing is a necessary part of Christianity and God will bless you if you tithe." I even heard one pastor say, "All are tithers; some give willingly, from others, God has to take it." In their book, "Pagan Christianity," Frank Viola and George Barna, make an interesting statement – "Tithing does appear in the Bible. So yes, tithing is Biblical. But it is not Christian. What does this mean? There were three types of tithing required by God of the Israelites in the Old Testament: a tithe of produce from the land to support the Levites or priests; one to support religious festivals; and the other to support orphans and widows. When tallied up, God commanded the Israelites to give 23.3% of their income every year. With the death of Jesus, all ceremonial codes that belonged to the Jews were nailed to the cross and buried."[62] Why then, do preachers continue to preach the "tithe?" There is truth in the fact, as we often hear from the pulpit, the tithe is required to "make sure His work continues," but there is no Biblical evidence where the believer is obligated and mandated to cover the costs for keeping a "cash cow" fed. It also begs to question, "what is it exactly we're funding?" – is it "His work," or our wants and comforts? There is no indication that I can find in the New

Testament where the true test for a Christian and his dedication to the cause has anything to do with tithing.

Tithing is only "referenced" on four occasions in the New Testament and in each instance, has no application to the Christian. So again, why is it "preached?" It is "preached" because money is necessary to cover the costs of "church," which includes the salaries of the ones "preaching" it. The New Testament explicitly teaches believer's giving is to meet needs and is benevolent in nature – *Acts 2:44-45* – *"All the believers were together and had everything in common. They sold property and possessions to give to anyone who had need."* It is also to be free from obligation or compulsion and given from the heart, rather than from a mandate (of 10% or more). Once again, Frank Viola and George Barna: "There is no doubt that it is imperative for believers to support the Lord's work financially and to give generously to the poor. Scripture enjoins both, and the Kingdom of God desperately needs both. The issue in question is the appropriateness of the tithe as a Christian "law" and how it is normally used: to fund clergy salaries, operational costs, and church building overhead."[63]

God does not need our money. In fact, God does not want our money. Churches need our money. Churches want our money. Why? Because most contemporary Christians view the church building and its accompaniments as a necessary part of "worship." Therefore, they never question the need to financially support a building, its maintenance and the professionals that oversee it. "In the US alone, real estate owned by institutional churches today is worth over $230 billion. Church building debt, service, and maintenance consumes about 18% of the $50 to $60 billion tithed to churches annually. Point: Contemporary Christians are spending an astronomical amount of money on their buildings."[64]

The Apostle Paul provides instruction to Corinthian believers regarding the offering for their famine-stricken Jerusalem brothers in *1 Corinthians 16: 2-4–"On the first day of every week, each of you should set aside a sum of money in keeping with your income, saving it up, so that when I come no collections will have to be made. Then, when I arrive, I will give letters of introduction to the men you approve and send them with your gift to Jerusalem. If it seems advisable for me to go also, they will accompany me."* Paul is not referencing "tithing." He is speaking of "grace giving" to meet a specific need.

"Tithing" means "ten" and in the Old Testament, it referenced a set amount of sacrificial giving – a tenth – as part of Old Testament Law requiring one to give a tenth of his bounty to the Lord, for the most part to support the priests and Levites (*Numbers 18:21 – "I give to the Levites all the tithes in Israel as their inheritance in return for the work they do while serving at the tent of meeting."*). Strange how many ministers today preach tithing and giving of the tenth, but in the same breath, preach the "end of the law" for the believer since he is now covered by the blood of Jesus Christ through the New Covenant (*Romans 10:4 – "Christ is the culmination of the law so that there may be righteousness for everyone who believes;" Hebrews 7:18-19 – "The former regulation is set aside because it was weak and useless (for the law made nothing perfect), and a better hope is introduced, by which we draw near to God; Hebrews 8:13 – "By calling this covenant "new," He has made the first one obsolete; and what is obsolete and outdated will soon disappear."*). In other words, we are willing to preach the blood of Jesus Christ covering our sins and how we are no longer bound by the Law and obligated to it through His New Covenant, yet we pull "tithing" out as the exception.

Paul spent fifteen chapters in his first letter to the church at Corinth discussing how "ALL" are stewards of the Gospel. In *1 Corinthians 16*, he approaches from a different side of stewardship – wealth redistribution for a need. He makes no apology for urging the Corinthians to follow through on their commitment to give to starving believers in Jerusalem. There are numerous words used in the New Testament, primarily by Paul, to define "grace giving" or giving from one's heart to meet a need:

a. *"Collection"* in the Greek is *"logia"* and means just that – "gather" (*1 Corinthians 16:1*).
b. *"Liberality,"* or *"gift,"* as he references in *Verse 3*, the Greek being *"charis,"* is our base word for "charity" – literally means "grace giving."
c. *Romans 15:26* references the word *"contribution"–"koinonia"* in the Greek, meaning "fellowship offering."
d. *2 Corinthians 9:5*, Paul uses the word *"eulogia"* – *"gift,"* which means "bounty or blessing."
e. *2 Corinthians 9:12*, he calls it a *"diakonia"–"service"* or "ministry."
f. *Acts 24:17* speaks of *"alms"* or *"offerings"* – *"eleemosune"* in the Greek, which means "kind act."

Putting these Scriptural references together, would lead us to surmise New Testament stewardship means "a kind act from one's bounty or blessings, of grace giving for a particular ministry or need." All instances reference missions giving, the key word being found in *1 Corinthians 16:3*–"*liberality*" or "*gift*"–"grace giving." Paul charges the Corinthians, as he did the churches in Galatia, regarding stewardship through "grace-giving." In *1 Corinthians 16:2*, he lays down a formula for sustained stewardship that is unequaled and should be taught to young and old alike as a regular Christian practice. We should be reminded – this is not the "tithe" – rather giving from the heart – not under obligation – but for specific needs. There is a distinct difference. He gives four principles as a guide:

1. "*On the first day of every week*" – Giving is to be regular and systematic, not haphazard and spasmodic.

2. "*Each one of you*" – Paul says there are no exceptions. Rich and poor are to come with their offerings for the needy. Paul assumes all believers understand they are to be givers. "Grace giving" is not a choice.

3. "*Should set aside*"–Some scholars interpret this to mean, laying one's offerings aside at home. However, the prevalent translation of this command is that the offerings be brought to the place where the Corinthians assembled for worship – homes–as an act of worship or service. These were not to be stored at one's private home until his arrival in Corinth. The later plan would have necessitated an offering when Paul arrived, and this is what he was seeking to avoid.

4. "*In keeping with your income*" – "Grace giving" was to be proportionate, based on one's ability; not on one's "gross adjusted income." It should also be noted in context: *Luke 12:48 – "From everyone who has been given much, much will be demanded; and from the one who has been entrusted with much, much more will be asked."* Paul further elaborates in *2 Corinthians 9:6-7* (referencing this same collection for the Jerusalem saints) – "*Remember this: Whoever sows sparingly will also reap sparingly and whoever sows generously will also reap generously. Each man should give what he has decided in his heart to give, not reluctantly or under compulsion, for God loves a cheerful giver.*" Bottom line, God doesn't want us calculating "gross or net," 10%, or fretting over an obligatory "tithe" we are told is required. "Grace giving" may

be less than 10%; on the other hand, it could be a lot more. Either way, we are all to give and we are to do it, not out of reluctance or requirement, but from the heart and joyfully. Just as there is no temple curtain, no earthly high priest, no temple tax, no animal sacrifices – all made obsolete by the coming of Jesus Christ – there appears no New Covenant requirement for a 10% tithe.

5. *"Then, when I arrive, I will give letters of introduction to the men you approve and send them with your gift to Jerusalem. If it seems advisable for me to go also, they will accompany me"–1 Corinthians 16:3-4.* Here Paul details good accounting and accountability procedures. He asked them to pick a committee to take the collection to Jerusalem with him. Scripture also tells us the churches at Berea, Derbe and Thessalonica sent delegates to present their gifts to the elders in Jerusalem, along with Paul, Timothy, Barnabas and Luke

There is much to learn from Paul's admonitions. Giving, as Paul describes it, is for a specific purpose and need and should be done so liberally and joyfully. Nowhere in the New Testament do we find "grace giving" applying to the funding of salaries for clergy and covering the overhead for iconic buildings and campuses. Regardless of what is being preached, it is just not Biblical. Beware an ulterior motive.

Chapter 4

WHY NOT TAX?

"Therefore, it is necessary to submit to the authorities. Not only because of possible punishment but also as a matter of conscience. This is also why you pay taxes, for the authorities are God's servants, who give their full time to governing. Give to everyone what you owe them: if you owe taxes, pay taxes; if revenue, then revenue; if respect, then respect; if honor, then honor" – Romans 13:5-7.

April 15th is a day all Americans are excited to see arrive – NOT! Ask people what day Columbus Day falls and most could not tell you; ask what day is "Tax Day," and all know – at least those who pay taxes. Since my dad was self-employed, I recall many times as a kid riding with him to the post office at 11:55 pm on April 14th to mail his tax returns. Trust me, they were not placed in the mail slot until 11:59 pm. I never understood that ploy, at least until I came of "tax-age."

There is a saying I believe attributed to Benjamin Franklin – *"The only thing sure in life is death and taxes."* That is not entirely correct. All of us will face death – that part is true; all of us do not pay taxes. There are five groups in the United States who do not pay taxes: foreign citizens; low-income taxpayers; those with many deductions; those with many dependents; and not-for-profit organizations.[65] Section 501©3, of the Internal Revenue Code notes a not for profit organization qualifying under this section is exempt from paying taxes. Churches, or "religious entities," fall under this section. Technically, one could invent a church, apply for a 501©3 deduction and not pay tax. Those entities qualifying as 501©3 are responsible for covering their own expenses.

According to the Internal Revenue Service, "the term "church" is found, but not specifically defined, in the IRS Code. With the exception of the special rules for church audits, the use of the term "church" also includes conventions and associations of churches as well as integrated auxiliaries of a church. Certain characteristics are generally attributed to churches. These attributes of a church have been developed by the IRS and by court decisions. They include: distinct legal existence; recognized creed and form of worship; definite and distinct ecclesiastical government; formal code of doctrine and discipline; distinct religious history; membership not associated with any other church or denomination; organization of ordained ministers; ordained ministers selected after completing prescribed courses of study; literature of its own; established places of worship; regular congregations; regular religious services; Sunday schools for the religious instruction of the young; and schools for the preparation of its members. The IRS generally uses a combination of these characteristics, together with other facts and circumstances, to determine whether an organization is considered a "church" for federal tax purposes."[66] It appears the basis for much of today's Protestant church structure and organization may be based on IRS mandates more so than the Scriptures.

In addition, members or contributors who donate to 501©3 organizations can claim tax deductions for contributions. According to IRS publication 526, one can generally claim up to 60% of one's adjusted gross income for charitable contributions which include tithes to a religious entity. The individual's taxes are reduced by the reduction of adjusted taxable income.

Code Section 107(2) also allows for a "parsonage exemption," applying only to "ordained ministers of the gospel" (not afforded to leaders of non-religious 501©3 organizations; "gospel" being loosely defined – "gospel" of what?). Qualifiers can exclude the cost of their housing when filing their taxes. In many cases this can also include property taxes – state and local.[67] According to the "New York Times," "this benefit saves clergy, including non-Christian leaders, $800 million annually in taxes, per the latest estimate from the congressional Joint Committee on

Taxation."[68] I might add, this deduction is a hot topic at present, based on the number of pending court cases. All in all, a qualifying religious leader making a "high five or six figure salary," coupled with perks (car expenses, travel allowance, housing allowance, etc.), along with these tax deductions, make religious leadership a pretty lucrative profession for "*peddling the gospel.*"

Matthew Branaugh, Editor, "Content and Business Development," notes the COVID 19 pandemic is "forcing many church leaders to assess their budgets and expenses. In some instances, decisions about cutting back on personnel – traditionally a church's largest expense – are surfacing. Those decisions are spawning another storm of significant consequence: employees laid off by their churches most likely are not allowed to apply for unemployment benefits. That is because the vast majority of states exempt churches from paying unemployment taxes. When churches do not pay in, employees who are let go are ineligible for any unemployment benefits associated with their previous ministry work." He also notes churches can voluntarily pay unemployment taxes, but quoting Robert Brockman Jr., a California based attorney representing numerous churches, "they are the minority; the vast majority do not participate."[69] The downside is the disadvantage to the employee should he/she be furloughed ; the upside, as shown, is churches rarely cut staff – it is the mission portion of the budget that takes the hit when budget restrictions become necessary.

Ask most churchgoers today who they consider the founder of today's "church of man," and most would likely answer, "why Jesus Christ of course." As earlier noted, today's church has little resemblance to the New Testament Church of the Apostles, since today's counterpart traces most of its formality, ritual, and ceremony to the Reformation and arguably to the founder of the modern-day church itself – the Roman Emperor Constantine. If one seeks a deeper challenge, similarities are traceable to the Jewish religion of the Old Testament abolished by Jesus Christ and affirmed by the Romans in 70 A.D. with the destruction of the Temple.

Constantine was the first to grant tax exempt status for all church property.[70] Tradition, with some historical basis, notes Constantine converted to Christ in 312 A.D., prior to the Battle of Milvian Bridge, when on the eve of that battle, he supposedly saw a sign of the cross in the sky foretelling of his impending victory.[71] With the positive result of that battle, he became Caesar of the Western Empire and later, in 324 A.D., Emperor of Rome itself. Whether his supposed conversion to Christianity was genuine or not, is the conjecture of many historians and theologians. Many believe his conversion was politically motivated since he continued to worship and honor his pagan gods, especially Mithras, considered the god of the sun; he also added the cross to his coins on one side, but kept the sun on the other side, apparently attempting to appease both deities.[72] Regardless, Constantine's contribution to the modern-day church was dramatic, timely (since it appeared to legitimatize Christianity) and everlasting. Shortly after becoming emperor, Constantine ordered the construction of church buildings – replacing the house churches established by the early apostles, attempting to gain acceptance and political legitimacy among the Christians. Since the pagans worshipped their gods in elaborate temple complexes, he felt it unfair the Christians be relegated to small house churches, even though this was God's way as established in *Acts 2:42-47*. It should be noted, Christianity has never experienced such magnitude of spiritual blessing since.

Christianity was ripe for the picking with the suffering and persecution that had been endured under earlier emperors, especially Nero. Constantine did not make Christianity the official religion of the empire and continued to support both Christianity and paganism, but without question, most of today's "church" traditions, including its furnishings, buildings, adornments, and formalities, etc., can be traced back to Greco-Roman pagan cultures and back to Constantine himself.

The early New Testament Church was opposed to the paganistic world system but appeared to change during the fourth century when many of these pagan practices were incorporated into the Christian church. By the third century A.D., evidence can be seen regarding worldly infiltration into the church as the church began to lose its influence in the world it was called to win. The Gnostic influence, in addition to persecution and the pressures of segregating oneself from the world, were all confronted by the early Apostles, and can be readily seen in their writings. Paul wrote to the young Timothy in his second Letter and encouraged him to guard the Gospel (*2 Timothy 1:14*), persevere, and continue proclaiming it (*2 Timothy 3:14; 4:2*) and to suffer, or if necessary, give his life for it (*2 Timothy 1:8; 2:3*). James wrote his Epistle encouraging Jewish believers who had been dispersed by persecution. As the Gospel began to come under increasingly intense fire from the outside world, Peter, in his first Letter, wrote to suffering believers—*"encouraging you and testifying this is the true grace of God" (1 Peter 5:12)*. In his second Letter, he warned believers on how to recognize and deal with false teachers and agents of Satan within the body who had infiltrated the church with their worldly doctrine – *"But there were also false prophets among the people, just as there will be false teachers among you" (2 Peter 2:1)*. Paul warns the Corinthian believers – *"Satan himself masquerades as an angel of light. It is not surprising, then, if his servants masquerade as servants of righteousness. Their end will be what their actions deserve" (2 Corinthians 11:14-15)*. In his three Letters, the Apostle John warned of the same false doctrines that had infiltrated the body and warned of the dangers of catering to the world at the expense of the Gospel's teachings – *"Do not love the world or anything in the world. If anyone loves the world, love for the Father is not in them" (1 John 2:15)*.

Paul issued a stern warning to Timothy as a young leader in the *"ekklesia"* of Ephesus, that the driving force of worldly influence within the church would be fueled by greed or the desire for monetary gain – *"For the love of money is a root of all kinds of evil" (1 Timothy 6:10)*. He warned him this desire would be so great, those so consumed would attempt to deceive true believers into believing what they were doing was Godly, putting agents of Satan into teaching positions to add a false sense of truth to their contentions – *"Everyone who wants to live a godly life in Christ Jesus will be persecuted, while evildoers and impostors will go from bad to worse, deceiving and being deceived. For the time will come when people will not put up with sound doctrine. Instead, to suit their own desires, they will gather around them a great number of teachers to say what their itching ears want to hear" (2 Timothy 3:12-13; 4:3)*.

Even Jesus warned, attempting to appease the world for the sake of money is "hatred" of God – *"No one can serve two masters. Either you will hate the one and love the other, or you will be devoted to the one and despise the other. You cannot serve both God and money" (Matthew 6:24)*. As individuals, when money or the desire for it becomes our impetus for life, it becomes our idol; the same holds true for the church. Compare how much time is spent in our churches regarding money and the need for it – stewardship committees, counting committees, trustees, business meetings, budgets, pledge cards, "love" offerings, "special needs offerings," raffles, yard sales, car washes, etc., etc. How does this compare to strategic planning sessions on how to win the community to Christ? By comparison, one can quickly see where a church's heart lies. From those fellowships–and they comprise the majority – beware and steer clear!

Nothing has gained the "church of man's" attention more than the issue of taxation. Forget false teaching, false leaders, false doctrine, worldly influence, or lack of spiritual outreach – just keep your hands off our money! As taxation is near and dear to the heart of the working individual, so it is with today's "church." As in the days of Christ's earthly ministry, the tax collector was the hated of the hated–the worst of sinners. Association of any type with the tax collector brought the wrath of the religious elite. Hence why Jesus was so assailed because of His calling and association with Matthew and his cohorts – *"While Jesus was having dinner at Levi's house, many tax collectors and sinners were eating with Him and His disciples, for there were many who followed Him. When the teachers of the law, who were Pharisees saw him eating with the sinners and tax collectors, they asked his disciples: 'Why does He eat with tax collectors and sinners'?" (Mark 2:15-16)*. Seems this hatred and bitterness for the tax collector and the tax is still evident today. No issue brings more "righteous wrath" from today's "church" than – "should it be taxed?"

Based on the initiatives of Constantine and their lasting influence, "Church property used for religious purposes was granted tax-exempt status in early England, *BASED ON THE RATIONALE THAT THE CHURCH RELIEVE THE STATE OF SOME GOVERNMENTAL WELFARE FUNCTIONS, THEREFORE DESERVING A BENEFIT IN RETURN. THE ENGLISH STATUTE OF CHARITABLE USES OF 1601, WHICH INCLUDED CHURCHES ALONG WITH ALL OTHER CHARITABLE INSTITUTIONS, FORMED THE BASIS OF AMERICA'S MODERN TAX EXEMPTION FOR CHARITIES."* Tax exempt status for the church was granted by English lawmakers in exchange for the church assuming welfare responsibility for the needy. By 1776, nine of the original thirteen colonies were offering varying types of tax relief to churches. However, all did not bode well; opposition was expressed by at least three presidents – Madison, Garfield, and Grant. Grant submitted a petition containing 35,000 signatures to Congress in 1875, demanding "that churches and other ecclesiastical property shall be no longer exempt from taxation." He further noted, "church properties resulted in approximately $83 million in lost revenue at that time and doubling by 1860. By 1900, the estimated sum exceeded $3 billion."[73]

U.S. churches have received official IRS tax exemption status since 1894, which includes property, donations and as a 501©3, other perks due to employees and staff. It should also be noted, this is another contribution to the tax system attributed to Constantine. In 313 A.D., he made Christian clergy exempt from paying taxes since pagan and Roman Catholic priests were also afforded the same privilege.[74] According to the "IRS, Parsonage Exemption, and Johnson Amendment" – "The United States IRS classifies churches as 501© 3 nonprofit charitable organizations, which are exempt from federal income tax and are able to accept tax-deductible donations. Unlike secular charities, churches are automatically considered to be 501© 3 organizations. As earlier noted, using a benefit known as the "parsonage exemption" (or "parish exemption"), licensed, commissioned, or ordained ministers of "religion" (this could include Satanic, Atheistic, or any entity classified as "religious" in nature) may deduct most of the money they spend on housing from their federal income tax and these properties are often exempt from state property taxes."[75] Ensuing legal battles have erupted from other charitable entities who cannot legally participate in these deductions, since at the present time, these tax perks are reserved for men and women of the cloth. There is no evidence to support that CEO's of any other 501© 3 organizations are afforded this perk. One wonders – since Scripture declares true believers an ordained priesthood in the body of Christ – *"But you are a chosen people, a royal priesthood, a holy nation, God's special possession, that you may declare the praises of him who called you out of darkness into His wonderful light" (1 Peter 2:9)* – if the rest of us would qualify for such an exemption? I might try that on my next tax return and see if the IRS agrees.

As with any issue, there are both proponents and opponents and taxing the church is no different. Opponents against taxing the church argue tax exemption is guaranteed under our constitution and therefore upholds the separation of church and state. Their basis for support of tax exemption is historical, going back to our English forefathers granting tax exemption in England, which is the basis for our judicial and taxation system in our country today – "CHURCHES DESERVE A TAX

BREAK BECAUSE THEY PROVIDE CRUCIAL SOCIAL SERVICES WITHIN THE COMMUNITY THEREBY TAKING THE RESPONSIBILITY FOR WELFARE OFF THE GOVERNMENT."

Proponents counterargue that giving churches tax exempt status violates the separation of church and state but are a right and not a privilege. They argue, churches overall have neglected their service to the community as a welfare monitor, forcing the government to take on the role originally mandated to the church, which has resulted in a subsidy worth billions of dollars annually the government cannot afford. With churches today spending an average of 85-95% of their income on themselves, as a card-carrying member of both the church and the IRS "taxpayers society," they may have a point.

Not surprisingly, according to the organization, "Debate.org," based on a web site survey, 74% of respondents said, "yes," to the question – "Should the church pay taxes?"[76] Some of the reasons provided by participants to support their premise were:

a. "The cost of government should be shared equally."

b. "Separation between church and State pertains to freedom of Religion; pay your taxes just like other businesses, which is what you are."

c. "Why should a church not be treated like any other business? It is a business plain and simple."

d. "Why would a church not want to pay their fair share? Seems hypocritical to me."

e. "Tax exemption for churches increases the amount of tax others have to pay and denies the government a valuable source of income."

f. "Churches tell parishioners who and how to vote; if they want to get involved in government, make them pay taxes."

Reasons provided for keeping churches tax exempt:

a. "Churches are not subsidized; they are non-profit and should be treated the same as other non-profit organizations."

b. "To tax the church would be forcing members to use their money to fund causes they do not support for religious reasons."

c. "If churches are forced to give up their 501©3 status, then the government can tell them and force them to do and say what the government wants."

d. "To tax the church is a clear violation of the concept of separation of church and State."

e. "Taxing the church will hurt and close many benevolent services they support due to lack of funding because of the tax requirement."

f. "Churches are not in business to make a profit; therefore, they should be treated as the non-profit entity they are."

According to the IRS website, it is "guesstimated" $1,118 billion is spent on "welfare" in the U.S. – federal, state and local. This includes $650 billion for Medicaid and $467 billion for "all other." It should be noted, these are strictly estimates and do not include welfare for illegal immigrants, since the numbers of illegals cannot be confirmed; additional estimates for that group range from $11 billion–$22 billion annually. Per the "Washington Post," "if churches paid their "fair share," based on standard IRS rates levied on businesses of similar size and income, it would amount to over $83 billion and would cover the $76 billion the government spends on federal welfare, with the remaining $7.3 billion covering housing for every homeless person in America."[77] It should be noted, this premise is debatable.

If the basis for granting the church freedom from taxation was its commitment to assume the welfare role from the state, thereby absolving the government of such responsibility, the question arises – is the church maintaining its end of the agreement, or has it chosen to switch its strategy to addressing its own wants and comforts rather than those it initially committed to serve? When a church chooses to spend a disproportionate amount of its monies on itself rather than the Great Commission and the needs of the world, it can be classified as "inwardly focused." Thom Ranier, former CEO of "Lifeway," says, "An inwardly focused budget is one where a disproportionate share of the budget is used to meet the needs and comforts of the members instead of reaching beyond the walls of the church."[78] "A dying church's solutions are always inwardly focused, not wanting to discuss reaching the lost and benevolence to the needy, but rather how they can make church more comfortable and palatable for its members."[79]

Reverend Brandon Ware's commentary on Ranier's book, "Autopsy of A Deceased Church," notes, "A fourth thing that these churches all had in common was that their budget moved inwardly. Jesus said, *'For where your treasure is, there your heart will be also' (Matthew 6:21)*. Not only is this true of individuals, it is also true of churches. Where the money of the church goes, there also goes its heart. In many of the deceased churches, the personnel portion of the budget steadily increased over the years. It was not that the churches were paying their staff more; rather the personnel portion of the budget increased proportionally to the declining total each year. Less and less money was available in the budget, but personnel costs were the last thing to be cut. Instead, they cut other operational expenses. They even cut missions giving down and ministry funding out of the budget. In dying churches, the last expenditures to be reduced are those that keep the members most comfortable. When a church has an inward focus rather than a missional focus, it will always be reflected in its budget. The church is on a death march when it cares more for its own needs than the lost community and world that surrounds it." [80]

So, what percentage spent on its own needs and desires constitutes a church that is considered "inwardly focused?" As reported in Chapter 2, "up to 95% of all church budgets in the US are spent on their own comforts and programs. Less than 1% is spent on evangelism."[81] Author and founder of "Group Publishing" and "Lifetree Café," Thom Schultz, reports—"Churches in America spend 82% of their average church budget on personnel, buildings, and administration. In comparison – for the same items – Red Cross 8%; World Vision 14%; Compassion International 16%. It's made worse by how funds are allocated – 3% children, 2% adults, & 1% benevolence."[82]

There are many arguable points pro and con for what genuinely goes to benevolent missions in a church budget and what does not. Performing a self-examination of the spending plan of one's own church may yield some surprises. From my own church budget (2018-19), I "liberally" identified my church as 14.6% outwardly focused or 85.4% inwardly attentive. It should be noted this outlay includes 10% of the operational budget dedicated to a denominational program where designated monies are funneled to the state convention for dispersion to pre-approved "mission" and organizational outlets.

Southern Baptist Churches consist of approximately 16 million members, 45,000 churches, 1174 associations, and forty-two state conventions.[83] According to the denomination's website, "individuals give tithes and offerings to their local church and participating churches forward a portion of their undesignated funds to their state convention. During the annual meeting of each state convention, messengers from local churches across the state decide what percentage of the gifts stay in the state to support local missions and what percentage goes to the Southern Baptist Convention to support U.S. and international missions. This is what the Southern Baptist Convention calls the "Cooperative Program."[84] According to the "ERLC" ("Ethics and Religious Liberty Commission") of the SBC, "approximately 38.7% of monies on average are allocated to the Southern Baptist Convention from the states – of which, 73% go to world missions, 22% to SBC seminaries, 3% to the denomination's operational budget, and 1.65% to the ERLC." [85]

In a recent blog, Matt Svoboda, a former Executive Pastor and President of his own services and consulting business – "ChurchOps"–shared this comment, "I have always had the philosophy that churches should aim for a budget that gave 50% of their income to missions, local and foreign. I know this is a lofty goal and for some churches, it just is not possible. Nonetheless, I think it is a healthy goal for every church to strive for. Your opinions welcome."[86]

Holy Toledo!!!! What a firestorm of response from religion's CEO's!!!!

. . .

Jeff

"My church's annual offerings total about $150,000 (which is not bad for a church as small as mine).

Are we supposed to pay for the following on $75,000?"

(1) Pastor's salary, health insurance, and retirement.

(2) Part-time secretary's salary.

(3) Custodian's salary.

(4) Part-time music minister's salary.

(5) $20,000 of building insurance (we are stuck with a very large building for a small membership).

(6) Other liability insurance.

(7) Utilities for a large building.

(8) Maintenance on the building.

(9) Local benevolence.

I suppose there will be people who would say that we should not own a building or have any paid staff but let us be realistic. We are stuck with both the staff and the building."

. . .

Brent

"Back a few years ago, I heard the missions giving should be 1/3 of the church budget. I have always considered that exceptional and a goal to work for.

Seeing as how average staff expenditures for a church are 40-60% of the budget, I do not think 50% is particularly realistic.

We moved this budget year from just under 7% missions giving to a little over 11%. I did emphasize that prominently to our church the Sunday before we approved the budget."

. . .

Rick

"With regards to budget only, our breakdown is as follows:

13% missions

50% salaries and benefits

12% ministries

5% administration

20% building maintenance

Every situation may be different, but we would be hard pressed to push missions giving to 50% of budget. It is so unrealistic we would be forced to fire half the staff, sell the building, cut most of our ministry events and basically cease functioning as a local church. Membership would be driven away to those churches still offering youth, children, and music ministries. It would truly wipe us out. I appreciate your heart for missions, but I think the 50% figure is generally unrealistic for most churches."

If I'm not mistaken, the New Testament church of *Acts 2*, contributed 100% to missions – *"They sold property and possessions to give to anyone who had need" – Acts 2:45*. What in the world has happened over the past 1900 plus years?

Those of us who have owned or managed a business would likely agree, the death of a business is "overhead." "Overhead" can be lightly described as those costs that are not related to the cost of producing a product. For example, if a company is making metal desks, direct costs would include steel, hardware, production labor, welding supplies, etc. "Overhead" costs would include all others – pencils, pens, administrative labor, insurance, etc., etc. One of the keys for making and keeping a business solvent is to limit overhead. In any business, including the church, the largest overhead expense is typically indirect labor, which contrary to many opinions within the church, is not a fixed cost (necessity). From a business standpoint, fixed costs must be monitored closely to make sure one is obtaining the most competitive rates., but they are most difficult to control since taxes and utilities do not lend themselves to negotiation. However, "indirect" or variable costs – those costs associated with "overhead"–must be adjusted accordingly to maintain solvency. Since personnel costs are typically a company's largest outlay and are considered variable, they are usually the first adjustment a business makes when they sense financial threats against profitability. Ironically, personnel positions and accompanying expenses within the church are considered taboo and are never addressed as a cost-cutting option; it is the mission portion of the budget that typically absorbs the impact.

What does all this have to do with taxing the church? There is a saying echoed from the past I have heard spoken many times – "if the church would fulfill its benevolent obligation to the community it serves, then there would be no need for the government to be in the welfare business." There is a world of truth in that statement. There is a difference between the benevolence assigned to the church and what the government calls "welfare." When we speak of benevolence, we are referencing true needs and assistance designed to put one back on his or her feet, so once standing, they are equipped to pay their own way. In other words, church benevolence should be designed as a means of assistance until one is able to supply their own needs; government welfare has arguably become government adoption, which in some cases, may be for life.

Church benevolence also differs from government benevolence in other ways, but the most important, the church offers both missions and ministry – addressing the spiritual need at the same time they are meeting the physical need. One cannot be properly addressed without the other. In other words, we cannot take care of the spiritual needs without addressing the physical needs, and vice versa – "*What good is it my brothers and sisters, if someone claims to have faith but has no deeds? Can such faith save them? Suppose a brother or sister is without clothes and daily food. If one of you says to them, 'Go in peace; keep warm and well fed,' but does nothing about their physical needs, what good is it? In the same way, faith by itself, if it is not accompanied by action, is dead*" – *James 2:14-17*. Government can offer the missions, but not the ministry.

As noted, government assistance may help one to stand but typically does nothing to teach and assist one to pay his own way once upright. The problem in many cases is, the government has neither the time, money, nor resources to verify each case. Adding to the problem, children born into welfare homes tend to be raised in this "entitlement" atmosphere, thereby growing up believing they are rightfully owed permanent assistance. Another important advantage to church benevolence within the community is the community served by the church should be known inside and out – the church intimately familiar with the need and able to verify the need is legit. It is much more difficult, if not impossible, for the government to adequately verify true needs from false ones.

So – has the church lived up to its end of the bargain with Uncle Sam? As noted, our judicial and legislative foundations (including our tax regulations) were adopted from our English forefathers, giving the church tax exemption, providing the church meet the social and economic needs of the community it serves, thereby removing that responsibility from the government. Has that responsibility and commitment been relegated back to the government being replaced with the church's attention to its own desires? According to the "Heritage Foundation," "the exclusively federal share of spending on government welfare programs is up 32% since 2008 and comprises 21% of federal outlays (more than Social Security, Medicare, or defense)."[87] With the church now spending 85-95% of its income on itself with less and less emphasis on missions outside its four walls, it would indeed appear the church has reneged on its obligation to pick up society's welfare tab it initially agreed to fund. One can see why proponents for church taxation are quick to note, "why not tax the church or force her to live up to what she agreed, but relinquished?"

Let us look at additional arguments for and against taxing the church and the possible results:

    a.   "Taxing the church will cause many churches to close and drive us into the dark ages of religion." Truth is many churches should have closed long ago. Numbers of churches within my own denomination have not baptized a single soul in the past several years.[88] If churches are not reaching the lost, why keep the doors open?

b. "Despite the numbers, churches do provide viable benevolent services." True. However, this still does not mask the fact that churches are spending 85-95% of their budgets on themselves.

c. "Less money will cause many churches to cut back on the services they offer to their members and community." There is truth and fallacy with this argument. It may force the "church" to cut back on its own extravagance which would draw it closer to a re-constituted New Testament Church of *Acts 2:42-47.*

d. "Young people and young couples either do not support the church financially or struggle to and by taxing the church and adding more financial burden, more of these young folks will leave." Young people, especially young couples, are smarter than most church people give them credit. Most live by budgetary restrictions at home and expect their church to do the same. When the church fails in its mission to do so, they choose not to support it.

e. "The government has no business taxing the church as mandated by the constitution." Well, possibly – and possibly not. If the church was given tax exemption because she assumed the responsibility of social benevolence from the government, but relinquished that responsibility, is the government not in its legal right to levy taxes? As some argue, the constitution may grant us the freedom of religion unregulated by government restriction, but does that take away our social responsibility for community benevolence? Are we setting the right example and testimony for what we say we stand for?

Most of us have elbows just as most of us have opinions. As with the size and shape of the elbows, opinions are just as varied. You are not interested in my opinion, nor am I necessarily interested in yours. What I think or you think is not important. What is of the utmost importance is what the Word of God says. *Matthew 22:21 – "So give back to Caesar what is Caesar's, and to God what is God's." Romans 13:1-4 – "Let everyone be subject to the governing authorities, for there is no authority except that which God has established. The authorities that exist Have been established by God. Consequently, whoever rebels against the authority is rebelling against what God has instituted, and those who do so will bring judgment on themselves. For rulers hold no terror for those who do right, but for those who do wrong. Do you want to be free from fear of the one in authority? Then do what is right and you will be commended. For the one in authority is God's servant for your good. But if you do wrong, be afraid, for rulers do not bear the sword for no reason. They are God's servants, agents of wrath to bring punishment on the wrongdoer."*

You be the judge – or once again – He will be – or may already have.

Chapter 5

WHY NOT
HOUSE CHURCHES?

"Day after day, in the temple courts and from 'house to house,' they never stopped teaching and proclaiming the good news that Jesus is the Christ" – Acts 5:42.

Several years ago, I was asked by a friend in Christ who is "Director of Missions" in our local association of churches[89] to serve as Associational Director of Sunday School or Small Group Bible Study. It was here I began to look and fixate on "church" numbers. During the past recording year (2017-18), it was noted of the twenty-four churches in our association, 25% had not led a single person to Christ based on baptisms; 80% had led zero to Christ ages 12-17, and 60% zero baptisms ages 18-29.[90] If rationalization helps, these numbers are in line with the denomination in general.

In a church Bible study group of around twenty couples I formerly led–ranging in age from 18 to 88–one young lady in her early twenties asked to speak to me after one of the sessions. She had started a Bible Study in her home. It began with family – cousins and relatives–who did not know the Lord or who may have been exposed to the Gospel, but never reacted. Cousins and in-laws began to invite friends and neighbors, ballooning the Bible Study to around eighteen participants at the time of this writing. She also shared there had been salvations.

Since we have already established the "church" is a business, and *if* this small home Bible Study were a business and I had finances to invest, where would I logically invest my efforts based on profitability – profitability being defined as "souls?" Here is a small group Bible Study meeting in a home – no music director, no children's director, no "preacher," no youth director, no minister of education, no associate pastor, no literature expense, no budget, no multi-million-dollar building investment with accompanying bank payments, etc., etc., etc. – yet, this home Bible Study had yielded a profit of eternal importance – SOULS. With an employment (membership) of 18 people and no overhead, it just exceeded the baptisms (spiritual profitability) of 75% of the twenty-four churches within the association of churches I represent – churches with an average membership of 393 members and an average annual budget of $250,000 or more. Where would you choose to invest? This is the New Testament Church of the *Acts of the Apostles*! It worked then – why would it not work today? To say it would not, is simply saying to God – "Sorry – but our way is better." Is it?

People are disheartened. They are disheartened politically, socially, economically and yes, spiritually. Professed Christians are not immune. People who are lost are just that – lost–blind. They are disheartened also, but in a different sense from the professed believer (*1 Corinthians 1:18 – "For the message of the cross is foolishness to those who are perishing....;" 1 Corinthians 2:14 – "The person without the Spirit does not accept the things that come from the Spirit of God, but considers them foolishness, and cannot understand them because they are discerned only through the Spirit."*). Many professed Christians tend to be disheartened because of religion. They have been disheartened and disillusioned with tradition, rites, formality, passive worship, entertainment, exorbitant budgets for buildings and salaries, to the point of being disenfranchised. The statistics prove it. They have been disheartened by a "Do Nothing" doctrine, where professed Christians sit idly by while the world around them goes to Hell. The sad problem is, the "Do Nothings" are oblivious to the fact they may be in hell with them – *"Not everyone who says to Me, 'Lord, Lord', will enter the kingdom of heaven, but only he who does the will of my Father who is in heaven" (Matthew 7:21).* Someone accurately stated that if the apostles had "acted" in this manner, there would be no *Acts of the Apostles*.

A recent article by Matthew Green, freelance writer and vice president of communications for "Pioneers," a global church-planting organization based in Orlando, Florida, emphasizes, "people who once attended church, are in a growing group who are classified as dropouts. Some quit because they may have been hurt by leaders or fellow brothers and sisters in Christ; others were disappointed by pastoral failure. However, statistics show the vast majority left and are leaving due to irrelevant church programs and the question of whether the ritual of sitting in a church pew, singing songs and listening to a sermon is what it means to obey the Scriptures."[91] Church planter and author Neil Cole adds, "of greater concern are those who don't drop out but remain in the pews as passive consumers of a religious product that never transforms their lives, convinced that the Sunday ritual somehow earns them favor with God and satisfies His radical call to discipleship."[92]

During my recent travels, I picked up a local pastor's sermon on a religious radio station in the Low State of South Carolina. His message was centered on "The New Testament Church." His opening oration stated, "he pastored a Bible believing New Testament Church built entirely on the early church as described in *Acts 2*, and he made "no apology" for the boast." The fact of the matter, he owed his entire listening audience an apology! His church, located at 000 Somewhere Street, Anytown, USA, was not a New Testament Church! New Testament churches were house churches and they reached people for the Lord Jesus Christ!

Jim Rutz of "World Net Daily" makes an interesting observation on "house churches" in the United States–"For the first time in 1700 years, simple churches meeting in homes are once again a factor in human events. Briefly stated, the number of house churches are about halfway between the Catholic church and the Southern Baptist Convention (the second largest denomination in the U.S.)."[93] George Barna, a leading U.S. church pollster, notes the following survey based on 5,013 adults, including, 663 African-Americans, 631 Hispanics, 676 Liberals and 1,608 Conservatives (with a sampling error of +/- 1.8%): "In a typical week, 9% of U.S. adults attend a house church; in real numbers, this roughly equates to 20 million people; in a typical month, about 43 million U.S. adults attend a house church; all told, 70 million U.S. adults have at least experimented with participation in a house church."[94]

Without question, the greatest growth in Christianity occurred within the first 200 years after the ministry of Jesus Christ. In the face of persecution and even death, the church grew in record numbers. With the growth and spread of Christianity in the early first century, came the first staunch efforts of Satan to destroy it. The first real slap in the face to the early Christians came with the martyrdom of Stephen. However, a major set-back it was not. In fact, it fueled the church's growth and resulting spread of the Gospel even more–*"On that day a great persecution broke out against the church in Jerusalem, and all except the apostles were scattered throughout Judea and Samaria. Godly men buried Stephen and mourned deeply for him. But Saul began to destroy the church. Going from HOUSE TO HOUSE, he dragged off men and women and put them in prison. Those who had been scattered preached the word wherever they went"* – Acts 8:1-4. Several important items to note in these passages: Saul went *"house to house"* – why? Because the early New Testament churches were just that–"house churches." He went to the places of Christian worship with intent to destroy. Secondly, with the scattering of the Christians due to the persecution, those who were scattered continued to proclaim the Gospel through the "house church" concept. In the face of the worse persecution imaginable, the Gospel continued to spread and grow through believers grounded in the faith!

"The church's greatest period of vitality and growth ended shortly thereafter with the implementation of large "church buildings" by Constantine around 300 A.D."[95] "After Christianity was acknowledged by the state and empowered to hold property, it raised houses of worship in all parts of the Roman Empire. There was probably more building of this kind in the fourth century than there has been in any period, excepting perhaps the nineteenth century in the United States."[96] David Norrington, English author and religious leader, states, "As the bishops of the fourth and fifth centuries grew in wealth, they funneled it into elaborate church building programs."[97] With the church building, arguably came the cap on spiritual growth. Darryl Erkel, author and pastor, states in his blog, "Church Buildings or House-Churches?" notes – "Whatever else church buildings were and are good for, they were not and are not essential either for numerical growth or spiritual depth. The early church possessed both these qualities – they met and worshipped in homes. In other words, the church grew fastest when it did not have the help or hindrance of church buildings."[98] "To attempt to apply New Testament church practices to our contemporary large churches is just as unnatural as pouring new wine into old wineskins (*Matthew 9:17*). Ironically, the institutional church structure has attempted to rectify this by abandoning the 'new wine' and holding on to the 'old wineskins.' Consequently, today's church more closely resembles Judaism or Catholicism than it does New Testament Christianity."[99]

The New Testament church, after the death and resurrection of Christ, brought to fruition the "house church." The New Testament never refers to the church as a physical building. In other words, there was no First Baptist of Corinth or Second Presbyterian of Ephesus. The Corinthian "ekklesia" was comprised of "house churches" – planted by Paul most likely in the home of Aquila and Priscilla after being tossed from the synagogue. It is also possible another "house church" was established in the home of Titius Justus, who lived next door to the synagogue and was one of Paul's first converts (*Acts 18:1-8*). Another possibility as a Corinthian "house church" was Crispus, the synagogue ruler who became a convert along with his entire household. *1 Corinthian 16:19* confirms another "house church" was started in Ephesus by Aquila and Priscilla where Paul was residing when writing this Letter – "*The churches in the province of Asia send you greetings. Aquila and Priscilla greet you warmly in the Lord, and so does the church that meets at their house.*" There was also a "house church" referenced in *Acts 12:12* – "*the house of Mary, the mother of John, also called Mark, where many people had gathered and were praying.*"

The early New Testament church did not invent the "house church." The very first followers of Jesus were Jews. As His influence grew, there were Samaritans (*John 4*), and maybe a few Gentiles (*Matthew 8:5-10; 15:21-28*), but the bulk were Jewish. Even after the beginning of the New Testament Church in *Acts 2*, the majority, of early Christians came from Jewish backgrounds. Many of the Gentiles who became Christians followed the practices and traditions of the Jews, which further complicated Paul's efforts in showing them the atoning blood of Jesus Christ wins out over religion, tradition, ritual and lineage. Because of this Jewish influence, early Christians based their decisions on how and where to worship on their roots. In synagogue worship members met several times per week. Typically, a synagogue met in a designated building in a community or town, but if it was new or located in a poor community setting, meetings were held in homes. Many Jewish synagogues still operate in this manner today. The early church adopted this pattern.

With the growth of the early church and a growing influence from its Gentile members, both internal and external persecutions occurred. The internal persecution was generated from devout Judaizers who remained true to the rituals of Old Testament Law. As Gentile growth continued, an attempt was made to move away from the synagogue and its Jewish influence, the new gathering places adopting the name "*ekklesia*" ("to assemble; come together") which is translated in the Greek as "church." *Acts 19:9* tells us when they outgrew homes, other gathering places for "*ekklesia*" were utilized, such as community and educational centers, but other "house churches" were created as a result. To the early believers, there was no imagination of any ornate structures or complexes which they tended to view as pagan. After all, this is what they had just escaped from through the blood of Jesus Christ.

There are two important advantages to "house churches" one must consider:

1. House churches are Biblical. Further Scriptural evidence of early Christians worshipping in their homes:
    a. *Philemon 1:2 – "To Philemon our dear friend and fellow work-er-also to Apphia our sister and Archippus our fellow soldier – and to the church that meets in your home..."*
    b. *Colossians 4:15 – "Give my greetings to the brothers and sisters at Laodicea, and to Nympha and the church in her house."*
    c. *Romans 16:5 – "Greet also the church that meets at their house."*
    d. *1 Corinthians 16:19 – "Aquila and Priscilla greet you warmly in the Lord, and so does the church that meets at their house."*
    e. *Acts 2:2 – "Suddenly a sound like the blowing of a violent wind came from heaven and filled the whole house where they were sitting."*
    f. *Acts 2:46 – "They broke bread in their homes and ate together with glad and sincere hearts, praising God and enjoying the favor of all the people."*
    g. *Acts 20:20 – "You know that I have not hesitated to preach anything that would be helpful to you but have taught you publicly and from house to house."*

h. *Acts 5:42 – "Day after day, in the temple courts and from house to house, they never stopped teaching and proclaiming the good news that Jesus is the Messiah."*

2. House Churches produce results. *Acts 2:47 – "And the Lord added to their number daily those who were being saved."*

"House churches" are not perfect, just as the institutional church is not. They are both made up of human beings and human beings who, *"Have all sinned and fallen short of the glory of God" (Romans 3:23)*. Imperfections in the New Testament "house churches" were addressed by the Apostles in their Epistles and Letters, prompting the establishment by Paul of elders and overseers to monitor the multiple groups and keep them unified in Christ. However, the Apostles believed in the concept of these fellowships and God's approval was upon them as well.

From "A Study of Denominations," "the house church movement in the United States began in earnest in the 1960's and early 70's. It began to flourish as a result of perceived abuses and failures within the institutional church, including its financial demands upon its membership to finance its operation."[100] According to George Barna, American pollster, "as many as 30,000 house churches existed in the United States as of 2009, with an estimated 6-12 million attendees."[101] Numbers cannot be confirmed due to government restrictions, but we know from reports, "house churches" in China and the Mideast are flourishing under the harshest of persecution. Per a close friend and former missionary to Indonesia, "the spread of the Gospel in Indonesia was and continues to be fostered by the "house church" in the face of horrendous Muslim persecution."[102] Worldwide, its influence is growing.

Many of today's "house churches" exist without connection to any religious denomination, although many denominations are beginning to see the relevance of the concept and are focusing more on small cell groups or "Small Group Bible Studies'" attempting to recapture those moving away from the traditional church. These small groups fostered by traditional churches can sometimes be successful, but one must be cautioned, they are not the same. The key to any "house church" or any meeting of believers for that matter, is the Word of God and Jesus Christ—*"Above all, you must understand that no prophecy of Scripture came about by the prophet's own interpretation of things. For prophecy never had its origin in the human will, but prophets, though human, spoke from God as they were carried along by the Holy Spirit" (2 Peter 1:20-21).* Belief in the inerrant, infallible, divinely inspired Word of God is the foundation for any group of believers, regardless the place of meeting. Otherwise it is of hell itself.

As we will discuss in deeper detail in a later chapter, spiritual gifts are reserved for those true believers who are both mind and heart committed to the Lord Jesus Christ. Scripture is clear the seal of the Holy Spirit is one's proof of salvation (*Romans 8:9; Ephesians 1:13-14; 1 John 3:24; 5:10*). Through the Holy Spirit the believer is blessed with a gift or gifts that are part of the Spirit's equipping power providing us with the means by which we carry out His individual plan for our lives to accomplish His universal will for the world – the Gospel for all. In his Letters to the Romans, Corinthians, and Ephesians, Paul lists a number of these gifts for bestowal. Some theologians contend certain of these gifts were reserved specifically for the Apostles, including but not limited to healing and prophesy. For sure I possess neither of these gifts, but what we may see happening today may be prophetic.

As I sit at my desk putting what I hope to be the finishing touches on this book, our world is facing the COVID-19 pandemic. Grocery shopping along with many other activities we typically take for granted, have become adventures. No human knows what the future holds, but for sure, if it is God's will for recovery to come, it will no doubt change the way we live, do business, school our children and even worship.

During a recent television news report on a local CBS station, the reporter noted, "COVID 19 has created instant home schools across the country. Looking ahead, some parents say the home school option is looking better and better. While home schooling is not for everyone, those who chose to do it have realized it opens the door of learning on a whole new level."[103] Speculation on my part, but once parents and administrators find children can be appropriately educated through computer outlets without leaving the home, it may open the door for more emphasis on home-schooling. With many school curriculums including or considering subjects that appear to be anti-Biblical, parents may have the confirmation they need to make the decision to educate their children and do it from the comforts of home. Think of the tax dollars that could be saved on transportation, buildings, and support staff should this happen.

On the same token, businesses will likely change their methodology. My background being business management, millions upon millions of dollars are spent annually to cover travel and lodging costs incurred to visit and entertain customers. Now that companies have negated their employee's travel due to the potential spread of the virus, many may find future travel and entertainment could potentially be reduced or even eliminated altogether, replacing with face to face meetings via computer. I was challenged when my doctor telephoned me to note an upcoming visit to his office for a six-month physical examination was being changed to a "virtual" office visit by cell phone.

So, what about formal religion? My family was watching a service on television this past Sunday morning from a large metropolitan church in a neighboring city. During his opening remarks, the pastor quipped, "now we know how the early New Testament believers felt being relegated to worship from home." I begged to disagree with his analogy – they were not "relegated" to the "house church"– they chose it because it was God's way and it worked.

As a result of the cancellation of many formal church services across our nation because of COVID-19, many may find worshipping through media from one's own den with one's own family and potentially a small group of neighbors and friends, is spiritually intimate and growth inducing. Rather than coming together in a non-participatory formal service in a building costing millions of dollars to construct and maintain, why not a small group Bible study where discussion rules rather than a one-man oration where no dialogue is encouraged?

The TV pastor was also quick to note, "the ministries of the church continue whether you are here or not, so please do not forget your monetary obligations." Those "obligations" include his salary, the Scriptural basis of which is arguably questioned. The "ministries," as we have already shown, are primarily "wants" and the obligations that accompany them. Think of the monetary savings that could be realized and redirected to meeting needs rather than sating desires. Utilizing the "house church" format would mean no staff, no building payments, no buses, no gyms, no coffee kiosks, no literature, no office equipment, etc., etc. Some argue this type setting would take away from the ministry of fellowship, but in a formal setting, how many people do we typically fellowship? In most formal settings, the fellowship is limited to the cliques and close friends within the cliques. "House Churches" could potentially open one's home to lost neighbors whose need for the Lord far outweighs our need for formal "fellowship." Small groups afford intimacy.

According to a television news report from an NBC affiliate in Greenville, South Carolina (March 29, 2020), the reporter relayed a familiar result from the Coronavirus pandemic–"Upstate South Carolina churches have been using online streaming platforms to share their messages. According to one pastor, 'Being in the ministry for 25 years, I've had a little saying I go by: 'Blessed are the flexible, for they shall not break.' Realistically we have found more people viewing and watching the videos of the sermon than attends our church, so it is an outreach. We've gotten shoutouts from different parts of the world'" (Dr. Michael Privett, Summit View Baptist Church, Travelers Rest, South Carolina).[104] Doctor Don Wilton (Pastor First Baptist Church, Spartanburg, South Carolina) noted in his television and on-line message of April 26, 2020, twenty-two souls outside the body contacted the church expressing a desire for salvation based on his Gospel message shared during the previous week's broadcast. A member of the body shared by video the baptism of his own daughter in the bathtub of their home after coming to know Christ during the previous week. Not being computer literate, it was nothing short of amazing to me, to see ninety-six musicians and choir members singing in unison from their individual homes and broadcast through on-line streaming.

According to the NBC affiliate report, another pastor from a sister fellowship noted, "The idea of having to preach a sermon to a computer is strange, to say the least. But views on our online sermons have been gaining steam. Members of the church have been sharing with their friends on Facebook and in turn have drawn some new eyes and ears to our messages, eyes and ears that may otherwise not have heard our message in the sanctuary. Honestly, in a unique way, it may be a view of evangelism that we never really thought about sharing. A friend of a friend type of thing. I think one of the most difficult ideas of not meeting as a church on a regular basis is, how do you continue to fund a church when you are in a situation when people aren't here to bring their tithes and offerings in?" Money aside, the pastor understands the issue – "At some point, I think people are going to realize what really is important, and especially in the case of fear of death or sickness with coronavirus, I think people are really going to say, 'Well, what's really important'? And it is a relationship with God, relationship with each other and how I can help other people." (Dr. Clay Faulk, Lee Road Church and Connect Church, Taylors, South Carolina and Greenville South Carolina).

Small group "house churches" would also restore the responsibility for the spiritual growth of our children to the parent as outlined by God Himself in Scripture, rather than being relegated to the Sunday School teacher or Children's Director, the latter coming with a substantial price tag – "*These commandments that I give you today are to be on your hearts. Impress them on your children. Talk about them when you sit at home and when you walk along the road, when you lie down and when you get up. Tie them as symbols on your hands and bind them on your foreheads. Write them on the doorframes of your houses and on your gates. Fix these words of mine in your hearts and minds; tie them as symbols on your hands and bind them on your foreheads. Teach them to your children, talking about them when you sit at home and when you walk along the road, when you lie down and when you get up. Write them on the doorframes of your houses and on your gates, so that your days and the days of your children may be many in the land the Lord swore to give your ancestors, as many as the days that the heavens are above the earth*" – Deuteronomy 6:6-9; 11:18-20.

Plus, and best of all, we have the Lord's own assurance of success – "*For where two or three gather in My name, there am I with them*" – *Matthew 18:20*. Perhaps God is truly moving us in His direction rather than seeking our own desires and self-centered methodologies. Is the "house church" a viable model for the 21st century? When one considers the distractions within a traditional church – money, programs, titles, committees, petty responsibilities, buildings, cliques, etc., and compares to the "house church" where spontaneity, dedication to the Word of God, prayer, intimate fellowship, mutual participation and addressing needs exists, it would seem to be a "no-brainer" when properly analyzed. Consider the results.

Chapter 6

WHY 'FORMAL' WORSHIP?

"The highest form of worship is the worship of unselfish Christian service. The greatest form of praise is the sound of consecrated feet seeking out the lost and helpless" – Billy Graham.

As discussed in Chapter 1, the typical definition of "church" rendered by most is – "a place of worship." We noted two fallacies involving this statement – the first being, "church" is not a place, but rather people – believers – the *"ekklesia."* The second fallacy with this definition is "worship." What do we mean by a place of "worship?" What is "worship?" "Formal worship" and its repetitive rituals steeped in tradition, died with the elimination of the Old Covenant through Jesus Christ and the destruction of the Temple by the Romans in 70 A.D. Why then has man resurrected what Christ came to destroy? What exactly is a "worship service?" Perhaps we have this backward – rather than referencing a "worship service," we should understand "worship *IS* service."

Most see the "worship service" as an event, supposedly in the name of the Lord involving coming to a "steepled" building on a weekly basis – usually on Sundays–to perform or participate in an "act" which we believe is directed to God on His behalf. This event is like ice cream; it comes in different flavors and can be served in a variety of ways to suit our tastes or satisfy our psyche. It can be composed of formalities and ritual, be charismatic or outwardly expressive, and culminate with spontaneous performances that tend to be growing among the masses; two completely different and in some instances, opposing "styles," designed to earn us some degree of "brownie-points" with God and all performed in His name. The interesting aspect of all this – "What resemblance, if any, does today's 'formal worship' have with the New Testament *'ekklesia,'* of *Acts 2:42-47*? And which 'worship style' do we believe they chose?"

Another question to consider is who participates in "formal worship?" Lost people reside outside the four walls of the "church" and being spiritually blind, do not "worship" because they haven't a clue whom to "worship." Therefore, "formal worship" in the traditional church consists overwhelmingly of professed believers who have heard the Gospel and supposedly accepted its message. What message then can be delivered to those who supposedly know the Way; and if the message is obsolete, what is left other than the entertainment value? The Gospel is delivered one on one to the outside world since this is where the lost reside and we are commanded to take it. Servicing each other in a building in the name of "worship" may be what Jesus was condemning in *Matthew 15:6-9 – "Thus you nullify the word of God for the sake of your tradition. You hypocrites! Isaiah was right when he prophesied about you: 'These people honor Me with their lips, but their hearts are far from Me. They worship Me in vain; their teachings are merely human rules'."*

"Hallucinogenic" drugs are known as "psychedelics," and are drugs that change the way a person perceives the world."[105] Per the "National Institute On-Drug-Abuse," "they are a diverse group of drugs that alter a person's awareness of their surroundings as well as their own thoughts and feelings; they can sustain a periodic emotional and sensational "high." They can cause sensations that seem real but are not and can cause users to feel out of control or disconnected from their body or environment."[106] At the risk of being offensive, but not intending to be, is this not, in perhaps the remotest of ways, descriptive of many of today's "formal religious" gatherings and the influence they wield through what some call, "worship services?" Just as the user selects his drug of choice to provide him with a temporary "high," in an eerily similar way, the "formal worshipper" chooses the "worship style" that appeals to his psyche. What we end up with are events ranging from charismatic acrobatics and exotic dances, to strict traditional ritual and formality – all in the name of "worship."

The "worship style" Jesus requires is our service to His commands and our response to the Great Commission–"*Does the Lord delight in burnt offerings and sacrifices as much as in obeying the Lord? To obey is better than sacrifice, and to heed is better than the fat of rams*" – *1 Samuel 15:22*; "*Serve wholeheartedly, as if you were serving the Lord, not people*" – *Ephesians 6:7*. In *Matthew 9:12-13*, Jesus quotes *Hosea 6:6* ("*On hearing this, Jesus said, 'It is not the healthy who need a doctor, but the sick. But go and learn what this means: "I desire mercy, not sacrifice." For I have not come to call the righteous, but sinners'*."), in response to accusations from the religious leadership of the Jews, who believed worship included formality, adherence to their rules, and was the "worship" God desired, not association with tax collectors and sinners. Today's "church" has turned "worship" into an event which is performed in the name of Jesus, but realistically is directed to us and satisfying our psyche, just as the "fix" satisfies the drug user. One must consider if, by design alone, it tends to alienate us from those "tax collectors" and "sinners" outside its four walls. The process appears to foster attention to ourselves rather than preparation for outreach.

Let us look at "worship" as it is performed in many churches today, especially among Protestants. We will begin with its participants and their "fix," or "style," that most appeals to their psyche. Some claim a "traditional" or less expressive approach; more reserved and self-attentive; a quiet, non-vocal style with no outward display of emotion; usually includes a conservative dress code – suits, ties, sport coats, etc., although waning in most church's today. The other group of "worshippers" prefer a more charismatic approach, quite the opposite from the "traditional" group; they are outwardly expressive, participatory, vocal, and usually accompanied by what some would say, wild antics. Their dress code is "come-as-you-are" – shorts, jeans, pajamas, etc.–all in the name of being "spirit filled" (We will discuss in-depth later, but let's be clear – Scripture never describes the Holy Spirit as a "cheerleader" or influencer of someone to "cheerlead"). Each of these "worshippers" believe their "style" is pleasing to the Lord to the point we cannot "worship" together as one group at risk of someone being offended. Ask participants in either group and the typical response is their particular "style" puts them in the correct frame of mind to "worship." In other words, it appeals to their psyche – just as the "fix" appeals to the druggie.

Let us not forget the music – most protestant churches now offer both a "traditional" and "contemporary" "worship service," the performances designed to suit the entertainment preferences of the attendees. The music of the "traditional" service is normally hymn-based with piano or organ accompaniment, offering a softer, more serene appeal. The music of the "contemporary" service is quite the opposite. The piano is rolled away, the organ unplugged–replaced by high-wattage amps, strobe lights–the decibel levels shaking the foundations of the building itself. It is normally accompanied by electric guitars, drums and wind instruments. The songs are usually "Seven-Elevens" (seven words, sung eleven times over), all designed to hype the crowds and once again, appeal to the psyche.

One common denominator between the two "worship styles" is the final hymn, which in some Protestant churches is called the "Invitational Hymn." Even in the contemporary service, the decibel levels are usually toned down for what some call the "altar call." The "Invitation" has its critics, some believing it is psychologically manipulative, the music playing a large part. According to Iain Murray, British pastor and author, "the invitation is dangerous because it utilizes psychological, peer, and social pressure on a potential convert, placing undue pressure upon them to step out from a pew, walk an aisle, shake a hand, utter a prayer, sign a card, and consider themselves saved." [107]

What do "worship" music styles have in common with ingesting hallucinogenic drugs? According to Frank Garlock, a recognized authority in church music, "I have personally watched teenagers and adults alike (and heard many testimonies), where music, regardless the words, but the beat itself, causes one to go into ecstatic gyrations, get a far-away stare in their eyes, and act as if someone had given them a dose of LSD."[108] Frank Zappa, lead singer of the band, "Mothers of Invention," says, "music's effects on individuals shocks even me; a person can incur the same effect from music he can get from dope."[109] I have personally seen and heard "preachers" – especially charismatic ones – often say after hearing a particularly upbeat choir rendition, they are "pumped" and ready to preach! In one service I attended at a "Freewill Baptist Church" in a neighboring state, after the band concluded a stirring rendition, the "preacher" ripped off his tie, jerked off his coat tossing it into the crowd, and screamed, "I feel the spirit! I am in the spirit! Bring on the devil; I'm ready to preach!" I was ready to take cover!

Are we going to extremes comparing man's "worship styles" and the influence of music over the masses to drug use? Possibly – but we must admit, we choose "worship" styles – traditional or contemporary – based on their personal appeal and putting us in the "correct frame of mind" to "worship." It is like the restaurant buffet – choose what suits your appetite. Hopefully, the result will be an emotional, feel-good religious "high" that will carry us through until the next Sunday. If "I" am happy and sated, isn't that what "worship" is all about?

Are these "worship" styles, and their accompanying musical entertainment wrong? Maybe not – necessarily. People have been saved as a result. But how is it "worship" today has no inkling of resemblance to the church of *Acts 2:42-47* – the *"ekklesia"* – whose "worship" consisted of joint interactive study of the apostles teachings, growth of the body, meeting needs, prayer, the sacraments, and fellowship in the home . Being intentionally redundant, this was the "worship style" that pleased the Lord as once again evidenced in *Acts 2:47–"And the Lord added to their number daily those who were being saved."*

A typical Sunday morning at the Ramseys' – two "worship" services – contemporary and traditional – which do I attend? I am always baffled why God's people cannot come together because of entertainment preferences. Either way, we choose the "traditional" gathering because the entertainment factor is a little more to our psyche. The problem is the gathering begins at 8:30 AM. 8:30 AM on Sunday morning! The wife and daughter rise at 6:00 AM. I am not sure why, but since I am not awake at that time of morning, I assume it has to do with all the primping that is required to look presentable. I usually get up around 7:00 AM, eat some cereal, let nature run its course, wash my hair, shave, brush my teeth, and when I was leading in Bible study, still had a few minutes to do some last-minute cramming. Wow! It is now 8:00 AM! We have 12 miles to drive and no one is in the car! The wife forgot her umbrella; the daughter forgot her glasses; I left my Bible. Back to the house! Everyone is upset so no one speaks for the entire twelve-mile trip. Our intentions were to arrive early enough to get our seat five rows from the front and get a decent parking space. Oh, those choir members! They put their Bibles, purses and coats on the pews, saving the best seats for when they come down during the offertory prayer. Why don't they just stay in the choir?

The gathering and entertainment start. I check the bulletin to review the announcements and the order of service – not sure why – it has not changed in my 63 years of attendance. Finally, it begins – opening prayer, song, announcements, another song, offertory song, solo, sermon, and invitation. I concluded if one studied church history, he or she would probably find it has not changed in the last 500 years. The songs I have enjoyed from birth and know most from memory, especially the melodies. The sermons–come to think of it – do not change either. They are delivered to a passive audience in a cultivated form of speech. In other words, they contain an introduction, three to five points, maybe a cryptic take-off on some letters of the alphabet and a conclusion. Most people pray during the entire ordeal because I see them with their eyes closed and heads nodding, which I guess means God spoke to them and they were agreeing with His revelation. Sometimes they suddenly jerk upward and look around to make sure others noticed that God just gave them a special message. Admittedly I cram for my Bible Study lesson during the sermon. I hate to admit, but I find most sermons shamefully boring and highly mechanical – this morning's is no different. There are a few – "'amens"–during the message, but little additional response, including the invitation. Extremely rare to see anyone react to the altar call, so the invitational hymn is usually limited to two verses max. I stop by the bathroom during the intermission and then head off to Bible Study to lead an adult couples' class. There's coffee and food, fellowship, announcements, prayer requests, prayer and Bible Study. Maybe it was because my leadership responsibility demanded it, but I received far more spiritual growth from the Bible Study hour than the entertainment hour or "worship service." At any rate, it is now 11:00 AM and it is over. Let us eat!

Can this be called "worship?" I feel not one bit closer to God than I did prior to leaving the house. Is this the way those early New Testament believers "worshipped?" Where was the Holy Spirit? Where was the spontaneity? Where was the encouragement? Where was the exhortation? In *1 Corinthians 14*, Paul describes a gathering of believers with open participation by *all* the members, sharing a teaching, a revelation, an exhortation and spontaneous prophesying by everyone – why do I

75

not see that at my formal gathering? Why do I not feel what they felt? Scripture says, *"Where two or three come together in My name, there I am with them" (Matthew 18:20)*; so, where is He? There are 400 or more of us here – I do not see Him! What am I missing? Is it me?

God does not need our "worship," but He expects it. Why? Because a loving, caring, compassionate, merciful, grace-giving God, who sacrificed His only Son for me and grants me eternity with Him, deserves it! In other words, "worship" is for us, not Him. For what God has done for me, I cannot help but offer him worship and praise! It is a natural outpouring! If I love Him I cannot help but "worship" Him – through obedience! True "worship" impels us to service – *"As for us, we cannot help speaking about what we have seen and heard"* – *Acts 4:20*. What am I missing when I substitute "formality" for "worship?" We dress up in our formal clothes, go to our formal church, sit in our formal pew, quote some formal creeds, sing some formal songs, hear a formal sermon (maybe), give a formal offering, pray a formal prayer–go home and say – "I have performed my formal spiritual duties and requirements for the week and have 'worshipped'." We conclude God has a gigantic grade book and by performing "worship," we just earned points applicable to our final grade, even though we have done nothing in service to Him.

There is no specific definition of "worship" found in Scripture. The word itself has several meanings based on the Hebrew and Greek base words. In the Hebrew, there are two words which describe "worship" – one means to "bow, kneel or lower one's face in submission and respect"; the other means "service" or "to serve." Put these together and it would seem to denote, "worship is our humble adoration and response to God for His goodness and blessings upon us and results in service to Him." In response to His love for us, we are to be as Isaiah when called by God – *"Then I heard the voice of the Lord saying, 'Whom shall I send? And who will go for us?' And I said, 'Here am I. Send me'!" (Isaiah 6:8)*. Service is the culmination of true "worship." Samuel told Saul that God desires it above sacrifice – "formal worship." *"Does the Lord delight in burnt offerings and sacrifices as much as in obeying the Lord? To obey is better than sacrifice, and to heed is better than the fat of rams" (1 Samuel 15:22-23)*. In *Jeremiah 7:22*, God says, *"For when I brought your ancestors out of Egypt and spoke to them, I did not just give them commands about burnt offerings and sacrifices, but I gave them this* command: 'obey me, and I will be your God and you will be my people. Walk in obedience to all I command you, that it may go well with you'."

Isaiah is even more pronounced that service is more important than formal rituals – Isaiah 1:11-17 – "The multitude of your sacrifices – what are they to me? Says the Lord. 'I have more than enough of burnt offerings of rams and the fat of fattened animals; I have no pleasure in the blood of bulls and lambs and goats. When you come to appear before me, who has asked this of you, this trampling of my courts? Stop bringing meaningless offerings! Your incense is detestable to me. New Moons, Sabbaths and convocations – I cannot bear your worthless assemblies. Your New Moon feasts and appointed festivals I hate with all My being. They have become a burden to me; I am weary of bearing them. When you spread out your hands in prayer, I hide My eyes from you; even when you offer many prayers, I am not listening. Your hands are full of blood; wash and make yourselves clean. Take your evil deeds out of my sight! Stop doing wrong, learn to do right! Seek justice. Defend the oppressed. Take up the cause of the fatherless, plead the case of the widow'."

Anything less than total obedience to His call is hypocritical – "worship" centered on each other through formality, tradition, ritual, and obligation–Micah 6:6-8 – "With what shall I come before the Lord and bow down before the exalted God? Shall I come before Him with burnt offerings, with calves a year old? Will the Lord be pleased with thousands of rams, with ten thousand rivers of oil? Shall I offer my firstborn for my transgression, the fruit of my body for the sin of my soul? He has showed you, O mortal, what is good. And what does the Lord require of you? To act justly and to love mercy and to walk humbly with your God." If we fail to honor Him with our service to the needs of the world, our "formal worship" is just that – a meaningless public spectacle.

Michael Morrison, of "Grace Communion International" notes: "Word meanings don't prove what worship is, but they do illustrate three kinds of worship. There is:

1. Worship that involves speaking, and
2. Worship that involves listening, and
3. Worship that involves doing.

There is worship that expresses the heart, worship that involves the mind and a worship that involves the body. There is a worship that is giving praise upward, a worship that is receiving instructions from above and a worship that carries out instruction in the world around us. We need all three types of worship."[110] Praise is a wonderful response to God and His love, but if all we do is praise without listening and following in His footsteps, this is not the "worship" He desires. "Worship" must affect our actions and actions speak louder than words

The Old Testament reveals a variety of "worship" methods used by God's people. The early Patriarchs were "worship" leaders for their families, their clans and supporting staff – servants, slaves, etc. "Worship" was the responsibility of the Patriarch. No priest or intermediary was required; there was no set day or time and there did not appear to be any set methods. He was the religious leader. It was his responsibility to make sure his people were obedient to God's directions and instructions for both spiritual and physical survival. *Genesis 4* reveals the first mention of offerings being brought before the Lord – Cain and Abel. Scripture is not explicit in explaining why this occurred but if "worship" is indeed a response by us to God's outpouring of blessings, one would assume this was a response for that goodness. Later we find Patriarchs constructing altars – some based on God's command to do so and in many cases, a natural response for God's blessing – i.e. Noah after the flood; Abraham's altars at Shechem, Bethel, Hebron and Mount Moriah; Isaac at Beersheba; Jacob at Bethel. In all instances the construction of the altars included prayer, offerings, sacrifices and anointings.

During the time of Moses, "worship" became more detailed and structured – a priest, who by law was a descendant of Levi per God's instructions, would lead and make live animal sacrifices on behalf of the people. Where, how and when these sacrifices were to be offered were also specified (*Leviticus* through *Deuteronomy*). "Worship" for the first time became formal. So why the change? How, and perhaps a better question – why did "worship" go from direct access to God to a formalized setting where there was now an intermediary between the worshiper and God? It is called "sin" – that inherited human trait that separates us from a Holy God. There were now holy places, holy people, holy times, holy rituals, and holy offerings being offered to a holy God. The tabernacle, constructed under the specific instructions from God Himself, was a symbolic message from God. God is holy! He could no longer be approached by just anyone. You must be of a holy calling and approach him in a holy way at a holy time. The tent tabernacle was a designated place established as a meeting place for the priests or inter- mediaries to meet God on behalf of the people and offer sacrificial atonement for their sins. God was holy – set apart – off limits and could only be approached through the proper designated means He detailed.

The tent tabernacle could be looked upon as a place of "worship," but it was primarily a place of meeting and atonement. "Worship" was out of fear. People came because they feared God and His wrath. After the destruction of Solomon's Temple and the scattering of the Jews, synagogue "worship" was established. The synagogue was a commu- nity institution for teaching, prayer, fellowship and support. Members typically met several times per week for prayer, teaching, meals and the meeting of needs. It was here the attention was transferred to the reading of the Scriptures with much less emphasis on sacrifices. No sacrifices were offered in the synagogue. Synagogue "worship" is the focus of Jews to this day. People could "worship" without a priest or a sacrifice. Even after the Temple was eventually rebuilt, synagogue wor- ship became the new focus.

When it comes to New Testament "worship" – "What did Jesus do?" As a child He attended annual festivals in Jerusalem but as an adult and active in ministry, His "worship" was performed away from the temple. We are also told He occasionally went to the synagogue where he read and explained Scripture. However, His message was not accepted by the ruling classes who in turn, were successful in stirring many of the peoples against Him. *Luke 4:14-30* describes His return to His boy- hood home of Nazareth where He attended the synagogue. As was the custom, guest teachers were invited to share in the service. As He read from the Prophecy of *Isaiah* concerning the coming and mission of the Messiah (*61:1-2*), announcing the fulfillment of this prophecy in their presence, He was expelled from their fellowship and His life threatened. Seeking the lost, beginning with His own people, Jesus on occasion visited the synagogues since this was the common gathering place for the Jews, but His focus was outside the four walls of buildings and on the masses of lost people needing a Savior. Hillsides, mountainsides, seashores, streets, homes of the depressed, pools, gardens, lakesides, watering holes, solitary places, public places – wherever people were hurting – this is where Jesus "worshiped" in obedience to His Father and the mission He had been assigned. This was His "style of worship." Should it not be ours?

The greatest and most prolific example of true "worship" occurred in the early church. Jews continued to participate in temple "worship" until it was destroyed in A.D. 70, but with Christianity came a new and better way – His way. *Acts 2* details how "worship" was performed based on the example set by Jesus and laid down by the apostles. As a result, New Testament believers devoted themselves to being taught and discipled in a new and different way. They understood – it is not about the place of "worship," the method of "worship," the creeds, the rites, the music, the money – it was about preparation and obedience to the call. It was not about them or anything accomplished in the eyes of the world – it was all about God! The New Testament worshippers also began a new and different focus on the "place" of "worship." As earlier noted, it is here we begin to see small-group worship occurring in the home.

Paul says little concerning formal "worship" in any of his epistles. In fact, only a few times does Paul even reference formal "worship." Perhaps, his most pronounced reference is to the Corinthian believers, whose "worship" meetings had been infiltrated by pagan influence, to the point they had become disruptive and out of control. He puts a totally different spin on "worship," proclaiming our service to God is not based on a time or a building, but is wherever we are, because we are the temple of God – *"Don't you know that you yourselves are God's temple and that God's Spirit dwells in your midst?" – 1 Corinthians 3:16.* "Worship" is shifted to the individual Christian and his manifestation of Jesus Christ through the Holy Spirit that resides within- not a formal service inside a temple or building. Sharing the Gospel is an act of "worship." In fact, it is the greatest act of "worship." Whenever the Gospel is shared, we are declaring the "worth" of God – we are saying – "He is worthy." That is "worship!" We are the temple of God! The Holy Spirit lives in us – not in a building. The true test of "worship" is not what happens at "church," but what happens outside of it.

Service through testimony to the lost and addressing the physical needs of the impoverished are the only acts of "worship" Scripture notes brings rejoicing in heaven – *"I tell you that in the same way there will be more rejoicing in heaven over one sinner who repents than over ninety-nine righteous persons who do not need to repent" – Luke 15:7.* Formality, ritual and tradition are not "worship;" compassion and action in meeting the needs of a lost world are. This is the "worship" that honors Him – not us.

Chapter 7

"WHY MONUMENTS?"

"However, the Most High does not live in houses made by human hands. As the prophet says: 'Heaven is my throne, and the earth is my footstool. What kind of house will you build for Me? Or where will my resting place be? Has not My hand made all these things?' You stiff-necked people! Your hearts and ears are still uncircumcised! You are just like your ancestors: You always resist the Holy Spirit!" (Acts 7:48-51)

"There does not exist a shred of Biblical support for the church building. Yet scores of Christians pay good money each year to sanctify their brick and stone. By doing so, they have supported an artificial setting where they are lulled into passivity and prevented from being natural or intimate with other believers. It is high time Christians wake up to the fact that we are being neither Biblical nor spiritual by supporting church buildings. And we are doing great damage to the message of the New Testament by calling man-made buildings "churches." If every Christian on the planet would never call a building a church again, this alone would create a revolution in our faith."[111]

"**H**ypocrisy" (*"hupokrites"*) is defined by "Webster" as "the feigning to be what one is not; acting or presenting a false part or making false professions."[112] We have all complained and heard others lambast college and professional sports teams, along with their administrators and owners, for paying coaches and professional players exorbitant amounts of money – millions upon millions of dollars – to play football or another popular sport. The SOP addendum is typically, "what if those millions were spent on medical research or some other life-altering program that could benefit the masses?" In the same vein, what about the church?

ROI (Return-On Investment), is an accounting template used by businesses to justify (or the opposite) capital expenditures such as equipment, buildings, or expansions. According to "Wikipedia," "(ROI) measures the gain or loss generated on an investment, relative to the amount of money invested. ROI is usually expressed as a percentage and is typically used for business financial decisions and to compare the profitability or pay-back to the efficiency of the amount of money and cost of the investment."[113] In other words, a company is trying to decide to expand or make a significant capital investment – does the investment outweigh the risks and will it add to its bottom-line profitability? The typical return on investment formula for business is: *ROI = (Net Profit / Cost of Investment) x 100.*

Let us ponder a hypothetical ROI regarding the church building. There are 8,760 hours in a year (24 hours times 365 days). Consider a church building, with adequate educational space to accommodate the average Protestant congregation, costs in the range of $3- 5 million (likely in today's economic climate). Consider also the average church utilizes the building for two hours on Sunday morning – Sunday School or Small Group Bible Study and "worship;" maybe an hour on Sunday evening (for the sake of calculation we will make this assumption since not all churches have Sunday evening services); and one hour on Wednesday evening – also for the sake of calculation since not all churches have mid-week services. This would calculate to 208 hours annual utilization. Let us once again, for the sake of calculation, throw in one funeral quarterly–two hours (receiving and service); one wedding per quarter–two hours (wedding and rehearsal); and again, for the sake of calculation – another hour per month for miscellaneous. This calculates to a total of 236 annual hours of use – or bottom line–a $3-5 million investment in an edifice that will potentially sit empty over 97% of its life!

As a businessman or woman, or better yet, as a card-carrying Christian, does it make sense to invest that amount of money in something you are utilizing less than 3% of the time, yet the cost of maintaining the investment remains intact and grows with age? This renders the concept of under-utilization unfathomable. From a business standpoint, the answer is without question, "absolutely not." Yet, today's church continues to invest in these elaborate monuments to themselves at an astounding rate and incurring debt beyond imagination and they see this as wise and even worse, pleasing to God! Some have even gone so far as to say, "the building is a monument to God and a lighthouse to a lost community." Since when does a building save anyone? *"Then they said, 'Come, let us build ourselves a city, with a tower that reaches to the heavens, so that we may make a name for ourselves...'"*- Genesis 11:4.

For lack of having anything to say in a unique situation, which was very "un-Peter like," Peter's experience at the Transfiguration left him speechless. After experiencing this heavenly reunion between Jesus, Elijah and Moses, Peter interrupted Jesus with the suggestion – *"Rabbi, it is good for us to be here. Let us put up three shelters – one for you, one for Moses and one for Elijah (He did not know what to say, they were so frightened)"*–Mark 9:5-6. In other words, "it is comfortable here, let us stay up here on the mountain, build a building, seal ourselves in it and "worship" and be happy." Our Savior knew it is not on the mountain or inside the four walls of a building where people are in need – it is in the valleys of life and the fields outside the four walls that are ripe unto harvest.

To cover the cost and maintenance of such an investment is huge. Building and maintenance costs, coupled with six figure salary packages for staff, can cripple and even bankrupt a fellowship. To cover this enormous debt load, today's church must be selective and seek people of financial influence. The church is forced to concentrate its efforts on those who can offer more dollars to the body than what they may take away. Hence the strategy for church outreach concentrates on programs inside its four walls, where the front doors are thrown open and the message rings out, "Here we are; this is what we have for you; y'all come." Some do and will. But what about those who cannot come, do not have a way to come, feel too intimidated to come, cannot afford to come, have nothing to offer if they did come, or may ask for more than they are able to contribute if they do come? This is contrary to the call of Jesus Christ but is the way of the 21st century church. Paul's words to Timothy have never been clearer – *"For the love of money (and the desire for it) is the root of all kinds of evil"–1 Timothy:6:10.* One can add to that – "deception." Could the church of today be guilty of the same deception in its quest for affluency through the financing of its buildings? Absolutely! In business it is called "COMPETITION;" in today's church, it is spelled the same way.

How do businesses compete? Easy–they wrestle business away from each other. Competing companies produce the same products but differ in how they market and present them to the public. If churches are adopting the same strategy, with whom and how do they compete? "Competition" is defined as, "contention of two or more for the same object or for superiority; rivalry."[114] A business needs income or money to survive. The church, being a business, also needs income to survive. The business makes its income by marketing its product. So does the church. The business markets its product to the masses. So does the church. – enticing affluent members from sister churches.

Pastor and teacher Dennis McCallum states, "While many believers today maintain that the evangelical church is growing and reaching large numbers, studies show that over 90% of so-called church growth in America is nothing but people transferring from other evangelical churches.[115] D.A. Carson, Emeritus Professor of the New Testament at Trinity Evangelical Divinity School and co-founder of "The Gospel Coalition," refers to research showing that only 2 to 4 percent of converts reached at evangelistic events in the U.S. are still involved in Christianity five years later. According to one denominational expert in church planting, nationwide church growth averages 3% by conversion. The rest is all transfer or biological growth (members having children)."[116] Author William Chadwick adds, "When people join one church after leaving another, experts call it transfer growth. People in the pew call it church shopping. I call it one of the most dangerous trends to face the body of Christ in decades. It is sheep stealing. All around us churches are seeking better and more creative ways to attract people-more dynamic preaching, better worship, more of the Spirit, better drama. Great effort is being expended, but few are turning to Christ for the first time. Instead, the faithful are mostly just changing churches."[117]

People move their "church" membership for varying reasons – relocation, doctrinal aberration, church issues, etc. But when financial obligations force the church to focus on transfers as a resource for income and "growth," then the reasons are apparent – money–and it becomes the overriding goal at the expense of the lost. Members in good standing at sister churches are usually "tithers," therefore, their move to a sister church is welcomed with open arms, especially if they come with their wallets. Unfortunately, those who are lost and not seeded in faith and doctrine, come with little to offer other than themselves. With the financial demands for funding the operation of the church including its edifices and monuments to itself, this is not enough. If you are unable to pay your own way, stay away. We do not need you nor do we want you.

Thom Ranier, CEO of "Lifeway Resources" comments, "In the recent past (15 to 20 years), transfer growth was rewarded. Churches and church leaders were recognized for the total number of new members who joined their churches. Thus, at least implicitly, transfer growth, was seen being as important as conversion growth (where a non-Christian becomes a believer and joins the church). The Millennials specifically seem to have an aversion to this type of church growth. Much of transfer growth has been the result of the consumer mentality creeping into churches. Many Christians have become church hoppers and shoppers to find the right church that meets their needs and preferences. They view a local congregation as a country club with perks for the members. It has not been uncommon for pastors to become competitive and antagonistic about members transferring from one church to another."[118]

Since it is all about the money, what else could one expect? Dennis McCallum also notes in his book, "Satan and His Kingdom," "We don't believe pastors are lying, but they appear to believe their church is doing better than what it actually is when it comes to growth. However, it is interesting to note that the same staff that can break its statistics down in a dozen different ways from memory is unable to give a statistic for the convert versus transfer composition of its people. So far, all we have interviewed noted that they don't study the question."[119] William Chadwick thinks "church leaders purposely conceal the truth about transfer growth by launching strategies only likely to win transfers."[120] While I do not necessarily agree with this argument, it does deserve consideration. The need for finances to cover overbearing debt can cause one to resort to unorthodox methods; the church is no different.

How does the church market its wares? During a recently attended Small Group Bible Study leadership training session, I was intrigued by the comments of our instructor, an Associate Pastor at a sizable Protestant Church, when he shared, "the number one reason strangers attend a church is because they were invited." Ok, I believe that. Next—"the number one reason (80% of those surveyed) they came back for a second visit was the fact they felt welcome during their first encounter." Ok, makes sense, I believe that also. Interestingly, the next most popular reason was the building complex and its appearance – size of the gymnasium, size of the nursery, convenience of parking, sound system, etc., etc. To fund the complexity of today's church requires cash and cash comes through membership growth from those affluent in nature. To attract those of this category requires "bells and whistles" and those "bells and whistles" come at significant cost. Otherwise, as a business, it will bankrupt. Unfortunately, this worship of finances is resulting in the worse bankruptcy of all – spiritual bankruptcy.

The greatest debt incurred by churches is obviously its building investments. Dave Ramsey, author, radio show host and businessman, notes "churches provide money-management seminars to individuals offering advice on how to become debt free but are not willing to follow their own advice." He believes churches should follow the same principles, even to financing church buildings, since the church that practices debt-free living is more effective in ministry. "Imagine what your church could do if it were not burdened by debt. You'd be able to give more to the community, and support missions and giving efforts within your church. Your leadership would not be stressed and diverted by the pressure of raising funds in order to pay the bills."[121] Unfortunately, this is not what today's church wants to hear. Many Protestant seminaries teach debt as the means for keeping a body focused on giving. Statistics rendered show people are quick to support building debt but are reluctant to finance a non-related cause for missions.

Patton Dodd, a writer from San Antonio Texas, wrote an article that was picked up by the "Washington Post" regarding inner city properties needed for low income housing. With many property owners against development for such in their neighborhoods, a pushback was occurring from suburban homeowners fearing possible repercussions such as crime, schools, commercial development, etc. One of the solutions suggested for consideration was the use of underutilized church properties. In many of the suburban areas in San Antonio it was found some of the oldest buildings were large underutilized churches surrounded by expanses of parking lots. Dodd noted "they are all over the suburbs." A study by the city's "Faith Based Initiative" estimated over 3,000 acres of underutilized church real estate. He notes, "I am not about to propose that church real estate is a silver bullet in the affordable housing crisis, but it is absolutely the case that many churches are holding underutilized real estate – parking lots, vacant lots, and empty or mostly empty buildings, especially in this era of declining religious affiliation."[122]

According to Jonathan Merritt of "The Atlantic Monthly Group," "Many of our nation's churches can no longer afford to maintain their structures – 6,000 to 10,000 churches die each year in America. Congregational participation is less central to many Americans' faith than it once was. Most denominations are declining as a share of the overall population, and donations have been falling for decades. Religiously unaffiliated Americans nicknamed the "none's," are growing as a share of the U.S. population. As donations and attendance decrease, the cost of maintaining large physical structures that are in use only a few hours a week by a handful of worshippers becomes prohibitive."[123]

The problem of underutilized and empty "monuments" is not just relegated to the United States. According to an article by Carrie Borden, church planter in Austria, more than 500 Catholic churches have closed in Germany alone in the past twenty years, over 30% of those demolished with the remainder sold for development. Thomas Begrich, head of finances for the Evangelical Church of Germany, stated the problem is not reserved for Catholics alone. He notes of the 340 Protestant churches closed between 1990 and 2000, 46 were demolished. He predicts an additional 1,000 church buildings are on the verge or will fall in the "very near future."[124]

Regardless one's religious preference, the "church" building is quickly becoming a relic of the past. Believers are beginning to recognize the futility of supporting such extravagance, financial irresponsibility, and unfathomable underutilization. For centuries, our desire for it has been so overwhelming we have come to believe one cannot have "church" without it. Then to maintain it and finance it, comes the need for affluency and the ensuing marketing ploys to attract those so identified. As a result, our mission becomes flawed and misguided at the expense of the lost. We find ourselves worshipping the monument at the expense of His Great Commission, all the time believing we are doing it in His name and to honor Him. This is the spiritual deception the Apostles warned us would happen. Is the investment of our monies, time, effort and focus on new and more religious edifices the best investment for growing God's Kingdom and reaching a lost and dying world? You make the choice but do so by seeking His face and His guiding hand. It is His resources we have been entrusted.

Chapter 8

WHY ACCEPT FAILURE?

*"When they had finished eating, Jesus said to Simon
Peter, 'Simon son of John, do you love Me more than
these?' 'Yes, Lord,' he said, 'you know that I love you.'
Jesus said, 'Feed My lambs.' Again, Jesus said, 'Simon
son of John, do you love Me?' He answered, 'Yes, Lord,
you know that I love you.' Jesus said, 'Take care of My
sheep.' The third time He said to him, 'Simon son of
John, do you love Me?' Peter was hurt because Jesus
asked him the third time, 'Do you love Me?' He said,
'Lord, you know all things; you know that I love you.'
Jesus said, 'FEED MY SHEEP'" (John 21:15-17).*

" ut Lord, I pastored five churches in my lifetime, I served the
ministry over forty-years; Lord, I taught Sunday School over fif-
ty-years; I served four terms as deacon, trustee, and elder; I chaired
the Nominating Committee ten years straight; I was head of the Church
Council five years; I led the Wednesday evening prayer service when
the pastor was away; I allowed myself to be available to lead the choir
when the music director was vacationing. I directed the Nursery for
twelve years; but Lord, but, but, but!"

We have already seen when Scripture references the "church," it is not
referring to a building, but rather to an *"ekklesia"*–"the whole body of
believers scattered throughout the earth."[125] What is its mission? Trevin
Wax, pastor and managing editor of "The Gospel Project" at LifeWay

Christian Resources, states, "The church is a sign and instrument of the kingdom of God, a people united by faith in the gospel announcement of the crucified and risen King Jesus. The mission of the church is to go into the world in the power of the Holy Spirit and make disciples by proclaiming this gospel, calling people to respond in ongoing repentance and faith, and demonstrating the truth and power of the gospel by living under the lordship of Christ for the glory of God and the good of the world."[126]

As a born-again believer, I can personally speak from profundity by noting God will never make a demand on one's life without providing a way. Both His demand and His way are found in *Matthew 28:19-20 and Acts 1:8–"Go and make disciples of all nations, baptizing them in the name of the Father and of the Son and of the Holy Spirit, and teaching them to obey everything I have commanded you. And surely I am with you always, to the very end of the age." "But you will receive power when the Holy Spirit comes on you; and you will be my witnesses in Jerusalem, and in all Judea and Samaria, and to the ends of the earth."*

Is the "church" failing in its mission? Researcher David Olson writes, "In reality, the church in American is not booming. It is in crisis...If trends continue, by 2050 the percentage of Americans attending church will be half the 1990 figure."[127] Julia Duin, American journalist and author, cites studies from both evangelical and secular sources showing "a large-scale exodus from churches and no recorded growth."[128] Within my own denomination – Southern Baptist–the largest single Protestant denomination in the U.S.–this decline is evident and concerning.

A recent article in the "Baptist Courier," a publication detailing activities of South Carolina Southern Baptists, Lee Clamp, South Carolina Southern Baptist Evangelistic Director, shared about D-Day and the courage and bravery of those soldiers who stormed the beaches of Normandy in a battle that changed the course of World War II in favor of the Allies. Defeat could have meant an entirely different world than what we experience today. Many of these young men paid the ultimate sacrifice allowing us the freedoms we now enjoy. To initiate such an onslaught against the enemy took much planning, preparation and training. Every conceivable angle had to be studied, including the habits and tendencies of the enemy – even down to the weather itself on that victorious, but bloody day.

In the same context, Paul emphasizes in *Ephesians 6,* Christians are indeed at war and provides us with intimate details regarding our enemy and the defense mechanisms we are to employ to repel the enemy's onslaughts and advance upon him. However, statistics verify, professed Christians are typically unprepared, ill-trained and completely oblivious to this spiritual war we have been called to fight on behalf of our Lord Jesus Christ. Lee Clamp reported over 400 Southern Baptist Churches in South Carolina in 2016 failed to baptize a single soul![129] That being the case, why not padlock the doors and utilize these facilities for civic or community activities? What inherent difference would it make in that community for the cause of Jesus Christ if those churches ceased to exist?

Late 2014, I felt God's calling to plant a new believers' fellowship. The reasons for not doing so seemed too easy but the challenges to heeding the call were overwhelming. After meeting and praying with a close friend in Christ and Director of Missions of my church association, we jointly felt the call to address the Hispanic community in our area. In early 2015, Fuente de Vida (Fountain of Life) Hispanic fellowship emerged, and we conducted our first meeting in an abandoned and refurbished liquor store and bar! Although I am not seminary or theologically trained and had no experience or clue how to "plant a believer's fellowship," through God's guidance and the help of other believers willing to commit their time, prayers and efforts, all things were made possible. I remind myself daily—"*I can do all things through Christ who strengthens me" (Philippians 4:13).*

Although not a fully self-supporting body, Fuente de Vida has grown and continues to reach out to other ethnic cultures in addition to Hispanics. Through the gracious gift of a caring family, we were afforded the blessing of securing a used church van. Most of our participants cannot or will not drive, so it is imperative a mode of transportation be provided other than personal vehicles. The fellowship has expanded, both ethnically and age-wise, with an influx of middle and early high-school age kids who are non-Hispanic. Since our Hispanics are led by a Spanish-speaking pastor and the Bible studies presented entirely in Spanish, it has become necessary for us to split the meetings with several of us gringos leading the youth.

Our youth are primarily coming from the "other side of the tracks" – low income areas where the traditional church will not venture. These kids and their families are totally ignored by the traditional church. It breaks my heart to pick up a load of kids directly across the street from a "church" representing my own denomination and no attempt has ever been made to reach out to them or their families. Based on experience, it boils down to the "$" sign – we are dealing with all "takers" and no "givers." The "church" of today cannot afford these "financial liabilities." But aren't their souls important also? Jesus said they were. Unfortunately for both, the "church of man" does not see it that way. One Sunday evening my wife was riding with me as my chaperone. We passed a small church – four cars in the lot–directly across the street from a large trailer park where many of our kids reside. The church sign noted – "God loves you!" Before I could open my mouth, my wife abruptly interrupted our silence with, "God does, but you sure don't." We proceeded to pick up sixteen kids within walking distance of this church.

Recently, I was enjoying a burger at a fast-food restaurant on a Sunday evening, when a pastor I know came into the restaurant accompanied by several family members and a small group from his fellowship. He approached our table and after exchanging pleasantries and a hug, began to share it had been an eventful evening at his church. He became emotional to the point of tears. He shared with me he had been praying, visiting, preaching his heart out, yet his church was in crisis and was struggling to pay their bills. I am not exactly sure what it meant but was told a "vote of confidence" was taken during the service that evening affirming the support of the members for his leadership. Following sports, especially college football closely, I did not have the heart to tell him a vote of confidence from a college Athletic Director is normally followed by a near-future firing of the coach. I did agree to make his church a matter of prayer. What I wanted to say but did not at the risk of being brutally honest and recognizing this was his livelihood, is his church has not baptized a single soul in years. That being the case, why not shut the doors, turn out the lights, close the curtains, gate the parking lot, trash the budget, go home and take the few true believers who have a heart for the lost, get down on your knees and commit your new "ekklesia" to God, work from the home, seek His will and see what happens. Could the results be any worse?

According to "Gallup News," "the percentage of Americans who report belonging to a church is at an all-time low, averaging 50% in 2018. U.S. church membership was 70% or higher from 1937 through 1976, falling to an average of 68% in the 1970's through the 1990's. The past twenty years have seen an acceleration in the drop-off, with a 20% decline since 1999 and more than half of that change occurring since the start of the current decade. This decline mostly reflects the fact that fewer Americans than in the past now have any religious affiliation. However, even those who do identify with a particular religion are less likely to belong to a church or other place of worship than in the past."[130] Thom Ranier in his blog "Hope for Dying Churches," says, "gone are the days when church attendance was a societal norm. It is tempting to blame secular culture, national politics, or church leaders for the declining evangelical influence in today's culture. But if outside forces were the reasons behind declining and influential churches, we would likely have no churches today. We are not hindered by external forces; we are hindered by our own lack of commitment, selflessness, and evangelistic urgency."[131]

In a May 29, 2014, post from Kate Tracy, "Christianity Today", entitled "Five Reasons Why Most Southern Baptist Churches Baptize Almost No Millennials," she addresses this issue as pertains to Southern Baptists in particular. We won't address all her reasons here, but instead look at her reference and comments regarding another interesting quote from Thom Ranier who states, "The heartbreaking slide in Southern Baptist baptisms has now entered its seventh year. While the loss of nearly 4,600 baptisms was not as steep as last year's drop, the continued decline is still enough for me to say I am grieved we are clearly losing our evangelistic effectiveness. According to a recent report by a special task force of pastors in the Southern Baptist Convention, the baptism drought in America's largest evangelical denomination – which counts 15.7 million members and 5.8 million Sunday worshipers – is worst among millennials. The only consistent growing baptism group was children under the age of five. While the number of Southern Baptist Churches increased, reported membership of those churches declined by 136,764, down 0.9% to 15.7 million members. Primary worship attendance declined 2.21% to an average of 5.8 million worshippers."[132]

Consider the following from the reporting year 2015-16 per the Southern Baptist Convention website:

...one –quarter (25%) of SBC churches reported "0" baptisms

...60% said they had baptized no youth (ages 12-17)

...80% reported one or fewer young adult baptisms (ages 18-29)

A task force of pastors was put together by the SBC president to identify the problem. Here are the results:

a. *Spiritual* – "Many of our pastors and churches are not effectively engaged in sharing the gospel and yet continue business as usual. There is no sense of brokenness over the spiritual climate of our churches and our nation." *We do not care.*

b. *Leadership* – "Most pastors have confessed to being overwhelmed in the operation and ministries of the church to the neglect of personal evangelism. This lack of leading by example has impacted our church members' engagement in personal evangelism." *We are too busy.*

c. *Discipleship* – "Most pastors have confessed to focusing on attendance while giving little attention to reproducing fruit-bearing disciples who are involved in intentional evangelism." *We are not equipping.* George Barna reports in his book, "Growing True Disciples", 3% or less of American evangelicals report ever being discipled.[133]

d. *The Next Generation* – "Although our churches have increasingly provided programs for children, youth and young adults, we are not being effective in winning and discipling the next generation to follow Christ." *No strategy.*

e. *Celebration* – "Majority of our churches have chosen to celebrate other things as a measure of their success, such as internal programs, capital improvements, etc., rather than new believers following Christ in baptism. We have drifted into a loss of expectation." *No purpose.*

Certain levels of quality control require businesses and organizations to adopt a "mission statement." It is typically a one or two sentence summarization of the entity's goals, direction, intent, products and markets served. It is usually posted as a reminder in a public place viewable by both employees and visitors alike. The Mission Statement for the church was authored by Jesus Christ and is found in *Matthew 28:19-20*

– *"We will go and teach all nations, baptizing them in the name of the Father, Son and the Holy Ghost, teaching them to observe all things whatsoever He has commanded us, knowing He will be with us, even unto the end of the world."* When a company digresses from its mission statement it results in confusion, chaos, lack of confidence in leadership, misdirection, and even to closure. The same scenario holds true for the church, but once again, the collateral is much greater. As a business owner or stockholder in a company, mediocrity is unacceptable. Why then does the "church" accept anything less from its leadership and its members?

Based on my personal lifetime sojourn within the traditional church, allow me to submit ten reasons I believe the church has lost its zeal for success through evangelism:

1. Lost in the minutia. Too busy with our own pettiness – meetings, committees, etc. *"These people come near to me with their mouth and honor me with their lips, but their hearts are far from me"*–Isaiah 29:13.
2. Lack of evangelistic leadership. It is all about the "preaching" but little about the "going." *"Where there is no revelation, people cast off restraint but blessed is he who heeds wisdom's instruction"* – Proverbs 29:18.
3. Lack of accountability. A business has a bottom line – profit; a church has a bottom line – salvations and baptisms. Just as the business CEO is accountable to his Board of Directors, so should the church staff answer for a church's lack of evangelistic outreach. Though they may not necessarily bear total responsibility, they are certainly accountable for creating the strategy and directing the mission. *"When I say to the wicked, 'You wicked person, you will surely die,' and you do not speak out to dissuade them from their ways, that wicked person will die for their sin, and I will hold you accountable for their blood"* – Ezekiel 33:8.
4. Lack of goals. Evangelistic objectives should be set for each staff member and their ministries; if the pastor as the CEO refuses, then the trustees, deacons, or board should do so – including for the pastor. Goals and status should be reviewed regularly and consistently, and those analytical reviews shared with the

body. *"But as for you, be strong and do not give up, for your work will be rewarded"* – 2 Chronicles 15:7.

5. Lack of strategy. War requires strategic planning. Striking out blindly results in striking out. A church needs to know its community – i.e., ethnic background, economic status, creed, religious background, customs, culture, etc. The strategy needs to come from leadership. *"Or suppose a king is about to go to war against another king. Won't he first sit down and consider whether he is able with ten thousand men to oppose the one coming against him with twenty thousand?"* – Luke 14:31.

6. Lack of preparation. Church is all about preparation for service. Church leaders have an obligation – not to preach, sing, baby sit, etc., but to train soldiers. *"So Christ Himself gave the apostles, the prophets, the evangelists, the pastors and teachers, to equip His people for works of service..."* – Ephesians 4:11-12.

7. Lack of spiritual growth. Too comfortable on the "milk" with no desire to gravitate onto the "meat" of the Word. When one depends on "pulpit preaching" as his or her only choice for spiritual growth, they may be in trouble. Intimacy found in organic small group Bible studies provide that opportunity. *"...so that the body of Christ may be built up until we all reach unity in the faith and knowledge of the Son of God and become mature, attaining to the whole measure of the fullness of Christ"* – Ephesians 4:12-13.

8. Lack of outward vision. Worshipping the facility and its programs–"the lost know we are here; if they want to come, they are welcome, but no need for us to reach out to them." *"You must go to everyone I send you to and say whatever I command you'."* – Jeremiah 1:7.

9. Lack of conviction and compassion. Favoritism; the mandate is to "go," but if we "go," the preference is to be selective on where we "go." Comfort outweighs need. *"As the Scripture says, 'Anyone who believes in Him will never be put to shame.' For there is no difference between Jew and Gentile – the same Lord is Lord of all and richly blesses all who call on Him, for, 'Everyone who calls on the name of the Lord will be saved'"* – Romans 10:11-13.

10. Lack of salvation. Those commanded to "Go" may not because they are lost themselves. One sealed with His Holy Spirit cannot help but channel His message–works will not save us, but they

are a genuine sign we have been saved. "Pew warmers" need to evaluate their status with Jesus Christ before it is eternally too late. *"As for us, we cannot help speaking about what we have seen and heard" – Acts 4:20.*

Our Mission Statement of *Matthew 28:19-20* is our formal summary of the aims and values of the *"ekklesia."* It identifies us and affirms our purpose. Let us examine it in detail:

a. *"Go"* – a 'word' of action–a verb. It literally means to act; do something; leave from a place; depart. "Go" is not an option. "818 unevangelized ethno-linguistic peoples have never been targeted by any Christian agency. Out of 648 million Great Commission Christians, 70% have never been told about the world's 1.6 billion unevangelized individuals."[134] Thom Ranier notes in his book, "Breakout Churches," "fewer than 15% of church members indicated they had shared with someone how to become a Christian in the past twelve months." Are we "going?"
b. *"Ye"* – You, Me – ALL of us. *1 Corinthians 12:7–"Now to each one the manifestation of the Spirit is given for the common good."* "EACH ONE"–the Greek is *"anthropos"* – meaning every man, woman, boy and girl. ALL are called. ALL are sent. Are we heeding the call (*Matthew 9:37–"The harvest is plentiful, but the laborers are few."*)?
c. *"Therefore"* – Why? Because of everything I have done for you and taught you through the written and spoken Word. Are we seeking Him through His Word?
d. *"And"* – there is more
e. *"Teach"* – Witness, proclaim; share the Gospel. *Acts 1:8 – "...and you will be my witnesses ...;"* *"Always be prepared to give an answer to everyone who asks you to give the reason for the hope that you have" – 1 Peter 3:15.* Are we proclaiming?
f. *"All"* – No favoritism. *Romans 10:12-13 – "For there is no difference between Jew and Gentile – the same Lord is Lord of all and richly blesses all who call on him, for, 'Everyone who calls on the name of the Lord will be saved'."* Are we prejudiced in any way – color, gender, rich, poor, nationality?

g. *"Nations"* – not just here at home but the world. *Acts 1:8 – "...and you will be my witnesses in Jerusalem, and in all Judea and Samaria, and to the ends of the earth."* Are we quick to travel to third world countries with the Gospel – as we should – but neglect the same peoples living across the street?

h. *"Baptizing them"* – Lead them to a saving knowledge of Jesus Christ. *Matthew 3:13-15 – "Then Jesus came from Galilee to the Jordan to be baptized by John. But John tried to deter him, saying, 'I need to be baptized by you, and do you come to me?' Jesus replied, 'Let it be so now; it is proper for us to do this to fulfill all righteousness.' Then John consented."* This baptism proved His consecration to God as it does for us who are saved. Profitability is the "bottom line for business; baptisms are the "bottom line" for the *"ekklesia."*

i. *"In the name of the Father"* – *1 John 4: 9-10 – "This is how God showed His love among us: He sent His one and only Son into the world that we might live thru Him. This is love: not that we loved God, but that He loved us and sent His Son as an atoning sacrifice for our sins."*

j. *"And the Son"* – *John 14: 6 – "Jesus answered, 'I am the way and the truth and the life. No one comes to the Father except through Me'."*

k. *"And the Holy Ghost"* – our seal as an officially commissioned soldier; the eternal, indwelling, personal presence of Jesus Christ in the believer's life. *John 15: 26-27 – "When the Advocate comes, whom I will send to you from the Father, the Spirit of Truth who goes out from the Father, he will testify about me. And you also must testify, for you have been with me from the beginning." Romans 8: 9 – "And if anyone does not have the Spirit of Christ, they do not belong to Christ."* Are we sealed by His Holy Spirit? If we are, we are saved and our actions will evidence our sealing; if there is no evidence of the Holy Spirit's work in one's life, he/she needs to examine themselves to be sure their salvation – regardless what they have been told from the pulpit.

l. *"Teaching them"* – discipling them to grow from the milk onto the meat of the Word. *1 Peter 2:2 – "Like newborn* babies, crave pure spiritual milk, so that by it you may grow up in your salvation, now that you have tasted that the Lord is good." Are we reaching them and leaving them; or are we reaching them and training them to serve Him?

m. "To observe all things" – the Scriptures. 2 Timothy 3:16-17 – "All Scripture is God breathed and is useful for teaching, rebuking, correcting and training in righteousness, so that the servant of God may be thoroughly equipped for every good work." Are we growing spiritually?

n. "Whatsoever I have commanded you" – It is not a request; it is His command to us for all to share the Gospel. 1 John 3:23-24 – "And this is His command: to believe in the name of His Son, Jesus Christ, and to love one another as he commanded us. The one who keeps God's commands lives in Him, and He in them. And this is how we know that he lives is us: We know it by the Spirit He gave us."

o. "And lo I am with you always" – this is His equipping; we make ourselves available; He does the work through His Holy Spirit. John 14:18-20 – "I will not leave you as orphans; I will come to you. Before long, the world will not see me anymore, but you will see me. Because I live, you also will live. On that day you will realize that I am in my Father, and you are in me, and I am in you."

p. "Even unto the end of the world" – until He returns. John 14:1-4 – "Do not let your hearts be troubled. You believe in God; believe also in Me. My Father's house has many rooms; if that were not so, would I have told you that I am going there to prepare a place for you? And if I go and prepare a place for you, I will come back and take you to be with me that you also may be where I am. You know the way to the place where I am going."

According to a study by Xenos Christian Fellowship, a non-traditional, non-denominational, institutional cell church system, "Over the past decade, Xenos leaders have led research teams to dozens of the most famous and rapidly growing churches around the country to study their methods and outcomes. These include churches from a wide variety of approaches – charismatic, seeker-sensitive, cell-based, emergent, house church, health and wealth, satellite churches, churches that plant churches elsewhere in the country, etc. During our early trips, team members often commented that virtually no members or staff they interviewed had met Christ as adults at that church. To our own amazement, we have found that the number claiming to have become believers at that church is invariably less than 10% of the sample – often less than 5%! So far, we have only identified three churches where more than 10% of their own people report that they were converted in that church. We continue this research today, still looking for other large groups where majority of growth comes from conversions. If you know of one, let us know!"[135] In fact, if you know of one, become a part! How do you recognize them – *"Thus, by their fruit you shall recognize them"* – *Matthew 7:20*. A church's salvation and baptismal records are a clear indicator of *"fruit-bearing."* Statistics typically do not lie.

Is today's traditional "church" accomplishing anything "good" on behalf of Jesus Christ? Absolutely! Churches, for the most part, are lighthouses in their communities. Many offer food – banks, build handicapped ramps, serve and offer soup kitchens, volunteer for various civic programs for hospice and delivering of meals to the sick and elderly. These are all wonderful mission opportunities and one should be applauded for taking part. But the bottom line is salvations! Missions without ministry will never work and vice versa. *James 2:14-17 – "What good is it my brothers and sisters, if someone claims to have faith but has no deeds? Can such faith save them? Suppose a brother or sister is without clothes and daily food. If one off you say to them, 'Go in peace; keep warm and well fed,' but does nothing about their physical needs, what good is it? In the same way, faith by itself, if it is not accompanied by action, is dead."* Our call is Gospel sharing; planting seeds (*Mark 4:14 – "The farmer sows the seed."*); missions sets the stage for ministry. If we fail to utilize the mission for the ministry, what have we accomplished except to meet a physical need. As James notes, meet the physical need but use that mission to address the spiritual need.

When a past President of the world's largest Baptist denomination and the largest Protestant denomination in the United States says – "Our pastors and churches are not effectively engaged in sharing the gospel and yet continue business as usual. There is no sense of brokenness over the spiritual climate of our churches and our nation" – then we must ask ourselves, "are we indeed failing in our mission?" Are we sure we understand our mission? There is no reward for failure. In fact, quite the contrary.

Chapter 9

WHY SERMONS?

"One living demonstration of the Gospel is far better than a hundred explanations of many sermons"– Jonathan Hayashi.[136]

Teaching is a necessary part of life. Those of us who are literate owe a tremendous debt of gratitude to teachers who have dedicated their lives to the betterment of others. In the same vein, Scripture notes there are those who by their belief in Jesus Christ and subsequent sealing by the Holy Spirit, are blessed with Spiritual gifts bestowed by that same Spirit. One of those gifts is teaching – *"We have different gifts, according to the grace given us. If your gift is prophesying, then prophesy in accordance with your faith; if it is serving, then serve; if it is teaching, then teach.." – Romans 12:6-7*. Obviously if there is teaching within the *"ekklesia,"* there must be teachers.

We will discuss more in detail in the next chapter, but among the hierarchy set forth by Paul for the New Testament *"ekklesia,"* was an individual of the body referenced by four different names – "pastor" (mentioned only once in the New Testament – *Ephesians 4:11*), "overseer," "bishop," and "elder." As noted, the New Testament *"ekklesia"* were a conglomeration of loosely fragmented "house churches" consisting primarily of reformed Jews with a smattering of Gentile converts. Whether there was an "overseer" or "shepherd" representing each "house church" is not likely, but at the very least, an "overseer" would shepherd a select group of "house churches" within a city or region – *"The reason I left you in Crete was that you might put in order what was left unfinished and appoint elders in every town, as I directed you"* – *Titus 1:5.*

Among other things (*1 Timothy 3:1-7; Titus 1:6-9*) the "overseer" must possess the gift of teaching – *"Now the overseer is to be ...able to teach" (1 Timothy 3:2; 2 Timothy 2:24).* "Teaching," as Jesus described in His Great Commission (*Matthew 28:19-20–"Go ye therefore and teach all nations...teaching them to observe all things whatsoever I have commanded you"*) appears to be twofold – the testimony of the Gospel to the world, and discipleship. Discipleship would then be the teaching involved in spiritual growth – weaning a new believer off the "milk and onto the meat" of the Word. The "overseer," as noted by Paul, was to possess the gift of teaching, but there is no Biblical indication the gift of teaching is reserved strictly for the "overseers." In fact, quite the contrary.

Teaching was a gift available to other qualified members of the body – *"Let the message of Christ dwell among you richly, as you teach and admonish one another with all wisdom.."* – *Colossians 3:16;* *"The student is not above the teacher, but everyone who is fully trained will be like their teacher"* – *Luke 6:40.* Teaching is a spiritual gift bestowed upon those so blessed, but it is not in any way descriptive of a titled position. Teachers were spiritually mature (some theologians believe "aged" hence the term "elders") members of the body and the faith itself and so gifted to explain the "mysteries of the Gospel." However, no Biblical passage describes their teaching methods as "sermonizing," at least as we understand that term today. As a word of caution, those who desire this gift should be warned – *"Not many of you should become teachers, my fellow believers, because you know that we who teach will be judged more strictly"–James 3:1.*

A good "laic" definition of a sermon is an oration or opine with three to four points, consisting of an introduction, some personal commentary from a select individual believed to be divinely inspired, and ending with a dramatic conclusion intended to "entice" one to "accept" Jesus Christ, or in the case of an apathetic "professed believer," "revive and renew." It is deemed appropriate and necessary in today's "church" for the "ministry of the Word."

According to Matthew Pierce, evangelical thought leader, "the sermon is the product of "professed" believers who do not wish to take the time to read, study and meditate upon His Word, choosing rather to create titled and compensated individuals to tell them what's there so they don't have to find out for themselves."[137] I personally define the "sermon" as an oral presentation by a titled individual – normally a "preacher" – to the same non-participatory audience on a consistent basis. There is no indication, based on *Acts 2:42-47*, of anything that resembles this performance in the New Testament church. From my own perspective, passive listening to a one-man oration fosters putting trust in one man's ideals rather than allowing believers an open forum to function and mature as believers as taught by Paul in *1 Corinthians 12-14*.

Per author Lon Martin, "the sermon is another of Emperor Constantine's contributions to today's "church of man." Constantine introduced the idea of a single man ruling, rather than elders serving so appointed by Paul. The earliest recorded Christian source for regular sermonizing is found during the late second century. Clement of Alexandria (150-215) lamented the fact that sermons did so little to change Christians. Yet despite its recognized failure, the sermon became a standard practice among Christians by the fourth century. Listening to eloquent public orators (*"sophists"*) was a popular form of entertainment in Greek culture. These celebrities were well paid. Constantine made professional oratory the norm, attempting to increase the attendance in the massive church buildings he built, replacing interactivity. "Sophistry" ("the use of fallacious arguments, especially with the intent of deceiving"[138]) evolved into "giving sermons." Sermons later fell out of use under Catholicism but were reintroduced during the Protestant Reformation."[139]

There is no indication Jesus, nor the Apostles, ever gave a "sermon," at least in the context we understand formal sermonizing today. They utilized "dialog" (*"dialegomai"*). According to "Webster," a church service is defined as, "a public religious worship according to prescribed form and order; a ritual or form prescribed for public worship."[140] As previously noted, it is the contention of the author the demands of formality, customs and tradition in this type setting, stifles spiritual growth; this includes the sermon. "The sermon reinforces the basis of brainwashing through repetition."[141] The Biblical way, as seen from the New Testament Church, promotes understanding by study of the

Scriptures (the "Apostle's teachings") in a free-flowing setting where dialog is encouraged, not quelled. This interactive style teaching was especially utilized by Paul and was arguably adopted from Greek philosophical methodology and was the basis for first century higher education teaching practices from which our educational teaching styles are based today. The Protestant church, however, chose a different methodology basing spiritual growth on one individual's sermonized message.

In Paul's admonition to the Corinthian *"ekklesia"* in *1 Corinthians 14,* his charge is addressed to the entire assembly, not to or through a specific individual. If there were one responsible for directing the entire assembly, we would assume the admonition would have been directed to that individual. There was no need to write to the "church" if a "ruler" was responsible for directing the church. Paul admonished worship practices that should be followed in the Corinthian church and should be heeded today:

1   Prophesy (*Verses 1,24*)
2. Speak in tongues (foreign languages) (*Verses 2,27*)
3. Interpretation of the languages (*Verses 5,28*)
4. Speak by revelation, knowledge, prophesying, or teaching (*Verses 6,29-31*)
5. Pray (*Verses 13-16*)
6. Sing psalms (*Verses 15,26*)
7. Bless with the spirit (*Verse 16*)
8. Teach the uninformed (*Verses 16,24*)
9. Give thanks (*Verse 17*)
10. Critique: reinforce, question, or refute via dialog the concepts and conclusions of that day's participants (*Verse 29*))

There is no indication in Paul's admonition of any formalized sermon or anything that might resemble such. Biblically speaking, the spiritual growth of early believers was facilitated through the processes of teaching, dialog, and discourse. Many carelessly assume Paul validates formal "preaching" as Luke describes in *Acts 20:9 – "Seated in a window was a young man named Eutychus, who was sinking into a deep sleep as Paul talked on and on* (was long preaching – KJV). *When he was sound asleep, he fell to the ground from the third story and was picked up dead."* [142] A closer look at the word "preaching" (*"dialegomai"*) reveals the word literally means "interactive dialog" – discussion.[143] It is doubtful Paul left many questions unanswered. "Dialogue" with his listeners was the natural interactive method of teaching used by Paul, patterned after the teaching methods of Jesus Himself:

1. Acts 17:2 – "As was his custom, Paul went into the synagogue, and on three Sabbath days he reasoned ("dialegomai" – discussed) with them from the Scriptures."

2. Acts 17:17 – "So he reasoned ("dialegomai" – conversed) in the synagogue with both Jews and God-fearing Greeks, as well as in the marketplace day by day with those who happened to be there."

3. Acts 18:4 – "Every Sabbath he reasoned ("dialegomai" – conversed) in the synagogue, trying to persuade Jews and Greeks."

4. Acts 18:19 – "They arrived at Ephesus, where Paul left Priscilla and Aquila, He himself went into the synagogue and reasoned ("dialegomai" – conversed) with the Jews."

5. Acts 19:8 – "Paul entered the synagogue and spoke boldly ("dialegomai" – vigorously debated) there for three months, arguing persuasively about the kingdom of God."

6. Acts 19:9 – "But some of them became obstinate; they refused to believe and publicly maligned the Way. So, Paul left them. He took the disciples with him and had discussions ("dialegomai" – verbal interaction) daily in the lecture hall of Tyrannus."

7. Acts 20:7 – "On the first day of the week we came together to break bread. Paul spoke to the people ("dialegomai" – verbal interaction) and, because he intended to leave the next day, kept on talking until midnight."

8. Acts 24:12 – "My accusers did not find me arguing ("dialegomai" – debating) with anyone at the temple or stirring up a crowd in the synagogues or anywhere else in the city."

9. Acts 24:25 – "As Paul was talking ("dialegomai" – verbal interaction) about righteousness, self-control, and the judgment to come, Felix was afraid and said, 'That is enough for now! You may leave. When I find it convenient, I will send for you'."[144]

If one blindly accepts human intuitive teaching without verification, one is leaving himself open for spiritual deception as warned by every single one of the New Testament Apostles. "Do not treat prophecies with contempt but test them all; hold on to that which is good, reject *every kind of evil" – 1 Thessalonians 5:21.* One can never be certain he understands a truth, even from the pulpit, unless he is willing to evaluate and consider other possible explanations. The contention among many today is "lay" people are not qualified and should leave these matters to people that are above questioning. This applies to the message or sermon generated through one voice and can lead to blindly following that individual and his message rather than the truth of Jesus Christ. "The truth can set you free but only when you have proven the truth to be the truth."[145]

One of the most dangerous heresies of the first century was the philosophy of Gnosticism, which is arguably the basis for today's New Age Philosophical thinking. Some believe it had its beginnings in *Genesis 3* in the Garden of Eden – *"Now the serpent was more crafty than any of the wild animals the Lord God had made. He said to the woman, "Did God really say, you must not eat from any tree in the garden'"? (Genesis 3:1).* This one statement introduced sin into the world and is the way of Satan today – questioning and distorting the Word of God and as a result, leading astray the souls of those who are Biblically uninformed and solely dependent upon one voice to explain its truth.

Gnosticism, in its most basic form, taught God made man and since man was imperfect, God excuses man's sin. Since man's imperfection is excused, God will not hold man responsible, making the threat of Hell null and void. The philosophy teaches God will not punish an individual for something he is ultimately not responsible. Gnostics also taught Jesus was never human and only seemed to be human and His divinity joined the man Jesus at His baptism but left Him before He died. The Gnostic way of salvation represented escape from the body, not by faith, but through special knowledge – *"gnosis"* – possessed only by the Gnostic himself and available at a cost. Although this is not the forum to intimately discuss Gnosticism in-depth, the question arises – "How did this philosophy spread so rampantly and so soon after the earthly ministry of Christ"? The heresy was so great, every apostolic writer addressed it in their writings, perhaps none more prominent that John, Peter and Paul.

Ironically, Gnosticism can trace its beginnings to the church itself and its spread was facilitated through false and deceptive teaching: *"But there were also false prophets among the people, just as there will be false teachers among you. They will secretly introduce destructive heresies, even denying the sovereign Lord who bought them – bringing swift destruction upon themselves. Many will follow their depraved conduct and will bring the way of truth into disrepute. In their greed these teachers will exploit you with fabricated stories. Bold and arrogant, these men are not afraid to heap abuse on celestial beings. But these people blaspheme in matters they do not understand. They are blots and blemishes, reveling in their pleasures while they feast with you. With eyes full of adultery, they never stop sinning; they seduce the unstable; they are experts in greed – an accursed brood! THEY HAVE LEFT THE STRAIGHT WAY. For they mouth empty, boastful words and by appealing to the lustful desires of the flesh, they entice people who are just escaping from those who live in error. They promise them freedom, while they themselves are slaves of depravity"* – 2 Peter 2:1-3; 10,12,13-15; 18-19. *"My goal is that they may be encouraged in heart and united in love, so that they may have the full riches of complete understanding, in order that they may know the mystery of God, namely, Christ, in whom are hidden all the treasures of wisdom and knowledge. I tell you this so that no one may deceived you by fine-sounding arguments"* – Colossians 2:2-4. *"See to it that no one takes you captive through hollow and deceptive philosophy, which depends on human tradition and the elemental spiritual forces of this world rather than on Christ"* – Colossians 2:8. *"They went out from us, but they did not really belong to us. For if they had belonged to us, they would have remained with us; but their going showed that none of them belonged to us"* – 1 John 2:19. *"Many deceivers, who do not acknowledge Jesus Christ as coming in the flesh, have gone out into the world. Any such person is the deceiver and the antichrist. Watch out that you do not lose what we have worked for, but that you may be rewarded fully. Anyone who runs ahead and does not continue in the teaching of Christ does not have God; whoever continue in the teaching has both the Father and the Son. If anyone comes to you and does not bring this teaching, do not take them into your house or welcome them. Anyone who welcomes them shares in their wicked work"* 2 John 7-11.

False teachers may have been the source of Gnosticism, but its spread was facilitated by naïve listeners who failed to examine, debate or question the teaching – *"Dear friends, do not believe every spirit, but test the spirits to see whether they are from God, because many false prophets have gone out into the world. This is how you can recognize the Spirit of God: Every spirit that acknowledges that Jesus Christ has come in the flesh is from God, but every spirit that does no acknowledge Jesus is not from God. This is the spirit of the antichrist, which you have heard is coming and even now is already in the world" – 1 John 4:1-3.* In truth, the naïve listeners were just as guilty as the false teachers. A setting where there is one message originating from one human source without the possibility of dialog, risks spiritual deception. When that message is anything other than the Gospel of Jesus Christ, it is based solely on human intuition and can be spiritually lethal.

"Had the early Christians begun listening to monologues (sermons) instead of being able to question whatever was being said, things would have fallen apart even quicker than they did. Why not personally evaluate your every belief with the brain you were given and the Holy Spirit in which you were blessed? Why leave your Biblical beliefs up to chance? That is your reasonable duty. There is an all too human response of people finding a charismatic individual who reveals to them a few remarkable truths, and then they just swallow everything they teach. They stop questioning everything. A façade of harmony appears to be present when only a few people are permitted to express their thoughts through a formal sermon. This was not at all what Jesus or the Apostles intended. We should not put some individuals on a pedestal and consider only their opinions concerning the Scriptures."[146] According to Reverend W.A. Criswell, who pastored the First Baptist Church of Dallas, Texas for over forty years, "When a man goes to church, he often hears a sermon that rehashes everything he has read in the editorials, newspapers and magazines. The listener says, 'Preacher, I know what the television commentator says – I hear him every day; I know what the editorial writer has to say – I read it every day; I know what the magazines have to say – I read them every week. What I really want to know is, how do I find Jesus Christ?'"

Preparing for a recent associational training session for Sunday School and Small Group Bible Study leadership, I visited with a gentleman I had met several years earlier who acquired the nickname, "Mr. Sunday School," due to his life-long dedication to formal Small Group Bible study. He was ninety-four years of age and in failing health, so rather than ask him to assist with the sessions which he had done in the past, I sat down with him at his home and video-taped an open-air conversation. I will never forget his response to one of the questions I posed regarding formal worship "sermons" in comparison to Small Group Bible Studies as relates to one's spiritual growth. Without hesitation he replied, "the problem with sermons is we have way too many individuals delivering them who love to hear themselves preach and that's all they want to do!"

Being on the plus side of sixty years of age and based on the fact my parents had me in church every time the church doors were opened, I suppose I began sitting through a formal worship service at the age of around five years. If this is correct, I calculate I could have sat through potentially 9,338 sermons. Considering I probably missed a few due to sickness or neglect, let us round that number off to 9,250 for discussion sake. If I take into consideration each sermon consisted of 30 minutes (and I can certainly recollect many being much longer – or at least they seemed that way), that means I have spent 4,625 hours, or 192.7 days (almost 6-1/2 months), listening to sermons in my lifetime. I can honestly confess I cannot remember a single-one! In fact, I am ashamed to say, I cannot remember what my pastor preached just this past Sunday! Some of that can be blamed on age or senility. I believe most can be blamed on the fact it is just not interesting and too reminiscent of a college classroom setting where emphasis is centered on media and note-taking. Clyde Reid, author of "The Empty Pulpit", a study in the art of "preaching" as a means of communication states, "Less than 1/3 of those attending a church service are able to reproduce the central message of the sermon clearly and accurately, while even in their general lives, very little is changed by the message they have heard."[147]

Is the sermon spiritually effective? Dutch theologian and journalist Klaas Runia notes, "If any part of the church's life and activities is under strong criticism, it is the sermon. Again and again the question is asked whether "preaching" has any meaning at all in our day and age. Many people, and among them there are quite a few theologians, believe that the sermon as we know it, is a relic of the past. It has become an antiquated means of communication."[148]

I personally categorize sermons in six ways:

1. *"Lullaby Sermons"* – these are sermons that are monotone in nature, boring and sleep inducing. I equate these to a 3:30 PM college class on a Friday afternoon with a professor who is

about as interesting, as my dad used to say, "a wart on one's posterior." The message may be sincere, but the presentation is in no way attention grabbing.

2.   *"Locker Room Sermons"* – the sermons that are typically called "old fashioned fire and brimstone." They almost want to make you slap your grandma if she is sitting next to you. These messages typically appeal to the emotions, but little to the intellect. They are exciting, but the excitement is typically short lived. They might fire us up for the "game," but once we leave the stadium, they tend to fade quickly.

During my business travels, I was blessed to meet a wonderful gentleman and his family from Eastern Tennessee. One Wednesday night, I invited he and his family to dinner. He agreed, on the premise I attend church with him. I was delighted! He warned me, knowing I came from a Southern Baptist Church, the service might be a little different from what I was accustomed. He let me know the pastor may "jump the pews" and "usher in the spirit." Since this was a freewill mountain church, I expected a little excitement, but being a Wednesday mid-week service, surely it would be toned down a notch. It was not. He was correct, but it was interesting to say the least. I will say one thing, I cannot recall what the message was about, but the pastor kept my attention. His sense of balance and acrobatics was astounding.

3.   *"Laboratory Sermons"* – these are "seminary" sermons typical of what are heard in most churches today and easily attainable from the internet, requiring limited preparation. There is a subject, Scripture reference, 3-4 points and a conclusion – as textbook as they come. Similar sermons are those which are cryptic in nature – where one takes a word and uses the letters of that word to make a point. In other words, one takes the word ACTS and expounds on the fact "A" stands for action; "C" stands for commitment; "T" stands for trust; and "S" stands for something or another. I am not sure the nature or the goal of these messages, but one can easily utilize that method to fill up 30 minutes – or longer.

4.   *"Get-On Board Sermons"* – these sermons are sales pitches and all about promoting the church and its leadership. They have

absolutely nothing to do with the Gospel but rather advertise the church and its programs. "We have 15 programs for kids, we have 12 programs for teens, we offer 15 coffee flavors at 2 of 3 of our kiosks, we have reduced our debt by over 50% in the last twenty years, and all under my leadership." These sermons are designed to appeal to potential new members and uplift the disenfranchised, attempting to convince them what a wonderful entertainment environment they possess and how blessed they are to have such wonderful "leadership." Paul describes this message as *"saying what their itching ears want to hear" (2 Timothy 4:3)*. If an altar call is rendered, one wonders who should respond, since no Gospel was ever presented, other than the Gospel of the "church."

5. *"Politically Motivated Sermons"* – these are sermons usually presented around a political election, where the preacher attempts to use Scripture to justify voting for a particular candidate. If you are a part of a typical southern conservative fellowship, you are usually told Republicans are the only one's Heaven- bound and heaven forbid you support a Democratic cause. This message, if it can be called such, has the same problem as the "Get-On Board Sermon" – the Gospel is never presented. When a "preacher's" political preferences are clearer than his proclamation of the Gospel, one has a major spiritual problem and can readily understand why the mission of the church is skewed.

6. *"Gospel Sermons"* – these are rarely ever presented, the reason being the vast majority attending formal services are professed believers who consider this message redundancy. It is far more popular for the orator to speak on the accomplishments of the church and how professed believers should live their lives in service to the body rather than arming the masses to take to the unharvested fields.

Perhaps in none of his letters did Paul express the style and manner of his proclamation better than in his letters to the believers at Corinth:

1. *1 Corinthians 2:1-5 – "And so it was with me, brothers and sisters. When I came to you, I did not come with eloquence or human wisdom as I proclaimed to you the testimony about God. For I resolved to know nothing while I was with you except Jesus*

Christ and Him crucified. I came to you in weakness and great fear and trembling. My message and my preaching were not with wise and persuasive words, but with a demonstration of the Spirit's power, so that your faith might not rest on human wisdom but on God's power." Paul did not proclaim with an outline, structured sermon, plays on the alphabet, or simply to hear himself preach. He proclaimed the Gospel! There should never be a message shared at any gathering of God's people where the Gospel is not the center of the testimony.

2. *1 Corinthians 1:17; 23 – "For Christ did not send me to baptize, but to preach the Gospel – not with wisdom and eloquence, lest the cross of Christ be emptied of its power." "But we preach Christ crucified..."* The Gospel must be proclaimed in the power of the Holy Spirit working through an empty vessel. A teaching shared through the Holy Spirit will not bore its listeners, especially those who are true to the Word.

3. *2 Corinthians 4:5 – "For what we preach is not ourselves, but Jesus Christ as Lord, and ourselves as your servants for Jesus sake."* It is all about Him and has nothing to do with us. When the message is anything other than Jesus Christ, it is self-centered and a waste of time for both the teacher and the listener.

Paul's proclamation was based on the teachings of Christ, with one major addition. Jesus proclaimed the love of God and salvation through the acceptance of that love. Paul built upon that same message, by not only proclaiming the same agape love Christ proclaimed, but went a step further – Jesus not only proclaimed love but gave His life to prove that love. And not only that, He arose from the grave and has prepared an eternal place for those who love Him to reside with Him for eternity. Paul's proclamation was a reminder of that sacrificial love and how to find it – *1 Corinthians 15:1-4 – "Now, brothers and sisters, I want to remind you of the gospel I preached to you, which you received and on which you have taken your stand. By this gospel you are saved, if you hold firmly, to the word I preached to you. Otherwise, you have believed in vain. For what I received I passed on to you as of first importance: that Christ died for our sins according to the Scriptures, that he was buried, that he was raised on the third day according to the Scriptures."* This is the Gospel. It is not Paul's Gospel, but he received it from the One who authored it and was duly obligated to share it, just as we are. This is what he proclaimed. No Christian should testify of anything else. Proclamation of this message – His Gospel – is not reserved for one man to share; nor is it reserved for a pulpit. In fact, nowhere in Scripture is there one individual mandated to be a "mouth" for believers – much less a paid one. We are all proclaimers and our lives are the only pulpit most will ever see–"*We are ambassadors for Christ*" *(2 Corinthians 5:20).*

There is a difference between "preaching" and "teaching." "Whether one is "preaching" ("*kerygma*" – proclaiming) to unbelievers or "teaching" ("*didache*" – doctrinal tutorage) believers, the message to both believer and unbeliever alike is Jesus Christ."[149] "They – the apostles – proclaimed a person. Their message was frankly Christocentric. Indeed, the Gospel is referred to simply as Jesus or Christ: 'He preached Jesus to him – Jesus the man, Jesus crucified, Jesus risen, Jesus exalted to the place of power in the universe; Jesus who meantime was present among His people in the Spirit.' The risen Christ was unambiguously central in their message."[150]

"The Christian family needs a restoration of the Biblical practice of mutual exhortation and mutual ministry. Granted, the gift of teaching is present in the church. But teaching is to come from all the believers (*"For you can all prophesy in turn so that everyone may be instructed and encouraged"* – 1 Corinthians 14:31) as well as those who are specially gifted to teach (*Ephesians 4:11; James 3:1*). The church needs fewer pulpiteers (and puppeteers) and more spiritual facilitators. We move far outside of biblical bounds when we allow teaching to take the form of a conventional sermon and relegate it to a class of professional orators."[151] If for any reason the Gospel is not the only message being shared in your fellowship or the one you might be considering, please find another. It is wasted effort, both for you and the one delivering the "so-called" message.

Chapter 10

WHY "SERMONIZERS"– WHY NOT MISSIONARIES?

"But when the apostles Barnabas and Paul heard of this, they tore their clothes and rushed out into the crowd, shouting: 'Friends, why are you doing this? We too are only human like you. Even with these words, they had difficulty keeping the crowd from sacrificing to them" – Acts 14:14-15,18. "But you are not to be called 'Rabbi,' for you have one Teacher, and you are all brothers. And do not call anyone on earth 'father,' for you have one Father, and He is in heaven. Nor are you to be called instructors, for you have one Instructor, the Messiah" – Matthew 23:8-10.

If Biblical support for the "sermon" is in question, then what about the titled and compensated position from which it originates? Every Protestant church is led by a "preacher," the Biblical justification of such arguably non-existent. The traveling Apostles never remained at any *"ekklesia"* for an extended period and deliberately left those believers so they could function as intended with Jesus Christ as their head. To remain would have resulted in total dependence on their leadership, thus hindering the cause of Christ amongst the body. The New Testament *"ekklesia"* knew nothing of a paid position with a titled head. Why would such be necessary? Why is it necessary today?

There is no specific definition of "preaching" in the New Testament. Dutch theologian Klaas Runia gives an interesting take on the word in his "Tyndale Biblical Theology Lecture." He notes there are over thirty-three verbs in the New Testament that reference "preaching," the most common being the following:

1. *"kerussein"* – meaning a message shared; an announcement; a herald; the most typical description of preaching when speaking of Jesus and the Apostles.
2. *"evangelizesthai"* – where we get our word "evangelistic." This word is used some forty-four times in the New Testament and means "the proclamation of good news." That "good news" is the Gospel.
3. *"marturein"* – means testimony of eye-witness events.
4. *"didaskein"* – meaning teaching or instruction.
5. *"propheteuein"* – warning of coming events.
6. *"parakalein"* – meaning an exhortation of the Gospel.[152]

We could then surmise a good New Testament definition of "preaching" to be, "an announcement of evangelistic importance, based on eye-witness events, exhorting through teaching and instruction, a path to eternal salvation proclaimed by all believers." "Eye-witness testimony" would include the apostles and those such as Barnabas and perhaps Timothy, who received direct testimony and affirmation from the apostles. Nowhere in the New Testament do we find a "call," mandate, or exhortation to "preach" formally for anyone other than perhaps the apostles and those assigned by them. Even so, it is debatable their methods of proclamation could even be classified as "preaching," at least as we understand it today. There is nothing "formal" about sharing the Gospel. Regardless, theirs were not paid or titled positions.

Paul is clear there were individuals gifted with leadership abilities in the early *"ekklesia"* – *"So Christ Himself gave the apostles, the prophets, the evangelists, the pastors* (elders) *and teachers, to equip His people for works of service, so that the body of Christ may be built up until we all reach unity in the faith and in the knowledge of the Son of God and become mature, attaining to the whole measure of the fullness of Christ" – Ephesians 4:11-13*. However, since there was no class or caste distinction in the early church between "lay people" and "clergy," there is no indication these gifts were bestowed on privileged individuals who were assigned formal positions – paid ones at that. They were of the body – the *"ekklesia"*–and served accordingly. These were not position's to be lorded over those who possessed "lesser" gifts (*"As it is, there are many parts, but one body" – 1 Corinthians 12:20*). To do such would have split the body into the "gifted" versus the "ungifted" and left those who were "ungifted" dependent on the "gifted" to expound the Scriptural truths, creating apathy and passivity eerily similar to what we see in the "church" today – one individual, one voice and one message, resulting in passive, and sometimes gullible and ignorant hearers.

Scripture appears devoid of titled positions in the early New Testament *"ekklesia,"* much less anything resembling the compensated positions we see today, the titled office of "preacher" being no exception. There are, however, several verses supporters use to bolster support for such a position:

A. *1 Timothy 5:17-18 – "The elders who direct the affairs of the church well are worthy of double honor, especially those whose work is preaching and teaching. For the Scripture says, 'Do not muzzle an ox while it is treading out the grain', and 'The worker deserves his wages'."* The key word in this passage is the word *"honor."* Supporters of a paid, titled office of "preacher" consider *"honor"* (*"times"*) to be money. Others believe Paul is referencing, if "oxen are worthy to receive food, and a hard-working laborer is worthy to receive his pay, so an "elder" or shepherd is worthy to receive "honor" or respect from those he shepherds. Also, referencing *Verse 3* of this same chapter, Paul notes – *"Give proper recognition* (single honor) *to those widows who are really in need"* – If we are confident that 'double honor' is the same as a laborer's wage, then all the true widows in the church should get half the salary that the senior pastor makes. The Greek word for *"honor"* (*"times"*) is used in both verses to literally mean, "respect." In other words, the godly people in the church deserve respect, especially if they teach and shepherd–and the widows should be respected too.

B. *1 Timothy 6:1 – "All who are under the yoke of slavery should consider their masters worthy of full respect* ("honor" – KJV) *so that God's name and our teaching may not be slandered."* The same word for "honor" (*"times"*) used in *5:17-18* is used here. If "double honor" means we should pay our elders a salary, then employing the same analogy, slaves should pay their masters a salary."[153]

C. 1 Corinthians 9:14 – "In the same way, the Lord has commanded that those who preach the gospel should receive their living from the gospel." Paul was a missionary and a church planter. He, along with the other apostles, traveled from town to town. They never served in a position of leadership drawing a salary from any of the "ekklesia." In his writings, he repeatedly says they may have the right to receive support for their efforts, but they did not pursue it. If support were to be offered, which on occasion was, they were under no obligation to accept, but the fact these were people traveling the world to share the Gospel, they were open for support to meet their physical needs. This is not a reference to a paid position.

D. Galatians 6:6 – "Nevertheless, the one who receives instruction in the word should share all good things with their instructor." Even though this verse is used to support the contention of paid positions within the body, it is arguably a flimsy premise. "If you teach the word, you can expect to reap spiritual blessings from that work. This has nothing to do with money."[154]

E. Philippians 4:14-19 – "Yet it was good of you to share in my troubles. Moreover, as you Philippians know, in the early days of your acquaintance with the gospel, when I set out from Macedonia, not one church shared with me in the matter of giving and receiving, except you only; for even when I was in Thessalonica, you sent me aid more than once when I was in need. Not that I desire your gifts; what I desire is that more be credited to your account. I have received full payment and have more than enough. I am amply supplied, now that I have received from Epaphroditus the gifts you sent. They are a fragrant offering, and acceptable sacrifice, pleasing to God. And my God will meet all your needs according to the riches of His glory in Christ Jesus." Though he did not seek support from the Philippians or any other "ekklesia", Paul gladly accepted it as a blessing. It was, however, as he noted – a gift – not a salary.

In turn, there are verses that contradict the notion of a paid position within the "ekklesia:"

A. *Acts 20:33-35* – *"I have coveted no one's silver or gold or clothes. You yourselves know that these hands ministered to my own needs and to the men who were with me. In everything I showed you that by working hard in this manner you must help the weak and remember the words of the Lord Jesus, that He Himself said, 'It is more blessed to give than to receive'."*

B. *1 Corinthians 9:18* – *"What is my reward? That, when I preach the gospel, I may offer the gospel without charge, so as not to make full use of my right in the gospel."*

C. *2 Thessalonians 3:7-10* – *"For your yourselves know how you ought to imitate us, because we were not idle when we were with you, nor did we eat anyone's bread without paying for it, but with toil and labor we worked night and day, that we might not be a burden to any of you. It was not because we do not have that right, but to give you in ourselves an example to imitate. For even when we were with you, we would give you this command: If anyone is not willing to work, let him not eat."*

D. *1 Peter 5:1-3* – *"Therefore, I exhort the elders among you, as your fellow elder and witness of the sufferings of Christ, and a partaker also of the glory that is to be revealed, shepherd the flock of God among you, exercising oversight not under compulsion, but voluntarily, according to the will of God; and not for sordid gain but with eagerness; not domineering over those in your charge, but being examples to the flock."*

Church history may substantiate the compensated office of the modern-day "preacher," but arguably Scripture does not. We must remind ourselves, the New Testament *"ekklesia"* consisted of loosely fragmented and randomly scattered groups meeting in homes. As a result, they were small and likely somewhat independent. With its impending growth, especially from differing people groups and sects, it became necessary to organize the body to allow for the uninhibited spread of the Gospel in addition to meeting the needs of its members. The Apostles began by choosing "deacons" – individuals assigned responsibility to oversee the daily distribution of provisions among the body to make sure needs were fairly and equally met, hence removing that responsibility from the Apostles allowing them to *"give attention to prayer and the ministry of the word" (Acts 6:1-4)*. Paul provides a list of qualifications for these individuals in *1 Timothy 3:8-13*. The Greek word for "deacon" is *"diakonos"* and means "one who serves."[155] Based on the fragmentation of the *"ekklesia,"* these individuals were likely chosen by the body through the oversight of the "elders" and assigned responsibility for specific groups of "house churches."

The only other leadership assigned in the New Testament *"ekklesia"* specifically established by Paul was the "overseer." Both "deacons" and "overseers" are referenced together in *Philippians 1:1*. It appears clear from this verse "deacons" and "overseers" were of the body – not lords over it or of a separate class or caste – *"Paul and Timothy, servants of Christ Jesus, to all God's holy people in Christ Jesus at Philippi, TOGETHER with the overseers and deacons."* It is also noteworthy he addresses the body first, not singling out one in a titled position of leadership. "Overseers" and "deacons" are also referenced together as a group in *Acts 6:1-4* and *1 Timothy 3*.

There appear to be three Greek words referenced in Scripture describing the "overseer" – "elder" (*"presbuteros"*), "overseer" (*"episkopos"*), and pastor or shepherd (*"poimaino"*). We find the use of all three words in *Acts 20:17,28*. Some translations substitute the word *"bishop,"* as in *Titus 1:7* (KJV), in place of "elder," but the Greek translation is the same and obviously references the same person. *Titus 1:6,7* reveals the "elder" IS an "overseer" – *"An elder must be blameless, faithful to his wife…"*; *"Since an overseer manages God's household…"* Both words appear to reference the same person. The Greek word for "elder" in *Verse 6* is *"presbuteros"* and for "overseer" in *Verse 7* is *"episkopos."* The word "elder" would appear to reference the individual's character and spiritual maturity (which would likely include the gifts of teaching and evangelism), while "overseer" references his duties and responsibilities within the fragmented body. An "overseer" is an "elder."[156]

In *1 Peter 5:1-2*, Peter addresses the "elders" and refers to them as "shepherds," even referencing himself as a *"fellow elder;"* he encourages them to *"shepherd God's flock."* The Greek word for "shepherd" or "pastor" is *"poimaino."* An "elder" therefore has two responsibilities – oversight and shepherding. All three terms – *"episkopos," "presbuteros,"* and *"poimaino,"* therefore reference the same individual. "Elders" are "bishops" who are also "pastors." "Those who oversee are to be elders who are spiritually mature. In the church, every "elder" performs the duties of a "shepherd." The one who is called a "pastor" must be an "elder," but he is not greater than other men."[157] "Deacons" and "overseers" were individuals of the body assuming responsibilities so assigned as confirmed by Paul in *1 Thessalonians 5:12 – "Now we ask you, brothers and sisters, to acknowledge those who work hard among you, who care for you in the Lord and who admonish you."* They were servant-leaders – working "among" the body–not of a separate class or caste. There appears not even the remotest indication in Scripture regarding the establishment of titles, positions, or offices in the early New Testament church, must less compensated ones. There is no indication such was even considered.

So, when and why did the contention arise purporting a paid cleric within the early church? Cyprian (200-258) is the first Christian writer to mention the practice of financially supporting a clergy. He argued just as the Levites were supported by the tithe, so the Christian clergy should be supported from the same source. But this is misguided thinking. Today, the Levitical system has been abolished. As noted, we are all priests now. Cyprian's plea was rare for its time and it was not until some 300 years later that Christian leaders began to advocate tithing as the means to support a clergy caste.[158]

Constantine, once again, can be assigned the dubious honor of being the Father of clergy salaries. He was the first to institute the practice of paying a fixed salary to the clergy from church funds and imperial treasuries.[159] As pagan priests were compensated, he saw it as being unfair that self-appointed Christian (including Roman Catholics) leadership be afforded the same privilege. Thus, was born the clergy salary, a harmful practice that has no root in the New Testament.[160]

Pope Leo X (1475-1521) continued and built upon this practice. He was a member of the elite de Medici family and noted for his assigning of elite church positions, especially those of bishops, to his close friends and relatives. He tapped into the Vatican treasury to support his extravagant lifestyle. When the treasury ran low on funds, he implemented an interesting new fund-raising scheme – selling forgiveness of sins for money. For a fee, relatives could get a deceased loved one out of Purgatory. At the right price, they could also save up for their own future sins – a sort of spiritual IRA.[161] His tastes were costly, and he was only too happy to spend lavishly on himself, his self-appointed positions of church leadership, and his desire for entertainment and the arts. His policy of selling indulgences – money for forgiveness – spread to

Europe and was met with disdain by Martin Luther. Reformation was born when Leo refused to see a problem with the disgraceful sales.[162]

The Reformation arguably did little to change the thought process of a paid cleric. John Calvin bemoaned the Roman Catholic Church because its practices were based on "human inventions" rather than on the Bible, but he did the same thing.[163] Luther also built on this premise making the office of "preacher" a separate and exalted office. He believed the sharing of God's Word belonged to a special order – "God speaks through the preacher. A preacher is a minister of God who is set apart, yea, he is an angel of God, a very bishop sent by God, a savior of many people, a king and prince in the Kingdom of Christ. There is nothing more precious or nobler in the earth and in this life than a true, faithful parson or preacher. You ought to listen to the pastor not as a man, but as God."[164] Luther's premise arguably borders on blasphemy and set a dangerous precedent of exalting and equating human intuition to the wisdom and power of God.

Calvin indirectly continued another policy implemented by Leo X himself. He emphasized that the "preacher" or the pastor had a duty to provide care and healing to the congregation.[165] He was to bring healing, cure and compassion to God's hurting people – for a price. This idea lives on in the Protestant world today. It is readily seen in the contemporary concepts of pastoral care, pastoral counseling, and Christian psychology. In the present-day church, the burden of such care falls on the shoulders of one man – the "preacher." In the first century church, it fell on the shoulders of the entire church and a group of seasoned, non-compensated, non-titled, non-positioned men called "elders." Today's "office" of "preacher" is the same as that of a modified Catholic Priest. The Reformation brought about the "preacher" or "minister," all with the help of Calvin and Luther. And what we have today is a direct result.

The traditional "church" would not survive without the "preacher." He "preaches," councils, sometimes teaches, CEO's, visits, conducts funerals and marriages, referees, and on occasion, tends to his family. The majority are dedicated men and women of sincere spiritual intent. This chapter is not an indictment or vendetta against any of these individuals. Many fine, Godly, dedicated and spiritually diligent men (and women in some arenas) have served the pastorate well. Some have dedicated their entire adult lives endeavoring to serve the Lord by serving others through pastoring. There are too many to name that have shaped my life in ways they perhaps will never know until we reach eternity. To them, I say, "thank you," and am convinced eternal rewards await them in Heaven. It is not to them as a person this chapter is directed – it is to the "titled" and "salaried" position they represent. As noted, it is Biblically true there are those of the fellowship who are assigned leadership responsibilities in the body, but no Scripture envisions the establishment of paid positions within His Church. In fact, quite the contrary.

Just as the Israelites clamored for a king against the wishes of God, ("...'now appoint a king to lead us, such as all the other nations have.' But when they said, 'Give us a king to lead us,' this displeased Samuel; so, he prayed to the Lord. And the Lord told him: 'Listen to all that the people are saying to you; it is not you they have rejected, but they have rejected me as their king.' But the people refused to listen to Samuel. 'No!' they said. 'We want a king over us. Then we will be like all the other nations, with a king to lead us and go out before us and fight our battles'"–1 Samuel 8:5-7, 19-20), so the "church of man" clamored for an individual to fight their battles because other religions, especially first century Roman Catholicism, adopted the same strategy. As the Israelites were dissatisfied with God as their "King," so the church became dissatisfied with Jesus Christ as its Head.

Recalling childhood events is a challenge, especially at my age and the fact I have difficulty recalling where I placed my wallet or phone thirty minutes prior. One event from childhood I do recall is my mom's penchant for cleaning. There was no set day, but when she cleaned, it was not just "hit and miss" – it was the real deal. To say she was OCD is an understatement. Saturday was the usual day for this "grand" event, especially if the "preacher" was coming to dinner (lunch; we call it dinner in the south) the following day. The menu was even special – fried chicken or roast beef, macaroni and cheese, mashed potatoes or rice, gravy, a veggie, and my mom's "out-of-this-world" desserts.

I wore the "clip-on" ties to church as a kid. I never attended church, at least on Sunday morning, without formal attire, even as a child. My dad always reminded me, "Put your best foot forward going to church, including the way you dress; wear your best – if it's a pair of overalls and "Brogan" shoes, wear them." The "clip-ons" were easy to remove, but it was frustrating because my mom made me remain in my church clothes during the "preacher's" visit. Once I purposely spilled gravy on the tie so moving forward, she would at least let me remove it if I kept all else intact. This "divine visitation" was equivalent to preparing for English "royalty." As a kid I could not help but wonder if this person was capable of walking on water, as I was taught Jesus did in my Bible story the previous Sunday.

On one occasion I dared asked the question of my father – "Why is this man so special?" My dad said it was because he was a "called man of God." I thought we were all "called," but dared not question further. I could not help but wonder (and still do) – where in Scripture is this "calling" found? What make this "titled position" so special? Is it his PHD's, DDS's, etc.? If it is, isn't that dangerous for the rest of us – insinuating religious education is a requirement for spiritual growth and for those of us who cannot afford, or choose not to participate, the Bible is off limits and needs to be handled only by paid professionals who can tell us what and how to decipher it so we won't have too for ourselves? What happened to the Holy Spirit – our seal of salvation – our "Teacher," "Counselor" and "Equipper?" What happened to the message of the Hebrew writer, in addition to Peter, who remind us as believers we are all priests and have direct access to the Father through our Great High Priest – His Son Jesus Christ? These were troubling concerns I was not prepared to discuss with my dad.

Another question I posed to my father – "What exactly is this man 'called' to do"? My dad's succinct answer was, "to preach." "Preach," as a child meant to stand on a pulpit behind a podium and yell at everyone (not so much today), wipe his brow a time or two, extend an altar call, pray and go home. If someone died or married, I might see him there also. "Preach," to a degree still means the same thing to me today and I still ask the same question – "Is this Biblical," and can such a position, rather than edify the body of Christ, have an adverse effect? Consider the following possible dangers:

First, it can cause division. Segregation of believers is not Biblical. To say that some are "called" to titled positions is saying there are those in the body possessing "privileged information" not relegated to the rest of the body. It says there are a few who are "gifted," but the rest are not

and must depend on the gifted ones for enlightenment. This is spiritually dangerous and minimizes the workings of the Holy Spirit in the individual believer's life and creates passivity in the pew. Early Christians
knew nothing of a clergy. *"ALL devoted; ALL called; ALL fellowshipped
together; ALL gave; ALL met together; ALL shared; ALL prayed; ALL
shared in the apostle's teaching."* The result – *"And God added..."* (Acts
2:42-47). From the lips of Jesus Himself – *"The greatest among you will
be your servant. For those who exalt themselves will be humbled, and
those who humble themselves will be exalted"* (Matthew 23:11-12).
His confirmation of no such religious hierarchy in His New Covenant
"ekklesia" should be a glaring message to the "church" of today.

Paul confirms in *1 Corinthians 12:12-14, 27* – *"Just as a body, though
one, has many parts, but all its many parts form one body, so it is with
Christ. For we were all baptized by one Spirit, so as, to form one body –
whether Jews or Gentiles, slave or free – and we were all given the on
Spirit to drink. Even so the body is not made up of one part but of many.
Now you are the body of Christ, and each one of you is a part of it."* We
are all one in the sight of God, and if saved, are sealed and taught by
the same Holy Spirit – *"There is one body and one Spirit, just as you
were called to one hope when you were called; one Lord, one faith, one
baptism, one God and Father of all, who is over all and through all and
in all"* (Ephesians 4:4-6).

Secondly, a titled and compensated position can cause contention.
Many in today's "church" choose to "worship" the person rather than
the Savior and Lord He is supposed to represent. This is seen on many
occasions when a pastor chooses to leave a fellowship and certain of the
membership choose to leave and follow. This is not new and occurred
in the church at Corinth, and was addressed by Paul – *"I appeal to you,
brothers and sisters, in the name of our Lord Jesus Christ, that all of
you agree with one another in what you say and there be no divisions
among you, but that you be perfectly united in mind and thought. My
brothers and sisters, some from Chloe's household have informed me
that there are quarrels among you. What I mean is this: One of you says,
'I follow Paul'; another, 'I follow Apollos'; another, 'I follow Cephas';
still another, 'I follow Christ'. Is Christ divided? Was Paul crucified for
you?"* (1 Corinthians 1:10-12). It was not the intention of the early
New Testament church founders to establish one man (or woman) as
the mouth of the church, but instead encourage the participation of

all who *"have a hymn, or a word of instruction, a revelation, a tongue, or an interpretation" (1 Corinthians 14:26).*

Thirdly, the position can be an unwarranted financial burden. One must consider the monetary burden positional leadership places on a fellowship. Considering an average Evangelical church has 150 or so active members, with an average of 50 or so families (three members per family); factoring in an average giving participation of 80% and considering a potential salary, including perks, insurance, housing, car expense, etc., of $75,000 annually, the annual burden per family for the "preacher" alone could reach upwards to $2000 or more – all in the name of having someone to "preach" to us. As previously noted, when one adds the cost for additional staff, capital investments, fixed costs, debt, utilities, etc., the family burden becomes staggering. These exorbitant numbers cannot help but leave little if any room for mission expenditures outside the four walls. The office itself is essentially that of a "spiritual CEO," with some earning CEO salaries beyond comprehension.

Some, who defend the office of "preacher" contend that Paul was a "preacher" and are quick to note he demanded payment for his services. Those that make that contention need to reexamine the Scriptures. Paul was an apostle. The abstract definition of an apostle appears to reference someone who had direct contact with Jesus and received a specific mandate from Him to deliver a specific message. This definition holds water, with Barnabas perhaps being the exception; he too was called an apostle (*Acts 14:14* – *"But when the apostles Barnabas and Paul heard of this..."*), but there is no indication he ever encountered Jesus Christ in a physical way. It is likely he was appointed an apostle by his peers.

We know the eleven disciples (less Judas) were considered the original apostles. Paul met Jesus on the Damascus road, even though he considered himself *"untimely or abnormally born"* or unworthy (*1 Cor. 15:8-9* – *"For I am the least of the apostles and do not even deserve to be called an apostle, because I persecuted the church of God."*). As earlier noted, the message of the apostle was the Gospel and their method of disseminating that message was through "preaching", but not in the context we understand positional "preaching" today. Theirs, as ours should be, was proclamation. Paul was a *"kerusso"* (Greek), which is the New

Testament word typically used for "preacher." *"Kerusso"* means "crier or proclaimer."[166] As children of God commanded to share the Gospel, all of us are *"kerussos"* – proclaimers of the Gospel of Jesus Christ.

Paul made at least three – possibly four – missionary journeys. It is highly likely, "he traveled over 10,000 miles during his lifetime on behalf of the Gospel."[167] He was a Pharisee (*Acts 26:5*), the son of a Pharisee (*Acts 23:6*), born in the seaport city of Tarsus, was a business-man – "tent-maker" (*Acts 18:1-3;26:5*), and was educated under the renown Jewish teacher – Gamaliel (*Acts 22:3*). It could be assumed he was a person of some wealth and means. Based on the scope of his travels – by foot, ship, etc. – his expenses must have been costly, which is why he never demanded but was open to support from his church plants. Support could have been in the form of clothing, food, lodging, monetary or all the above. In fact, Paul refused support from the church at Corinth, explaining to them how he funded his ministry while there and why he refused help from them for his living expenses (*2 Corinthians 11:7-15*). To the elders of the church at Ephesus he echoes this same contention – *"I have not coveted anyone's silver or gold or clothing. You yourselves know that these hands of mine have supplied my own needs and the needs of my companions. In everything I did, I showed you that by this kind of hard work we must help the weak, remembering the words the Lord Jesus Himself said: 'It is more blessed to give than to receive'"* – Acts 20:33-35.

The Philippian church was probably the most supportive of his ministry, sending assistance while he was ministering at Thessalonica (*Philippians 4:16*) and while in prison in Rome (*Philippians 4:10-20*). Nonetheless, Paul was clear – he was not in it for any monetary gain but was receptive only for support to help with his needs – *"Unlike so many, we do not peddle the word of God for profit. On the contrary, in Christ we speak before God with sincerity, as those sent from God" (2 Corinthians 2:17).* He held no titled office; held no paid leadership position; did not adorn himself with any flashy robes, phylacteries, or tassels; sat in any chair upon any altar; nor stood behind any pulpit. He simply proclaimed the Gospel – house to house, in the marketplace, the streets, or wherever lost people were found – *"But we preach Jesus Christ crucified" (1 Corinthians 1:23).* There is no indication that any New Testament apostle even remotely considered serving in or assigning a titled office before God's people, let alone a paid position.

Fourthly, titled positions can foster "pew warmers." We have already noted the worn-out cliché – 15% of church members perform 100% of the work. We also affirmed there is no business that can be successful, let alone survive, with that type of inaction; the church is no different. When we attend a typical church service where we sit passively through performances that include a human generated and delivered oration, what exactly does this do for us in the pew? The answer is absolutely nothing, other than we have been entertained and sated to the point of "spiritual satisfaction." We are programmed; programmed to listen and hear, but nothing else. Formality has turned into entertainment directed to and for me – "my" music style, "my" preaching style, "my", "my," "my." As Reverend David Platt so aptly puts it–"And now the danger is that, when we gather in our church buildings to sing, and lift up our hands, in worship, we may not actually be worshiping the Jesus of the Bible. Instead we may be worshipping ourselves."[168] With this comes spiritual laziness; we are lulled to sleep spiritually and many times physically. We believe by attending a service, listening to a song and a message, and putting a dollar bill in the alms plate, we have worshipped and much of this has been fostered by the "one-man system." Nothing could be further from the truth.

Fifth, the message – what exactly does the "preacher" preach? "What message can he "preach?" In the most general sense of the word, the Old Testament Scriptures foretold and prepared the Jews for the coming of Messiah. The New Testament Scriptures revealed His coming, told of His ministry and message of salvation through a new and everlasting covenant ("*But in fact the ministry Jesus has received is as superior to theirs as the covenant of which He is mediator is superior to the old one, since the new covenant is established on better promises. For if there had been nothing wrong with that first covenant, no place would have been sought for another" – Hebrews 8:6-7*) and prophesied regarding His second coming. The message of the New Testament is the Gospel – the message Jesus brought into the world and commanded His followers to take to the lost (*Matthew 28:19-20*). It is the same message Paul proclaimed during his eleven-year mission. If the message to be "preached" or proclaimed is the Gospel, and the overwhelming majority warming pews in today's "church of man" are "professed" believers, then what is there to "preach?" "Preaching" is "proclamation" of the Gospel. True "preaching" occurs outside the church building and is the duty of every born-again believer; none of us are paid a monetary reward for this proclamation; our reward is eternal.

Sixth, it typically stifles spontaneity. It is a one-horse show. The "preacher" speaks, the people hear (sometimes), and that is that. There is no open means for interaction. If someone has a question or would like to discuss a verse or an issue in depth, there is no means for this to be accomplished. This was not the way of the early church. Today's "church" makes one man a "mouth" and the rest of us "ears." It makes us a spoon-fed inanimate object. This is dangerous – as Paul stresses in *Philippians 2:12-13 – "Continue to work out your salvation with fear and trembling, for it is God who works in you to will and to act in order to fulfill His good purpose."* It is you and I as individuals that will stand before Jesus Christ to answer for our actions or inactions.

Seventh, it completely goes against the message to the Hebrews. Whether it be Paul, Barnabas, Priscilla, Apollos, or whomever, that penned the Letter to the Hebrews, that person not only had a strong faith in Jesus Christ, but also a wealth of knowledge of the traditions and rituals of the Jewish people. That person was likely a Jew himself. Many of the Jewish believers made a complete lifestyle change and rebirth when they stepped out of the bonds of tradition and ritual into a fresh new life under the blood of Jesus Christ. But that change came with a cost. It came with persecution from their own families and coun-trymen who remained faithful to the old covenant and its traditions. The writer encouraged them to persevere and emphasizes the word *"better"* in describing Christ as the divinely human prophet, priest and king. Another interesting word used in this letter, and one the writer chooses to build upon in describing the New Covenant based on our relationship through the blood of Jesus Christ, is the word *"priest."*

The duties and qualifications of the Old Testament priest are well doc-umented in the Books of Law – Genesis, Exodus, Leviticus, Numbers, Deuteronomy. The Hebrew priest was to be in the family line of Levi and was the mediator between the people and God. He had access to the Holy of Holies within the temple and could venture where no com-moner could go. With the coming of Jesus Christ came a New Covenant – a new relationship (*Hebrews 1:1-2 – "In the past God spoke to our ancestors through the prophets at many times and in various ways, but in these last days he has spoken to us by his Son, whom he appointed heir of all things...*"). With this New Covenant relationship, Jesus Christ became our "high priest" and as believers, gave us direct access to His throne of grace (*Hebrews 5:1-6 – "Every high priest is selected from among the people and is appointed to represent the people in matters related to God, to offer gifts and sacrifices for sins. He is able to deal gently with those who are ignorant and are going astray, since he himself is subject to weakness. This is why he has to offer sacrifices for his own sins, as well as for the sins of the people. And no one takes this honor upon himself, but he receives it when called by God, just as Aaron was. In the same way, Christ did not take on himself the glory of becoming a high priest. But God said to him, 'You are my Son; today I have become your Father.' And He says in another place, 'You are a priest forever, in the order of Melchizedek'."*).

As a result of His New Covenant, we have no need for any individual to act on our behalf before our Lord (*Hebrews 8:1-2 – "Now the main point of what we are saying is this: We do have such a high priest, who sat down at the right hand of the throne of the Majesty in heaven, and who serves in the sanctuary, the true tabernacle set up by the Lord, not by a mere human being."*). The modern-day pastoral office has arguably upended this main point stressed by the *Hebrews* writer. The teachings of *1 Corinthians 12-14* that every member has both the right and the privilege to minister in a church meeting and the message of *1 Peter 2* that every member of the "*ekklesia*" is a functioning priest, has been made null and void by this "office." The position of "preacher" blocks that direct access to Christ and actually encourages just the opposite – a non-functioning body that believe it is their obligation to leave everything to the work of this one individual. This system not only encourages spiritual laziness, it facilitates it. Early Christians knew nothing of a clergy, which should serve as a message to the modern-day church–*1 John 2:20,27 – "But you have an anointing from the Holy One, and all of you know the truth..." As for you, the anointing that you received from Him remains in you, and you do not need anyone to teach you."*

Eighth, it shifts all spiritual responsibility for spiritual growth for the entire body onto one man. But how can one man be expected to assume this overbearing responsibility? "The contemporary pastor not only does damage to God's people, he does damage to himself. For this reason, 1400 ministers in all denominations across the U.S. are fired or forced to resign each month. Over the past twenty years, the average length of a pastorate has declined from seven years to just over four years."[169] Even Paul acknowledged the overwhelming burden he bore for the *"ekklesias"* under his apostolic responsibility – *"Besides everything else, I face daily the pressure of my concern for all the churches"* – *2 Corinthians 11:28.* Did Christ or the Apostles ever intend for one person to assume such responsibility?

In business there is a system utilized by quality control analysts referred to as a "Root Cause Analysis." The premise of this method is to intently research an issue where a quality failure has occurred. The method demands one continue to investigate and reverse drive the issue through all production processes to find the initial cause of the problem. For instance, a company is producing widgets and a batch of widgets are rejected. A Root Cause Analysis is initiated. Phase one notes the widgets were formed wrong; why? Phase 2 says they were formed incorrectly because the machine was set up incorrectly; why? Phase 3 says the machine was set up incorrectly because the operator was improperly trained; why? Phase 4 says the operator was improperly trained because his supervisor was unqualified; why? Phase 5 says the supervisor was unqualified because he was not trained himself for the position; why? Phase 6 says training was not mandated in the job description; why? Phase 7 says this failure to mandate training falls on management and is the ultimate responsibility of the Plant Manager who in turn, answers to the President of the company, who did not feel it necessary to invest time, finances and attention to the proper training of employees. Bottom line, the root cause of the widget failure is traced back to the owner of the company. In this example, if something needs to be changed to implement the proper corrections, it needs to start at the top.

What does this have to do with the traditional church of today? If a church is failing in its mission, a "spiritual root cause analysis" is mandated. If the people of today's church are failing to heed their calling to take the Gospel outside its four walls, then either they are ignorant of their calling or ill-equipped; if they are ill-equipped, then they are improperly trained; if they are improperly trained, then those responsible for the equipping are either ill-prepared or are ignorant of their responsibilities, and if they are ignorant of their responsibilities or ill-prepared, they serve a broken system that needs to be fixed or replaced; and if the system is broken, then the one ultimately responsible as the CEO of that system is at fault.

James warns – *"Not many of you should become teachers, my fellow believers, because you know that we who teach will be judged more strictly" – James 3:1.* Not meaning to be condescending in any way, but by assuming a position of spiritual responsibility for someone other than one's self, one has set himself up as a type of "savior." Only One can claim that position. It may lend new credence to Jesus warning in *Matthew 24:4-5 – "Jesus answered: 'Watch out that no one deceives you. For many will come in my name, claiming, "I am the Messiah," and will deceive many'."* At the risk of being judgmental but not intending to be, if one chooses to put himself in that "position," he may be assuming accountability beyond human comprehension. Nowhere is this more prominently shown than through the prophetic warnings of Jeremiah and Ezekiel regarding the Lord's retribution against hypocritical religious leadership and its subsequent accountability for a wayward people:

a. *Jeremiah 7:4 – "Do not trust in deceptive words and say, 'This is the temple of the Lord, the temple of the Lord, the temple of the Lord'!"*

b. *Jeremiah 7:8-10 – "But look, you are trusting in deceptive words that are worthless. Will you steal and murder, commit adultery and perjury, burn incense to Baal and follow other gods you have not known, and then come and stand before Me in this house, which bears my Name, and say, 'We are safe' – safe to do all these detestable things? Has this house, which bears My Name, become a den of robbers to you? But I have been watching, declares the Lord'!"*

c. *Jeremiah 23:10-11 – "The land is full of adulterers; because of the curse the land lies parched and the pastures in the wilderness are withered. The prophets follow an evil course and use their power unjustly. Both prophet and priest are godless; even in my temple I find their wickedness,' declares the Lord."*

d. *Jeremiah 23:13-14 – "Among the prophets of Samaria I saw this repulsive thing: They prophesied by Baal and led my people Israel astray. And among the prophets of Jerusalem I have seen something horrible: They commit adultery and live a lie."*

e. *Jeremiah 23:16-17 – "This is what the Lord Almighty says: 'Do not listen to what the prophets are prophesying to you; they fill* you with false hopes. They speak visions from their own minds, not from the mouth of the Lord. They keep saying to those who despise me, 'The Lord says: You will have peace.' And to all who follow the stubbornness of their hearts they say, 'No harm will come to you'."

f. Jeremiah 23:21 – "I did not send these prophets, yet they have run with their message; I did not speak to them, yet they have prophesied."

g. Jeremiah 25:34-38 – "Weep and wail, you shepherds; roll in the dust, you leaders of the flock. For your time to be slaughtered has come; you will fall like the best of the rams. The shepherds will have nowhere to flee. The leaders of the flock no place to escape. Hear the cry of the shepherds, the wailing of the leaders of the flock, for the Lord is destroying their pasture. The peaceful meadows will be laid waste because of the fierce anger of the Lord. Like a lion he will leave his lair, and their land will become desolate because of the sword of the oppressor and because of the Lord's fierce anger."

h. Ezekiel 13:1-12 – "The word of the Lord came to me: 'Son of man, prophesy against the prophets of Israel who are now prophesying. Say to those who prophesy out of their own imagination: 'Hear the word of the Lord! This is what the Sovereign Lord says: Woe to the foolish prophets who follow their own spirit and have seen nothing! Your prophets, Israel, are like jackals among ruins. You have not gone up to the breaches in the wall to repair it for the people of Israel so that it will stand firm in the battle on the day of the Lord. Their visions are false and their divinations a lie. Even though the Lord has not sent them, they say, 'The Lord declares,' and expect Him to fulfill their words. Have you not seen false visions and uttered lying divinations when you say, 'The Lord declares,' though I have not spoken? Therefore, this is what the Sovereign Lord says: 'Because of your false words and lying visions, I am against you, declares the Sovereign Lord. My hand will be against the prophets who see false visions and utter lying divinations. They will not belong to the council of my people or be listed in the records of Israel, nor will they enter the land of Israel. Then you will know that I am the Sovereign Lord. Because they lead my people astray, saying, 'Peace,' when there is no peace, and because, when a flimsy wall is built, they cover it with whitewash, therefore tell those who *cover it with whitewash, that it is going to fall. Rain will come in torrents, and I will send hailstones hurtling down, and violent winds will burst forth. When the wall collapses, will people not ask you, 'Where is the whitewash you covered it with'?"*

Placing oneself in the position of being accountable for another individual's spirituality, in addition to facing the daily challenges of worldly influence upon one's own life, seems unrealistic. Assuming that responsibility for an entire body is unfathomable. Again – one must question if it is even Biblical.

Ninth, putting the responsibility for one's spiritual growth in the hands of one individual is also dangerous from another perspective – false teaching. In fact Paul warns in *1 Corinthians 2:4* of the danger in trusting man's intuition – *"My message and my preaching were not with wise and persuasive words, but with a demonstration of the Spirit's power, SO THAT YOUR FAITH MIGHT NOT REST ON HUMAN WISDOM, BUT ON GOD'S POWER."* Assigning one person to be the so-called spiritual leader of an entire body renders an open opportunity for Satan to influence masses of people with a deceiving message (*"But there were also false prophets among the people, just as there will be false teachers among you"–2 Peter 2:1; "For such people are false apostles, deceitful workers, masquerading as apostles of Christ. And no wonder, for Satan himself masquerades as an angel of light. It is not surprising, then, if his servants masquerade as servants of righteousness"–2 Corinthians 11:13-15; "For the time will come when people will not put up with sound doctrine. Instead, to suit their own desires, they will gather around them a great number of teachers to say what their itching ears want to hear. They will turn their ears away from the truth and turn aside to myths"–2 Timothy 4:3-4).* One must be willing to *"test every spirit to see if they are from God" (1 John 4:1)*, rather than accept any and everything that comes from a pulpit (*"The Spirit clearly says that in later times, some will abandon the faith and follow deceiving spirits and things taught by demons. Such teachings come through hypocritical liars, whose consciences have been seared as with a hot iron" 1 Timothy 4:1-2).* False hope, false teaching, and false religion was prevalent in the time of the Apostle's; it is epidemic today.

James Warren Jones (1931-1978) was an American ordained "preacher", faith healer and cult leader who conspired with his inner circle to direct a mass suicide and mass murder of his followers in his jungle commune at Jonestown, Guyana.[170] His message and antics sounded sincere and in line with the "religious system" of the day – love and peace. This man was a pawn of Satan and one whom Paul warned the Corinthians to be wary (*2 Corinthians 11:13-15*). 918 souls, including 304 children, paid the ultimate price for following one misguided individual.

David Koresh was an American cult leader of the Branch Davidians sect, claiming to be its final prophet. The Branch Davidians were a movement led by Ben Roden that splintered off from the Davidian Seventh-day Adventist Church.[171] Just as Jones' "church" in Jonestown, 79 souls plus David Koresh violently sacrificed their lives in a worthless endeavor in the name of religion and a misguided message through one man and his "titled position."

There were four major sects of Jewish religion and politics – Pharisees, Sadducees, Essenes, and Zealots – the foremost being the Pharisees and Sadducees. The Pharisees were noted for adding to the Scriptures, the bulk of their rules and regulations contained in the Jewish Talmud. The Sadducees were the opposite, taking away from the Scriptures – possessing no belief in the spirit world, angels, or the resurrection. Even though they bitterly opposed each other, they were united in their opposition against Jesus. The entirety of *Matthew 23* is addressed to these apostate religious leaders. This religious system and its accompanying leadership were so hated by Jesus, He pronounced eternal judgment upon them direct to their hypocritical faces. *Matthew 23* details the reasons for His disdain and should serve as a warning for us of the potential dangers of putting our confidence in man-made positions. It was dangerous then – it can be equally dangerous today:

1. Positional leadership is comprised of human beings and thus imperfect. *"The teachers of the law and the Pharisees sit in Moses' seat. So you must be careful to do everything they tell you. But do not do what they do, for they do not practice what they preach" (Verses 2-3).*
2. Positional leadership tends to breed self-indulgence. *"Everything they do is for people to see" (Verse 5).*
3. Positional leadership positions are of man and not from God. *"You are not to be called 'Rabbi,' for you have one Teacher and you are all brothers. And do not call anyone on earth 'father,'*

for you have one Father and He is in heaven. Nor are you to be called instructors, for you have one Instructor, the Messiah" (Verses 8-10).

4. Positional leadership tends to stress obedience to a system rather than the Gospel. *"You shut the door of the kingdom of heaven in people's faces. You yourselves do not enter, nor will you let those enter who are trying to" (Verses 13-14).*

5. Positional leadership tends to espouse service within and selective ministry without. A system that has no concern for the spiritual and physical needs of those on the outside, is not of God. The false message is, "it's ok to stay busy and serve yourselves; you are fulfilling your calling. Don't worry about those on the outside; they know we're here; but reaching out to them is not a viable option." Intentionally or unintentionally, this appears to be the church of today's mission statement and we are teaching others by word and deed to do the same. *"You travel over land and sea to win a single convert, and when you have succeeded, you make him twice as much a child of hell as you are" (Verse 15).*

6. Positional leadership can be a breeding ground for false teachers. *("Israel's watchmen are blind, they all lack knowledge; they are all mute dogs, they cannot bark; they lie around and dream, they love to sleep" – Isaiah 56:10; "Those who guide this people mislead them, and those who are guided are led astray" – Isaiah 9:16).* Fruitlessness within a body is a clear indication of false leadership. Our supposed commitment to Him becomes worthless when we become "fruitless." When leadership by example fosters camping out within the "church," all the while believing we are serving Him, we eventually convince ourselves evangelism really does not matter. This type teaching is heretical, blasphemous and straight out of hell. *"Woe to you blind guides! You say, 'If anyone swears by the temple, it means nothing; but if anyone swears by the gold of the temple is bound by that oath. You blind fools! Which is greater: the gold or the temple that makes the gold sacred?' You also say, 'if anyone swears by the altar, it means nothing; but if anyone swears by the gift on the altar is bound by that oath'. You blind men! Which is greater: the gift or the altar that makes the gift sacred? Therefore, anyone who swears by the altar, swears by it and everything on it. And anyone who swears*

by the temple swears by it and by the one who dwells in it. And he who swears by heaven, swears by God's throne and by the one who sits on it" (Verses 16-22).

7. Positional leadership tends to foster service to "mammon." It tends to neglect the "free-from-obligation," cheerful, from the heart, free-flowing giving purported by Jesus Christ and later by Paul, to support the needs of the truly needy and the mission that partners with the ministry. It focuses on its own wants and associated expenditures. *"You give a tenth of your spices – mint, dill, and cumin. But you have neglected the more important matters of the law – justice, mercy and faithfulness. You should have practiced the latter, without neglecting the former. You blind guides! You strain out a gnat but swallow a camel" (Verses 23-24).*

8. Positional leadership tends to purport submission to formalities, rules, regulations, obligations, and traditions – suggesting external appearance is more important than inward change. Pharisaic rules and regulations required the cleaning of eating utensils, not because they were dirty, but in case they had been used by a Gentile or sinner. But their rules did nothing to change the heart of their religious bigotry. *"You clean the outside of the cup and dish, but inside they are full of greed and self-indulgence. Blind Pharisee! First, clean the inside of the cup and dish, and then the outside will also be clean" (Verses 25-26).*

9. Positional leadership tends to substitute Christ-like compassion with joy, comfort, and satisfaction–all at the expense of the lost. It makes one appear as if he genuinely cares on the outside but overshadows what is on the inside or in the heart – hypocrisy – "we want you to think we care, but we really don't." *"You are like whitewashed tombs* (so painted as to be visible at night so as to not be stepped on or desecrated), *which look beautiful on the outside but on the inside are full of the bones of the dead and everything unclean" (Verse 27).*

10. Positional leadership tends to foster religious pride – a sin that can easily beset a position of leadership and one which Jesus takes all occasions to condemn. *"You build tombs for the prophets and decorate the graves of the righteous. And you say, 'If we had lived in the days of our ancestors, we would not have taken part with them in shedding the blood of the prophets. So, you testify against yourselves that you are the descendants of*

those who murdered the prophets. Go ahead, then, and complete what your ancestors started!" (Verses 29-32).

Lest I incur the wrath of traditional church goers everywhere, let me once again be clear; this is not an indictment against any individual, rather the titled, salaried office he/she represents with arguably no Scriptural evidence to support. Quite the contrary, when Jesus says we are *ALL* called, we are *ALL* "one," with no member being any more important than another – *ALL* means *ALL*; not "one," who supposedly has a "higher calling." This class distinction fosters division and apathy among us who are "not called" since we see ourselves incapable of understanding the Word of God and therefore do not even try. Where does Scripture say there is "one" who possesses extra-Biblical abilities and understanding over any other and is dutifully "called" to "formally preach" to me for a price what I am not capable of understanding as I sit passively and silently taking it all in as complete and total truth?

It was deviously amusing during the pre-selection build-up for the 2018 College Football Playoffs, when the head coach of Clemson University – Dabo Swinney – attempted to build his teams resume among such heavy-weight football powers as Alabama, Notre Dame, and Oklahoma, by noting his team was relegated to riding the *"ROY"* bus, while the other schools were being treated as "royalty." His reference to the *"ROY"* bus meant the other teams were headlining all the playoff discussions, while his team was forced to ride the "Rest of Y'all" bus. In other words, it was all about "them" and little to do with "us." His team did win the 2018 College Football Championship, proving "the rest of us" can be a powerful entity.

The apostles never designated an "us" versus "them" segregation in the New Testament *"ekklesia,"* never designating a cleric or laic class distinction. Nor should there be one in today's "church." Do we not all have the same "Teacher" – the Holy Spirit? Are we not priests with direct access to His throne of grace through our Great High Priest and Intermediary – Jesus Christ? Is what we do today with the modern-day "preacher," a "throw-back" to the Old Testament religion of the Pharisaic Jews based on its rites, rituals, traditions, regulations and obligations in service to men, rather than to Jesus? Was that religious system not what Jesus destroyed during His earthly ministry and affirmed by the Romans by their destruction of the temple in 70 A.D.? No doubt when

He returns, He will once again destroy another 2000 years or more of the same organized religion man has resurrected along with the titled positions that accompany it.

While today's "church" leadership sit in their carpeted, air conditioned offices behind their oak desks preparing their Sunday orations or agendas on their Mac computers for their passive and entertainment-starved Sunday morning audiences, individuals called missionaries are serving in hot humid jungles of Southeast Asia or other hostile spiritual arenas, ministering to those battling disease, starvation, persecution, and poverty – both physical and spiritual. Paul Akin of the "International Mission Board," states in a recent article, "when one considers all that goes into this monumental task, you realize global missions is some of the most difficult work on the planet." He lists five challenges these individuals typically face: sacrifice – leaving behind family, friends, jobs, familiar environment, modern conveniences, etc.; foreign context – new people, tastes, sounds, and smells; language learning – communication; worldview clash – religious, spiritual and physical; and environmental challenges – health, climate, geography."[172] Yet, "for the sake of more than a billion people today who have yet to even hear the gospel, they want to risk it all; for the sake of 26,000 children who will die today of starvation or preventable disease, they want to risk it all; and for the sake of an increasingly marginalized and relatively ineffective church in our culture, they want to risk it all."[173] They are without doubt the modern-day Great Commission leaders for the Gospel of Jesus Christ.

We have already noted how easy it is in today's "church" to become engrossed with service to ourselves – our programs, our positions, our committees, our business, our leaders, etc., etc. But the fact of the matter, there is a lost and dying world right outside our doors and beyond. Consider the following:

a. "There are 6.7 billion people in the world; 2.3 billion are professed Christians (748 million are Evangelical Christian); 1.5 billion are Muslim; 971 million are Hindu; 703 million are non-religious; 626 million are Buddhist; 553 million are Ethnic Religions including Chinese Religion; 33 million 'other'. Of the 6.7 billion people in the world, 2.7 billion live among unreached people groups of the world and 1.6 billion are completely unevangelized."[174]

b. "90% of foreign missionaries work among already reached people groups. Only 10% work among unreached people groups."[175]

c. "Despite Christ's command to evangelize, 67% of all humans from A.D. 30 to the present day have never heard the name of Jesus Christ."[176]

d. "91% of all Christian outreach/evangelism does not target non-Christians, but other Christians."[177]

e. "In the last 40 years, over 1 billion people have died who have never heard of Jesus and around 30 million people this year will perish without hearing the message of salvation. 70,000 plus people die every day in the unreached world without Jesus."[178]

f. "Christians make up 33% of the world's population yet earn 53% of the world's annual income and spend 98% of it on themselves. Less than 1% of all Christian giving is directed toward mission efforts in the 38 most unevangelized world countries."[179]

g. "American Christians spend 95% of offerings on home-based ministry, 4.5% on cross-cultural efforts in already reached people groups, and less than 1% to reach the unreached. There are 430,000 missionaries from all branches of Christendom. Only between 2 and 3% of these missionaries work among unreached peoples."[180]

h. "Christians spend more time and money on the annual audits of their churches and agencies ($810 million) than on all their workers in the non-Christian world."[181]

i. "The average American Christian gives only $.01 per day to global missions. Approximately 85% of all missionary finances are being used by Western missionaries who are working among the established churches on the field rather than being used for pioneer evangelism to the lost."[182]

j. "It is estimated that Christians worldwide spend around $8 billion per year going to more than 500 conferences to talk about missions. That equals more than twice the total spent doing missions."[183]

k. "818 unevangelized ethno-linguistic peoples have never been targeted by any Christian agencies ever."[184]

I.   "Out of 648 million Great Commission Christians, 70% have never been told about the world's 1.6 billion unevangelized individuals."[185]

Paul, as a missionary and church planter, took the Gospel away from Jerusalem and Judea and moved it to the uttermost parts of the earth. All of us as believers are essentially missionaries. However, there are some who have dedicated their entire lives and the lives of their families to the mission field. They are to be commended! All have given up the comforts of home, family, financial security and physical safety to serve the Lord by being living examples and testimonies of the love of Jesus Christ for all people, including many who are not receptive. More than 70% of all Christians now live in countries where they are experiencing persecution. Over the last 20 centuries, and in all 238 countries, more than 70 million Christians have been martyred – killed, executed, murdered – for Christ.[186] More Christians have been martyred in the last 100 years than all other years since A.D. 30 combined. Over 160,000 believers will be martyred this year alone.[187] One can readily see why up to 50% of all new missionaries do not last beyond their first term on the mission field.[188] Our men and women are serving in these hotbeds of evil and face these issues twenty-four hours a day, seven days a week. They do it because they love the Lord! They do it because the *"fields are ripe unto harvest"* and they truly take Christ's message of the Great Commission seriously. They certainly do not do it for the money.

We have already discussed the church as a business entity, but how much does today's "church" support foreign missions and those serving in that arena? As noted earlier, the American church today gives a whopping 2% on average to foreign missions.[189] When the annual budget is prepared by the Stewardship Committee, Deacons, or elders and placed on-line or in the vestibule of the local church for the members to review and approve, the first line item usually critiqued is the pastor and staff salaries. The ultimate question – "did the preacher get a raise.?" This usually creates a great deal of discussion around the dinner table or even at the Sunday School Christmas party, but is seldom challenged at business meetings. How many times do we hear the question asked, "What about the foreign missionaries; did they get a raise?" That is an excellent question and helps narrow down where our priorities truly lie as a traditional, modern-day "church." Our financial tendencies tend to focus on what keeps us comfortable, sated, and satisfied.

What is the average pay scale for a typical foreign missionary versus a traditional church pastor of today? Surprisingly, with all the business computations and record keeping in today's church, this information is not easily obtained and there is much differentiation of numbers. Based on independent analysis, the average salary for a pastor of a church with a membership above the median (341 members), is $89,977 per year, excluding perks. This includes a range of between $73,970 up to $102,007 annually. Once again, data varies and is dependent on church membership and affluency. Churches that fall below the median number have a pay scale ranging from $0 (volunteer and bi-vocational pastors) to around $40,000 annually.[190] As noted, the base salary numbers do not include perks that usually accompany a competitive salary package – parsonages or housing allowances, cars or car expense, insurance, bonuses and other incentives akin to what a business would offer its CEO. Bottom line, for churches above the median membership average, it is not unheard of a competitive inclusive package for a pastor of between $125,000–$150,000 annually.

What about the missionary? Once again, statistics are somewhat difficult to obtain, depending on the denomination and the country being served. According to a study by "Bethany Global University," the average annual missionary salary is $30,000 annually based on the "Bureau of Labor Statistics."[191] Dana Stevenson, writer for the "Houston Chronicle," somewhat confirms saying the average annual pay for a foreign missionary is $31,600, which is all inclusive.[192]

How about church budgets in general? According to a study by Mark Chaves of "Duke Divinity School," the average Protestant church is small with a median weekend attendance of about 76 people. The average annual budget is about $85,000. Most churchgoers attend large churches with a median attendance of 400 people and an average annual budget of $479,000.[193] According to a close friend and brother in Christ who has served, along with his wife, on the foreign mission field in Southeast Asia, a parcel of land could be purchased and a small church constructed for under $5,000 American dollars in Indonesia.[194] What does this mean? It means the average Protestant church, with an average budget of $479,000 and up to 95% of it earmarked for themselves, could literally build close to 100 small house churches annually in Indonesia or other Southeast Asian countries with a similar economic status. Or, how about a well in the jungles of Honduras where there is no fresh drinking water and disease abounds. If a well could be dug for less than $1,000, that would mean the average church COULD dig up to 479 wells annually in Honduras and plant the seed for the Gospel!

"What one needs to see regarding church budgets is the percentage of money allocated to foreign missions or local missions that go away from the church itself. The only way to give adequate percentages of money to foreign missions is to keep church 'simple.' That means not going much beyond what is called for in scripture, an old reformation principle, called the 'regulative principle of worship,' that has kept the church protected from vanity and greed but doesn't sit well with American evangelical sanctified commercialism and consumer demand. 'Simple' means that church is primarily about the gathering of God's people to worship. Then, it is about proclaiming the gospel to the lost all over the globe. Then, if there is a little money left over, we might spend some on ourselves and our own comforts."[195] I am afraid most churches have their priorities exactly backwards. Our "us" budget items dwarf our "others" budget items by significant amounts.

What is the issue here? I will let you be the judge. We pay a salary and incentive package for leadership in a local church and support a budget which gives almost total attention to our entertainment and comforts, but for a person or persons risking their lives and those of their families in a foreign country planting churches and carrying out the Great Commission, where no peace, no security, and little comfort exist, they receive less than 2/3 the pay of a domestic "preacher" living life in a completely different setting.

Paul's defense of his missionary efforts to false teachers among the Corinthians who were challenging his personal integrity and apostolic authority is worth noting: – "Let no one take me for a fool. But if you do, then tolerate me just as you would a fool, so that I may do a little boasting. In this self-confident boasting I am not talking as the Lord would, but as a fool. Since many are boasting in the way the world does, I too will boast. You gladly put up with fools since you are so wise! In fact, you even put up with anyone who enslaves you or exploits you *or takes advantage of you or puts on airs or slaps you in the face. Are they servants of Christ? (I am out of my mind to talk like this.) I am more. I have worked much harder, been in prison more frequently, been flogged more severely, and been exposed to death again and again. Five times I received from the Jews the forty lashes minus one. Three times I was beaten with rods, once I was pelted with stones, three times I was shipwrecked, I spent a night and a day in the open sea, I have been constantly on the move. I have been in danger from rivers, in danger from bandits, in danger from my fellow Jews, in danger from Gentiles; in danger in the city, in danger in the country, in danger at sea; and in danger from false believers. I have labored and toiled and have often gone without sleep; I have known hunger and thirst and have often gone without food; I have been cold and naked. Besides everything else, I face daily the pressure of my concern for all the churches" – 2 Corinthians 11:16-20, 23-28.*

Paul may have indeed been a "church planter," but he lived a "missionary" lifestyle; his bio has no resemblance to any titled "church" position I am aware. It seems ironical how today's "church" orators can stand in the pulpit and "preach" missions, when the overwhelming majority have never set foot on the foreign mission field. Corrie Ten Boon states, "98% of so-called Christian evangelists, live and minister in the United States, where less than 1% of the world's population resides." How can you "preach" it if you have never experienced it first-hand?

I cannot remember where, but recall reading the following prayer: "Forgive us Father for forsaking the calling of your Son Jesus Christ, and instead, building more and more barns for ourselves. Cause us to possess the hunger and desire to see the lost saved and healed, regardless where they might be or how they might appear. Take from us our sinful proclivities, to a concern for the Gospel message. Let us decrease, so that you may increase – Amen." Missionaries of the Gospel of Jesus Christ pray this prayer daily in places of evil and insecurity we can only imagine. They are truly on the front lines of the battle between good and evil. Oh, that we could pray this same prayer from our padded pews and pulpits! God bless and protect those who understand and forgive those of us who do not!

Chapter 11

WHY SALVATION?

"If we are absolutely sure that our beliefs are right, and those of others' wrong; that we are motivated by good, and others by evil; that the King of the Universe speaks to us, and not to the adherents of very different faiths; that it is wicked to challenge conventional doctrines or to ask searching questions; that our main job is to believe and obey – then the witch mania will recur in its infinite variations down to the time of the last man."
Carl Sagan[196]

"Salvation," as found in Scripture, has as its Greek base the word – *"soteria."* The word literally means "deliverance, preservation and safety."[197] It is found forty-four times in the New Testament. As it is typically used, it means "God's rescue which delivers us as believers out of destruction into His safety."[198] Webster defines "salvation" as "preservation from impending evil."[199] In *Acts 4:12*, Peter and John standing before the Sanhedrin – the Jewish Supreme Court – answered accusations with – *"Salvation is found in no one else, for there is no other name under heaven given to mankind by which we must be saved."* Salvation comes through Jesus Christ. Christ Himself states in *John 14:6* – *"I am the way and the truth and the life. No one comes to the Father except through me."* We could then surmise "salvation" means, the saving Grace of our Lord and Savior Jesus Christ from eternal destruction that awaits the unbeliever in a place of torment called Hell. How do we obtain this "salvation?"

As Fuente de Vida, the Hispanic fellowship we were instrumental in establishing in 2015, continued to grow in the nurture and guidance of God's leadership, I recall a teenager who at one time attended on a semi-regular basis. She came with her mother; her father had died several years prior. She spoke fluent English but her mother only a broken version. She was in her late teens when she attended Fuente de Vida. A year or so earlier she was a passenger in a horrific car accident. The driver escaped the overturned vehicle, but she was trapped and severely burned. She incurred severe facial burns, her right arm so horribly seared, it resulted in her losing a portion of her hand. Numerous spiritual, physical and emotional battles came about as a result.

Our goal as a body of Christ, was to make sure the Gospel was shared, heard and hopefully accepted, and in this teenager's case, the love of Jesus Christ poured into her so she would feel and experience that love in a mighty way and learn to share it. As evangelicals, our natural tendency was to share the Gospel through what Southern Baptists call the "plan of salvation." This is a structured monologue along with a set of Bible verses and commentaries and is usually contained in what most call a "tract." Tracts are convenient and many times can be successful when placed in a lost person's hand, even with little to no commentary. Included in most tracts, at least Southern Baptist generated ones, is a page with what most call, "the sinner's prayer", which is a recitable confession where one admits he/she is a sinner and by praying the prayer and subsequently signing the attached commitment page, one is declared "saved."

The purpose here is not to deny or challenge the validity and potential success of tracts regarding the "plan of salvation" and the "sinner's prayer." Have people been led to a saving knowledge of Jesus Christ through such means? Absolutely! The Word of God, by its own power, is the best source capable of leading a lost soul to a saving knowledge of Jesus Christ: "*So is My Word that goes out from my mouth: it will not return to Me empty, but will accomplish what I desire and achieve the purpose for which I sent it*" *(Isaiah 55:11)*. The Gideon Ministry referenced earlier, teems with thousands of testimonies worldwide from those who found salvation through a copy of God's Word conveniently placed in a hotel room, doctor's waiting room, business lobby, and in the hands of military personnel, nurses, college students, and where allowed, elementary school students.

What is this "plan of salvation" and the "sinner's prayer?" This was the very question the young teenager posed to us in one of our fellowship meetings at Fuente de Vida: "Where do I find this 'sinner's prayer' in Scripture – chapter and verse please? Where does it say, if I utter this prayer I am saved? And where do I find the 'plan of salvation' in my Bible? I understand there are different verses that speak of salvation, but where specifically do I find 'the plan'?" Wow! The cat had truly grabbed our Christian tongues!

It could easily be argued the modern-day church has come dangerously close to turning salvation into something man-made and easily attainable. In some denominations, a simple walk down an aisle, a prayer, a shake of the pastor's hand, maybe a hug and you are signed and sealed forever. The purpose here is not to question the genuineness of one's salvation attained through such means. But we must also understand, it is not the "aisle," the handshake, the hug, the altar, or the "blessing" from a titled individual that saves us – it is strictly between Jesus Christ and the one to whom He is speaking. In this setting, there is always the danger the emotional aura of the moment playing on the psychological, leading to a decision made solely on atmosphere, emotions, or peer pressure. We must at least consider everything connected with a "public profession" of faith in a Protestant church, where one must walk an aisle to prove his/her commitment and is surrounded by soft, enticing music (called an invitation hymn) and other enhancements, could potentially play on one's emotions. Once again, this is not to imply the "light of the Gospel" cannot be found in these scenarios, but simply suggesting playing on the psychological can be a strong influence and is usually evidenced by those who's commitment is short-lived.

J Vernon McGee, in his, "Commentary of the Hebrews," makes an interesting statement on *Hebrews 12:24 ("You have come to God, the Judge of all, to the spirits of the righteous made perfect, to Jesus the mediator of a new covenant, and to the sprinkled blood that speaks a better word than the blood of Abel.")* – "Today, we have an epidemic of easy 'believism.' Many folks have made salvation a simple mathematical equation: if you can say 'yes' to this, 'yes' to that, and 'yes' to a half-dozen questions, then you are saved. This type of approach leaves no room for the work of the Holy Spirit and for the conviction of sin. It just means a nodding assent, a passing acquaintance with Jesus. It does not mean that you are born again. There is a word that is being overworked today: 'commit' your life to Christ. What kind of life do you have to commit to Christ? If you are coming to Christ as a sinner, you do not have any life – you are dead in trespasses and sins. The Lord Jesus is the one who said, '*I have come that you might have life.*' You do not commit a life, but He committed His life for you, and He died for you. You are dead in trespasses and sins, and He has life to offer to you: '*I am come that they might have life, and that they might have it more abundantly.*' We also hear people say, 'Give your heart to Jesus.' Well, my friend, what do you think He wants with that dirty, old heart? Read the list of things He said come out of the heart (*Matthew 15:19*). They are the dirtiest things that I know. He did not ask you to give your heart to Him. He says, '*I want to give you a new heart and a new life.*' We need the conviction of sin, to know that we are sinners. We have made salvation a very jolly affair. An evangelistic crusade today is just too ducky; it is so sweet, and it is so lovely. I don't see people come weeping under conviction."[200]

So, if a person is totally ignorant of God (lost) and inquires of us as believers on how to find salvation, what exactly do we tell them and how do we go about it? Truth is, most of us tell them absolutely nothing. Consider the following:

a. "Slightly less than 1 out of 4 professed Christian adults in the US (15%) have shared the Gospel with a non-Christian in the past 12 months, leaving 85% who did not."[201]

b. "Only 2% of born-again Christians regularly share their faith with others."[202]

c. "95% of evangelical church members have never led anyone to a saving knowledge of Jesus Christ."[203] Unless they are fortunate enough to find someone in the five -percentile of Christianity, a lost person's search for salvation will most likely go unheeded due to neglect or the simple fact the "professed" believer has no clue himself how to be saved.

We have already discussed the huge discrepancies regarding the number of denominations in the world today. The "World Christian Encyclopedia" states–"Christianity consists of six major ecclesiastic-cultural blocs, divided into 300 major ecclesiastical traditions, composed of over 33,000 distinct denominations in 238 countries."[204] Per a post by

Scot Eric Alt, freelance writer and blogger, "the most recent estimate is there are 51,314 world denominations."[205] Whatever the actual number, Paul warned us of their formation in his charge to Timothy regarding the "*last days*" (the time between the death and resurrection of Christ and His second coming) – "*For the time will come when people will not put up with sound doctrine. Instead, to suit their own desires, they will gather around them a great number of teachers to say what their itching ears want to hear. They will turn their ears away from the truth and turn aside to myths*" (2 Timothy 4:3-4).

Whether it is 33,000 or 50,000, every single one of these sects or denominations have their own "plan of salvation" or way to heaven and they are passionate, believing their way is the only way. To say there is massive confusion regarding salvation is a huge understatement! Let us look at some of the major denominations, sects, cults and religions, and briefly examine their road to salvation and eternal life:

1. What do Methodists believe about salvation?

United Methodists beliefs were descended from John Wesley. Here are their basic beliefs regarding salvation:

a. "When a person repents of sin and trusts in Jesus Christ as Savior and Lord, he is forgiven of sin and receives the gift of eternal salvation. The Holy Spirit takes up residence in that person, teaching and equipping him or her to be a disciple and confirming him or her as a child or God."

b. "Methodists believe God reaches out to the repentant believer in justifying grace with accepting and pardoning love. The process of justification and new birth is referred to as conversion."

c. "Methodists believe sanctification is the work of God's grace through the Word and the Spirit, by which those who have been born again are cleansed from sin in their thoughts, words and acts, and are enabled to love in accordance to God's will and to strive for holiness without which they will not see the Lord."

d. "Methodists believe good works are the necessary fruits of faith and follow regeneration, but they do not have the virtue to remove our sins or direct divine judgment."[206]

2. What do Presbyterians believe about salvation?

    a. "We believe there is a danger that threatens true life of every person which is sin. Sin is not just what we do, but what we are. The results of sin are spiritual death and a separation from God and human-kind's depravity. There is not a single part of our being not affected by sin."

    b. "We believe we are rescued from the dangers of death and total depravity. We believe salvation is reconciliation with God, others and ourselves. Salvation is an act of God, a gift that comes from God's love for us."

    c. "We are to respond to God's proclamation of love for us by faith in Jesus Christ."

    d. "By placing our faith in Jesus Christ, we are trusting in God's promise that He loves us, and we are lovable; He forgives us, and we are forgivable. We are reckoned by God as righteous (not by our own doing)."

    e. "Trusting that God loves us and forgives us enables us to love and forgive each other and to make peace among ourselves. This is salvation."[207]

3. What do Episcopalians believe about salvation?

Episcopalians originated from the Anglican Church of England. They believe, one is saved by "faith" alone; salvation, in no way, is based on works. From their creed book, "The Thirty-Nine Articles of Religion," it is stated, "wherefore that we are justified by faith only is a most wholesome doctrine and very full of comfort (Article XI). The baptism of young children is in any wise to be retained." (Article XXVII). Infants are born into sin inherited from their parents. When the child who was baptized (sprinkling or pouring) as an infant, grows of age, he or she is confirmed. Baptism is not essential to salvation or forgiveness of sins. Episcopalians claim salvation and forgiveness of sin before and without baptism."[208]

Interestingly the Presiding Bishop of the Episcopal Church stated, "Jesus is '*A*' way to heaven, but not '*THE*' only way. We who practice the Christian tradition understand Him as our vehicle to the divine. But for us to assume that God could not act in other ways is, I think, to put God in an awfully small box."[209]

My point in sharing differing and confusing religious roads to Heaven is to prove just that – the confusion that abounds regarding salvation. I am purposely not commenting on each view, but here I must stop and interject. Two issues with what is said here by the respected Bishop: First – "I think" – this is unacceptable. Previously stated – no one cares what "I think." People want truth. Truth does not come from a human being regardless of their title. Truth comes from the Word of God (*2 Peter 1:20-21 – "Above all, you must understand that no prophecy of Scripture came about by the prophet's own interpretation of things. For prophecy never had its origin in the human will, but prophets, though human, spoke from God as they were carried along by the Holy Spirit." 2 Timothy 3:16-17 – "All Scripture is God breathed and is useful for teaching, rebuking, correcting and training in righteousness, so that the servant of God may be thoroughly equipped for every good work."*). Bottom line, if God inspired it, then it is the holy, divine, inspired, inerrant Word of God and our source for truth.

Secondly – "But for us to assume God could not act in other ways is to put God in an awfully small box"–one must again be reminded, it's not that God "could not act" in other ways, rather God's chose to act in One way – *John 14:6 – "I am the way and the truth and the life. No one comes to the Father except through me."* As for the "small box," the 'box' is indeed small – *Matthew 7:13-14 – "Enter through the narrow gate. For wide is the gate and broad is the road that leads to destruction, and many enter through it. But small is the gate and narrow the road that leads to life, and only a few find it."*

4.   What do Catholics believe about Salvation?

"In a nutshell, Catholics believe to get to Heaven one must repent, have faith and be baptized. If you commit mortal sin, you must repent, have faith and go to confession. If you do these things you will be in a state of grace and as long as you remain in this state of grace, you will go to Heaven. It is still possible, however, to use our free will and turn our backs on God and fall from grace (*Galatians 5:4 – "You who are trying to be justified by the law have been alienated from Christ; you have fallen away from grace."*). To turn away from God and commit mortal sin is the opposite of repenting, so when one falls into mortal sin, he/she needs to turn back to God – to repent again. Going to confession is based on *John 20:22-23 – "And with that He breathed on them and said, 'Receive the Holy Spirit. If you forgive anyone's sins, their sins are forgiven; if you do not forgive them, they are not forgiven'."* Ministers or priests are empowered to forgive sins – also based on *John 20:22-23.* For a priest to know whether he is to forgive or retain a sin, he needs to know about the sin and whether we have repented of it. That means one must go and tell him, which is the Sacrament of confession."[210]

5.   What do Southern Baptists believe about Salvation?

   a.   "God desires a personal relationship with us."
   b.   "Sin separates us from that relationship. Sin is defined as our failure to measure up to his holiness."
   c.   "All are sinners regardless of works" (*Romans 3:23*).
   d.   "Our sins demand punishment." (*Romans 6:23*)
   e.   "God sent His Son to die for our sins" (*John 3:16*).
   f.   "Salvation comes from God, not from us. There is nothing we can do to obtain it. It is through His mercy and grace that this gift is offered to us" (*Ephesians 2:9; Titus 3:5*).
   g.   "Jesus paid the debt for our sins on the cross" (*Romans 6:23*).
   h.   "One must accept this salvation gift to be saved" (*Romans 10:9-10*).
   i.   "The sinner's prayer: acknowledge I am a sinner; believe in one's heart God raised Jesus from the dead; He paid the full penalty for my sins; confess Jesus is God by surrendering control of my life to Him; receive him as my Savior forever; accept that God has done this for me and He will do what He promised."[211] You are now signed, sealed and delivered to heaven! (Warning – this "sinner's prayer" is not found in Scripture.)

6.   What do Lutherans believe about Salvation?

From the writings of Martin Luther, we read: "Baptism gives the forgiveness of sins, redeems from death and the devil, gives eternal salvation to all who believe this, just as God's words and promises declare. Confession has two parts: first, a person admits his or her sin; secondly, a person receives absolution for forgiveness from the confessor (bishop, priest, minister, etc.), as if from God, without doubting it, but believing firmly that his or her sins are forgiven by God in heaven through it." From Luther's – "Large Catechism" – "a person must practice the sacrament of baptism and Holy Communion to become a Christian. These words tell us, 'given for you' and 'shed for you to forgive sins.' Namely, that the forgiveness of sins, life and salvation are given to us through these words in the Sacrament. Salvation as well. Our prayer should include the mother of God – what the Hail Mary says is that all glory should be given to God, using these words, 'Hail Mary, full of grace. The Lord is with thee; blessed art thou among women and blessed is the fruit of thy womb, Jesus Christ, Amen.' You see these words are not concerned with prayer but purely with giving praise and honor. We can use the 'Hail Mary' as meditation on which we recite what grace God has given. He who has no faith is advised to refrain from saying the 'Hail Mary'."[212]

    a.   "Lutheran belief is centered on Jesus Christ. He is the way to the Father."

    b.   "Lutherans believe Jesus Christ is both true God and true man in one person."

    c.   "Lutherans believe Jesus Christ came into the world to save sinners."

    d.   "Lutherans believe Jesus Christ truly died and was buried and rose and ascended heaven where he rules all things for the good of his work in this world to make disciples and save souls."

    e.   "Lutherans believe he will come again on a final day of judgment and recreate the universe in its pristine nature before the fall of man."

    f.   "Lutherans believe no work is too great for him. Jesus works through preaching, baptism and communion and is present and works through these means to create faith."[213]

7.   What do Pentecostals believe about Salvation?

The Pentecostal faith is an offshoot of evangelical Christianity. The defining characteristics of the Pentecostal faith are:

    a.   "Belief in the literal interpretation of the Bible and the belief supernatural gifts and events mentioned in the New Testament should be a part of today's church experience."

    b.   "Belief that those who have received salvation will spend eternity in heaven while those who have not will spend it in hell."

    c.   "Belief that salvation is a gift from God, available to all who received it and salvation can be received by being 'born again' through repentance (acknowledging and turning from sin) and faith in Jesus Christ."

d. "Belief in the possession of the Holy Spirit making it clear to believers that they have truly received salvation as they mature in their faith."

e. "Belief that those who die in their sins without seeking forgiveness through Jesus Christ will spend eternity in hell, which is a literal place of torment."

f. "Belief people's souls consciously exist eternally whether in the bliss of heaven or punishment in hell."

g. "Belief those who go to heaven will be completely sanctified (made Holy)."

"A significant offshoot of the Pentecostal movement is the Apostolic Pentecostal, which believes one must repent, be baptized in Jesus name and speak in tongues to be counted saved."[214]

8. What do Jews Believe about Salvation?

"Christianity maintains all men are doomed to sin and hell unless they accept Jesus Christ as their Savior. Judaism says we do not need that sort of salvation for we are not damned at birth. We are not doomed to sin. The basis for this contention is found in *Genesis 4:7* ("*If you do what is right, will you not be accepted? But if you do not do what is right, sin is crouching at your door; it desires to have you, but you must rule over it.*"). As the Jew translates this verse – 'if you do good, won't there be a special privilege? And if you do not do good, sin waits at the door. It lusts after you, but you can dominate it.'

The Torah ("Teaching" or "Law" – it can mean the first five books of Moses or the Hebrew Bible. It can also mean the totality of Jewish teaching, culture, and practice, whether derived from Biblical texts or later Rabbinic writings) teaches free-will – we are not doomed or obligated to sin, but free to choose. Per the Jewish belief, 'it is up to us.' 'We' children of Israel are righteous – the Torah says so (*Isaiah 60:21* – "*Then all your people will be righteous, and they will possess the land forever. They are the shoot I have planted, the work of my hands, for the display of my splendor.*" Isaiah 26:2 – "*Open the gates that the righteous nation may enter, the nation that keeps faith.*").[215]

Examples of men noted in Scripture to be righteous according to Jewish belief are, Noah (*Genesis 6:9,7*); and Moses (*Numbers 12:6-8*). Righteousness, per the Jewish belief, does not mean one has never sinned (*Ecclesiastes 7:20* – "*Indeed, there is no one on earth who is righteous, no one who does what is right and never sins.*"). Rather, the definition is taught in *Proverbs 24:16* – "*For though the righteous fall seven times, they rise again, but the wicked stumble when calamity strikes.*" Being righteous does not mean one never sins. It means after you sin you get back up again, repent and try again. You keep trying. That is being righteous (according to Jewish belief). Even if you keep trying and fail, you can still be forgiven and go to heaven (*Job 33:23*). Christianity, to the Jew, is a debunked theology or religion, since they believe it teaches there is no repentance after sinning (*2 Peter 2:20-21*). The Jewish belief is entirely about works.

What then, is the advantage of Jesus? God (Hashem) accepts repentance and loves those who turn away no matter how many times they have sinned and repented (*Ezekiel 33:14-16* – "*And if I say to a wicked person, 'You will surely die,' but they then turn away from their sin and do what is just and right – if they give back what they took in pledge for a loan, return what they have stolen, follow the decrees that give life, and do no evil – that person will surely live; they will not die. None of the sins that person has committed will be remembered against them. They have done what is just and right; they will surely live.*"). The Jew believes sin has not separated us from a Holy God. All we need to do is repent. Christians say we cannot be close to a Holy God without Jesus Christ, but Jews do not believe faith is gained through atonement in Jesus. Jews believe we are masters of our own faith (*Habakkuk 2:4* – "*See, the enemy is puffed up; his desires are not upright – but the righteous person will live by his faithfulness.*"). Jews ask the question – 'Did David not sin? Did Moses not sin?; Did Abraham not sin? Were they not near to God?' Saying, as Christians, many are called but few are chosen, to the Jew is not merciful nor would a merciful God make such a proclamation. In Judaism, it is entirely up to the individual. If you do good, you will get good."[216]

9. What do Muslim's Believe About Salvation?

"A Muslim is one who accepts Islam as the religion of God (Allah). Islam means, 'submitting peacefully in worshipping and believing in the One

True Living and Undivided God Almighty (Allah).' If one believes in Allah Almighty as One God, and believes Muhammad is his one true messenger, then, that person is a Muslim (*Quran 3:19*). Islam is the religion of Allah and the religion we must follow. Allah is not to be feared (*Quran 2:112*) and is most merciful and forgiving (*Quran 2:163, 173, 3:89*). Allah is our real friend (*Quran 5:55*). He is close and hears our prayers (*Quran 2:186*). He forgives almost all our sins, except idol worship, and 'trinity beliefs' (*Quran 4:48*). Therefore, Islam forms the direct relationship between a Muslim and his creator, so long as the Muslim believes in a One True God. There is no 'middle-man' between a Muslim and his creator (*Quran 50:16*). The Muslim's faith and righteousness will both make him live in perfect harmony with Allah. The Islamic concept of salvation is based on faith. Good works or unbelievers are worthless in the hereafter because of lack of faith in Allah. Islam abrogates all other religions (*Quran 3:85*). There is agreement among all Islamic scholars concerning the abrogation of previous religions like Judaism and Christianity, and that believing in their validity is a form of 'kufr.' Muslims use *Psalms 116, 117, 118, 91* and *Isaiah 53* as a basis Jesus Christ was never crucified or resurrected."

"A 'kufr' is one who denies the truth of Islam – an infidel. It can also mean one who is 'ungrateful to God.'"[217] "Considered the opposite of 'iman' or faith, 'kufr' is considered a grave sin punishable in the hereafter by hell-fire."[218] There are various types of "kufr" and too involved to adequately cover here, but to some "radical" sects of Islam, one can gain status in the hereafter by eliminating those who are considered "kufr" or infidels. As a result, the use of intimidation to grow its ranks is utilized.

"Regarding heaven, spiritual rewards in paradise for a good Muslim will be the same as they are now (*Quran 2:25*). Big spenders are pleasing to Allah since they keep the economy going (*Quran 3:132-133*). Muslims must maintain their duty to Allah to reach paradise (*Quran 13:35*). Muslims will have additional heavens to acquire through duty to Islam (*Quran 39:20*). Muslims doing good deeds will be entertained in paradise (*Quran 32:19*). Muslims will have a couch and all the fruits they can eat in paradise (*Quran 36:55-57*). Muslim men who keep their duty to Islam will have young women in paradise (*Quran 78:31-34*)."[219] I am not sure what the eternal reward for women dedicated to Allah might be – I suppose to entertain the men.

10. What do Jehovah's Witnesses believe about salvation?

According to the "Watchtower" and an article by Jason Barker, JW's teach *Acts 16:31 ("Believe in the Lord Jesus and you will be saved–you and your household.")* is the roadmap to getting saved. However, the "play" on the word *"believe"* is the key. Essentially JW's define "belief" as, "taking in accurate knowledge of God's purposes and his ways of salvation. Faith must be exercised in Jesus Christ, placing the Christian in a saved condition, but he must persevere in doing God's will and adhere to all of God's requirements (and those of JW's) for the rest of his life. Only then will he be saved to eternal life." JW's provide four requirements that must be fulfilled for one to be saved:

a. Accurate knowledge – knowledge of Christ's role as "earth's new king." This kingdom includes the 144,000 of *Revelation 7 and 14*, who are select folks who will rule over submissive JW's. It should be noted members of the Governing Body of JW's are members of the 144,000; following their leadership is therefore mandatory for earning one's salvation.

b. Avoid debauchery – refrain from an immoral way of life. JW's reference *1 Corinthians 6:9-10* as an incomplete list of immoral actions and add to the list other activities such as smoking, blood transfusions, boxing, raffles, voting and military or civic service.

c. "Watchtower" membership – one must become a JW to be saved and associate with his people – namely the Society. "By means of his organization, including the elders, he provides us with direction and protection."

d. Proselytism – being the most manifest means of loyalty. Members of the Society must support his government (JW's) by loyally advocating his kingdom (and theirs) to others. This includes their own literature. The status of the individual JW is measured by their activity in distribution of the literature.

"The list of requirements for salvation as a JW is extensive" and cannot be dealt with in necessary detail here. The Society claims, "We have to do more than merely accept the Kingdom message in order to be saved." They then act upon this claim by providing a specific list of works with which JW's must build upon the foundation of faith in the 'Watchtower Society'."[220]

It is a buffet!!!! You want eternal life in heaven, choose what appeals and is most closely related to your present lifestyle. Now that you are thoroughly confused, let me remind you once again, there are approximately 33,000 Christian denominations. That is not a mis-read – 33,000 – and some say the number is closer to 50,000. If that number is remotely correct, it means there are 33,000 – 50,000 differing views on how to reach heaven, and the participants and followers of each denomination are passionate and absolutely convinced, their "way" is the right "way." Please choose one, then sit back and enjoy what this life has to offer! If that one does not work, then you are free to switch preferences and select another, providing it is not too late.

In Luke's analogy of the early Church in the *Acts of the Apostles*, early followers of Christ were simply called *"disciples" (Acts 9:1)*; *"believers" (Acts 5:11)*; *"brothers" (Acts 9:30)*; *"saints" (Acts 9:13)*; and *"those belonging to the Way" (Acts 9:2)*. John calls followers of Christ *"Children of God" (1 John 3:1)*. Luke also describes these early Christians as devoted to the apostle's teaching, together and having everything in common, charitable, and enjoying the favor of one another in praise and service *(Acts 2:42-47)*. These were brothers and sisters, united for one common purpose – growing in the grace and knowledge of our Lord and Savior Jesus Christ. The result – *"and God added to their number daily those who were being saved" (Acts 2:47)*. Thankfully the "selection process" does not end here!

Chapter 12

WHY JESUS?

"Salvation is found in no one else, for there is no other name under Heaven given to mankind by which we must be saved" – Acts 4:12.

There is a saintly hymn written by William True Sleeper (1819-1904,) entitled – *"Ye Must Be Born Again."* The musical accompaniment to the lyrics were penned by George Stebbins, who wrote them accompanying Dr. George Pentecost in an evangelistic meeting in Worcester, Massachusetts. The lyrics go as follows:

1
"A ruler once came to Jesus by night,
To ask Him the way of salvation and light;
The Master made answer in words true and plain,
"Ye must be born again!"
"Ye must be born again!"
"Ye must be born again!"
"I verily, verily say unto thee,
Ye must be born again!"

2
Ye children of men, attend to the word
So solemnly uttered by Jesus, the Lord,
And let not this message to you be in vain,
"Ye must be born again."

3
Oh, ye who would enter that glorious rest,
And sing with the ransomed the song of the blest;
The life everlasting if ye would obtain,
"Ye must be born again."[221]

William True Sleeper penned these words based on *John 3:1-21*. A man by the name of Nicodemus, a ruler of the Jews, came to Christ with questions regarding the salvation message being proclaimed by Jesus and His followers. He was a learned man but coming to the Author of salvation Himself to seek answers. Interestingly, John is the only Gospel writer who records the story of Nicodemus and does so in much detail. For us to fully understand the salvation process, regardless our religious preferences, the message shared here by Jesus gives us the road map to eternal life.

Nicodemus was a Pharisee – a religious and political ruler of the Jews – and a member of the Sanhedrin, the highest court of the Jews. The Sanhedrin was a group of seventy aristocrats – all Jewish – with the high priest as its proclaimed head. The court consisted of clan leaders, scribes, Pharisees and Sadducees. The Pharisees were legalistic in their thinking, believing keeping the law of Moses and the traditions of their elders was the true way to Heaven. In other words, work-based religion. Devout Jews still hold on to this belief today.

The Pharisees were noted for adding to the Scriptures – numerous rules, regulations, and laws authored by them to supplement the Scriptures. For instance, regarding the Sabbath, *Exodus 20:8-11* states, *"Remember the Sabbath day by keeping it holy. Six days you shall labor and do all your work, but the seventh day is a sabbath to the Lord your God. On it you shall not do any work, neither you, nor your son or daughter, nor your male or female servant, nor your animals, nor any foreigner residing in your towns. For in six days the Lord made the heavens and the earth, the sea, and all that is in them, but He rested on the seventy day. Therefore, the Lord blessed the Sabbath day and made it holy."* The Pharisees, who considered themselves the holiest of the holy, expounded on these verses, eventually dedicating twenty-four chapters in the Talmud (Jewish document including the Mishnah – first work of Rabbinic law; and the Gemara – an after-publication of the Mishnah) to the adherence to the Sabbath. It was not the Scriptures they were always accusing Jesus of breaking, but their own rules and regulations. This religion bred hypocrisy. The Sadducees, another Jewish religious leadership sect, were quite the opposite – taking away from the Holy Scriptures and having no belief in angels, the resurrection, the soul, the afterlife, or spirit world.[222] Both were divided against each other, but united against Christ.

John refers to Nicodemus on three occasions in his Gospel. He is first mentioned in *John 3:1-3 – "Now there was a Pharisee, a man named Nicodemus, who was a member of the Jewish ruling council. He came to Jesus at night and said, 'Rabbi, we know that you are a teacher who has come from God. For no one could perform the signs you are doing if God were not with him."* These verses tell us several things about this man. First – he came at night – not wanting to be seen. Jesus was not a popular person with the ruling class of Jews. To be seen with Jesus could have cost him clout with his peers, threatening his ruling position. He could have also come at night to avoid the crowds since he desired a one-on-one dialogue with Jesus. The other interesting note, Nicodemus recognized Jesus as a "teacher" (Rabbi), one of influence and spiritual insight and even miraculous powers, but not as the Messiah. Being a Pharisee, Nicodemus knew the Old Testament Scriptures and the prophesies concerning the coming of the Messiah. It took boldness and courage for this man to risk his political standing, including his life, to come seeking Jesus, but it shows he was sincere in his quest. As it is with us, it will always take courage to seek the Savior.

Another interesting fact is evidenced by Nicodemus' confession he knew Jesus was from God. However, this is a far cry from believing he was the prophesied Messiah, most likely considering Jesus as a prophet. As with many today, they may know Him intellectually – but do not know Him as Savior and Lord – therefore noncommitted to His commands.

Verse 3 – "Jesus replied, 'Very truly I tell you, no one can see the kingdom of God unless they are born again'." This a statement we often hear from believers witnessing to non-believers. Arguably, there has been more commentary written about this one verse than any other in Scripture. If one wants to see Heaven, the requirement unequivocally stated by Christ Himself is, one *"must be born again."* What does this mean? Nicodemus, being a learned man, was himself confused and did not understand (*Verse 4 – "How can someone be born when they are* old?' Nicodemus asked. 'Surely they cannot enter a second time into their mother's womb to be born!'"). He did not understand Jesus was speaking of spiritual rebirth.

God created the world in perfection. In *Genesis 1-3,* He continually revealed his pleasure in his creation – "*And God saw that it was good...*" It was perfect. How glorious it would have been to have communed face to face with God in the Garden of Eden (*Genesis 3:8*). Yet, when sin entered the world through Adam, this communion with God ended and death, both spiritual and physical, was introduced to mankind. This is what we as humans are born into and inherit when we enter this world. (*Romans 3:23* – "*...all have sinned and fall short of the glory of God...*") Nicodemus was a good and powerful Jew, believing his works, his religion, his tradition and his family line, were enough to gain him heavenly entry. He did not understand forgiveness of sin and heavenly acceptance comes by grace from God Himself through faith in His Son, Jesus Christ. There is no other way.

The problem with Nicodemus is the same we experience today – not recognizing the need of a Savior in our lives. He saw himself as a self-righteous person, this self-righteousness enough to gain him Godly acceptance. Unfortunately, salvation cannot be earned (*Ephesians 2:8-9* – "*For it is by grace you have been saved, through faith – and this is not from yourselves, it is the gift of God – not by works, so that no one can boast.*"). Paul tells us it is a gift from God – a "grace" gift – but as with all gifts that are offered, it must be accepted. Being re-born means you have accepted His gift and your God is no longer the world, but the Lord Jesus. You no longer serve the "world," you serve the Lord (*1 John 2:15* – "*Do not love the world or anything in the world. If anyone loves the world, the love of the Father is not in them. For everything in the world – the lust of the flesh, the lust of the eyes, and the pride of life—comes not from the Father but from the world. The world and its desires pass away, but whoever does the will of God lives forever.*").

During one of my Youth Bible Study meetings at Fuente de Vida with a group of unchurched middle-school kids, I shared this event and expounded on this "*rebirth.*" One of the more outspoken boys laughingly said, "that doesn't make sense; how can one go back inside his mother's belly and be reborn?" This brought a round of embarrassing laughter from the rest of the group, but it was a wonderful teaching moment for me. I had expected the question and replied accordingly, "Your point is a good one. In fact, it was the same question Nicodemus posed to Jesus." It was then I read *verse 4* – *"'How can someone be born when they are old?' Nicodemus asked. 'Surely they cannot enter a second time into their mother's womb to be born!'"* In turn, I posed this question to the group, "Suppose one *could* be physically reborn; what would be the result?" Several interesting answers were rendered – "We might be reborn a different gender, different hair color, different appearance, different desires, different tastes in food, different, different, different." "Exactly," I noted; "You would be different; the same occurs when you give your heart to Jesus; you are reborn spiritually; you ARE different – different desires, different hangouts, different friends, different interests, etc. Salvation changes you; everything about you; it is as if you have been completely re-formed – a new you. You are not the same and the change is noticeable. There is a reason for that – you have a changed heart that results in a different *YOU* – a spiritually *reborn* "you!"

Most of these kids recognize a Bible when they see one but have no clue what message it contains or how to find it. Locating Scripture is a challenge – typically being relegated to page numbers. However, they are learning, and some have even mastered from memory the books of the New Testament. A far greater challenge is helping them to understand what they read. One of the best ways I have found that seems to have struck a nerve is to dwell on our commonalities. Despite our differences, there is one thing we all can agree – we are all going to face death, unless Jesus comes for us first. We know death is a reality because we experience it – pets, relatives, friends – it is a fact of life. In fact, the Bible confirms death as something all of us will face – *"Just as people are destined to die once, and after that to face judgment, so Christ was sacrificed once to take away the sins of many; and He will appear a second time, not to bear sin, but to bring salvation to those who are waiting for Him" (Hebrews 9:27-28).* The question that mankind wrestles – including these kids – "What happens next – Where do we go when we die? Do we just cease to exist?" It has been and continues to be the subject of many a book, movie and documentary. It has always been a historic enigma for unbelieving man. Paul addresses this question with those of the Corinthian *"ekklesia"* who were in danger of succumbing to the pressures of their pagan peers in denying the resurrection – *"If only for this life we have hope in Christ, we are of all people most to be pitied"* – *1 Corinthians 15:19*. In other words, if this is all there is to life, what a waste of precious time.

Regardless what the agnostic or atheist claim, we are all born with an innate belief in a higher power. Explorers of the deepest jungles of Africa and the Amazon region note finding tribes who have never seen an outsider or set foot outside the realm of their abode, yet they are worshipping something – the moon, stars, nature, sun, animal, etc. Paul notes in *Romans 1:20* – *"For since the creation of the world God's invisible qualities – His eternal power and divine nature – have been clearly seen, being understood from what has been made, so that people are without excuse."* It is puzzling how any human being can experience the birth of a child, see the mountains in full Fall color, see the waves of the ocean crash the shore, see and experience the fragrance of a beautiful rose blossom, see the different shapes and brilliant colors of fish in an aquarium, and try to count the stars in the night sky, but deny the existence of a higher power who created all this. Yet, this question of post-earthly existence remains a puzzle – to most.

Discussing this issue with our kids, I was asked, "What do you believe, Mr. Bobby, happens when we die?" "Well, let me see. Most people, especially those who are lost – do not know Jesus Christ – are not interested in what I think or believe. People want truth and evidence of that truth. We know Jesus is Truth because the Bible tells us, but providing the evidence becomes more of a challenge. But since you asked, here goes. Seems to me when we die–and we all agree we will face death – if we just cease to exist and end up as particles of atoms and just disappear, God wasted a huge investment of time and effort to create us and give us a mind, soul and spirit, and watch over us and love us–to just let us disappear into the cosmos – just doesn't make sense. For me personally, to know what awaits me after I close my eyes for the final time and breathe my last breath, someone – someone I trust – would need to go there – wherever – and come back and tell me what's there and how to get there. Make sense? In other words, if my mom or dad, who are both gone, came back and told me about this place called 'Heaven' and how wonderful it is, I would believe them because they love me, and I would trust their instructions on how to get there. One has done exactly that. One I trust. His name is Jesus."

David Ring is an unusual evangelist. He has cerebral palsy. He has an interesting introduction – "My name is David Ring and I have cerebral palsy; what's your problem?" I had the opportunity to hear David Ring speak years ago at a local college. He shared a personal testimony of when he was a small boy – a "mama's boy". David loved his mother dearly as she taught him to love and serve God. His mother died when he was young, and he grieved to the point of rejecting and even denying the God she lovingly taught him about. David recounted a vision – not a dream – but a literal living vision. His mother appeared to him. "David", she said, "You know I love you more than anything in the world. I taught you of a place Jesus created for us – those that trust in Him – and I am now there. I miss you more than words can share. If I chose to come back to you, God would indeed send me back. But the truth is, as much as I love you, I do not want to come back. I am waiting on you to come be with me. You know how to get here; I'm waiting on you."[223]

Truth is, One and only One – the One – has gone to the other side and come back and told us how to get there. In fact, from His own words – *"Do not let your hearts be troubled. You believe in God; believe also in Me. My Father's house has many rooms; if that were not so would I have told you that I am going there to prepare a place for you? And if I go and prepare a place for you, I will come back and take you to be with me that you also may be where I am. You know the way to the place where I am going" (John 14:1-4).*

"Trust" is a word salvation-seekers hear a lot from believers. The first time I took swimming lessons as a child, I remember the instructor standing in the deep end of the pool with arms open wide imploring me to dive in – "Just trust me! I promise I will catch you!" Several times I walked away, only to return and finally take the plunge. Following Jesus is similar. He is standing in the pool imploring us, "I have been there; I have created a place for you; come, let me show you how to get there; trust Me." It is our choice – trust Him or walk away. When He said to Thomas, the "doubting disciple" in *John 14:4, "You know the way to the place where I am going"*, Thomas was confused. He had seen every miracle, heard every teaching, saw Him calm creation, and raise the dead, yet he still did not understand where He was going and how to get there – *Verses 5-7 – "Thomas said to Him, 'Lord, we don't know where you are going, so how can we know the way'? Jesus answered, 'I am the way and the truth and the life. No one comes to the Father except through me. If you really know me, you will know my Father as well. From now on, you do know Him and have seen him'."* The place is Heaven; the "way" is Jesus Christ!

Two basic points that must be established to understand salvation:

First – the Bible is our fixed, unmovable, unchangeable foundation. It must be accepted as what it is – the "holy, divinely inspired, inerrant Word of God." It contains the truth we seek – *"Above all, you must understand that no prophecy of Scripture came about by the prophet's own interpretation of things. For prophecy never had its origin in the human will, but prophets, though human, spoke from God as they were carried along by the Holy Spirit" – 2 Peter 1:20-21.*

Secondly, Jesus is the only way to Heaven. The Bible says so. Some believe that is discriminatory. It may be, but if one has an issue, he/she needs to take it up with the Lord Himself – it is His plan. It is not a denominational edict – it is from the lips of Christ Himself *(John 14:6)*. John expounds on this claim in *1 John 5:1,5,10-12 – "Everyone who believes that Jesus is the Christ is born of God, and everyone who loves the father loves His child as well." "Who is it that overcomes the world? Only the one who believes that Jesus is the Son of God." "Whoever believes in the Son of God accepts this testimony. Whoever does not believe God has made Him out to be a liar, because they have not believed the testimony God has given about his Son. And this is the testimony: God has given us eternal life, and this life is in His Son. Whoever has the Son has life; whoever does not have the Son of God does not have life."*

This truth of Jesus being the only means to Heaven is not a Baptist, Presbyterian, Methodist, Lutheran, Episcopalian, or any of the other 33,000 denominations' contention – it is from the Author of salvation Himself. Since He is the only one who knows the way to the place He prepared, we must trust Him on how to get there. There are some that equate Heaven to a city on a mountain; they note there are different roads that lead up the mountain to its top. From the standpoint of religion, these roads could represent Islam, Buddhism, Hinduism, etc. – any number of religious roads. Unfortunately for them, the One who overcame death and came back to give us directions makes clear – *'He is the only Way'.* We must trust Him and follow His road to the top! He proved His love for us by giving His life for us – and then arose from the grave to prove there is indeed life after death – something no other religious "icon" has ever done!

Some say they are monotheistic – believe in god – a god – one god – but do not believe in Jesus. *"You believe there is one God. Good! Even the demons believe that – and shudder" James 2:19.* In his Epistles, most likely written late first century, John wrote to believers who were being influenced by philosophies where some professed belief in "god" – but denied Jesus as the Son of God and the Messiah and Savior of the world. John's reply – you cannot trust in "The God" without "The Son" – *"No one who denies the Son has the Father; whoever acknowledges the Son has the Father also. Everyone who believes that Jesus is the Christ is born of God, and everyone who loves the father loves His child as well. And this is the testimony: God has given us eternal life, and this life is in His Son. Whoever has the Son has life; whoever does not have the Son of God does not have life" (1 John 2:23; 5:1, 11-12).* Issue settled!

"Ok, Mr. Bobby, so we know Jesus died on the cross – based on historical and Biblical fact – we know the Roman soldiers confirmed His physical death by their own verifications – but how can we trust the Bible's contention that He was raised back to life the third day; the Bible says that, but give us evidence; how do we know?" "Funny you should ask." "Paul addressed this same question with members of the church in the city of Corinth twenty or so years after Christ's crucifixion. Paul basically says, "you want proof? I'll do better than that – I'll give you eye-witness proof!" *1 Corinthians 15:3-8 – "For what I received I passed on to you as of first importance: that Christ died for our sins according to the Scriptures, that He was buried, that He was raised on the third day according to the Scriptures, and that He appeared to Cephas, and then to the Twelve. After that, He appeared to more than five hundred of the brothers and sisters at the same time, most of whom are still living, though some have fallen asleep. Then He appeared to James, then to all the apostles, and last of all He appeared to me also, as to one abnormally born."* Bottom line – Paul provided the Corinthians with over five-hundred or more eyewitnesses who personally saw Him! He is alive! Risen indeed!

My wife has a fixation on the HGTV cable show – "House Hunters." We lie in bed at night watching real estate representatives showing prospective homes to potential buyers who have a wide range of home-owner tastes. In the end, the couples (or individuals) sit down and evaluate their options, eventually arriving at a decision to purchase or not. On one of the recent shows, a couple from San Diego, California, were looking at beach-view property and finally settled on a potential home. It was over budget, but after considerable discussion decided to proceed with the purchase. One thing instinctively caught my ear. As they strolled the beach in deep discussion, the wife made an interesting statement to her husband – "are you ready to make the most important decision of your life; are you ready to make a decision we must live with the rest of our lives?" Buying a home is not the most important decision of our lives. Deciding where our eternal home will be is our most important decision. It is that decision that has eternal, not lifetime, ramifications!

Salvation can be confusing. An entire chapter has been dedicated in this book on how different denominations believe one can find eternal life. In my own denomination, most believe if one reads a few verses of Scripture and/or some stereotyped "ABC's of Becoming a Christian," utters a simple prayer ("sinner's prayer"), he/she are saved. It is a fact some have indeed found salvation in that manner. But we must be eternally cautious. As Reverend David Platt in his book "Radical" puts it – "This is the gospel. The just and loving Creator of the universe has looked upon hopelessly sinful people and sent His Son, God in the flesh, to bear His wrath against sin on the cross and to show His power over sin in the Resurrection, so that all who trust in Him, will be reconciled to God forever. So how do we respond to this gospel? Suddenly, contemporary Christianity sales pitches, do not seem adequate anymore. 'Ask Jesus to come into your heart. Invite Jesus to come into your life. Pray this prayer, sign this card, walk down this aisle, and accept Jesus as your personal Savior.' Our attempt to reduce the gospel to a shrink-wrapped presentation that persuades someone to say or pray the right things back to us, no longer seems appropriate. That is why none of these man-made catch phrases are in the Bible. You will not find a verse in Scripture where people are told to 'bow your heads, close your eyes, and repeat after me.' You will not find a place where a superstitious sinner's prayer is even mentioned. Surely more than praying a prayer is involved. Surely more than religious attendance is warranted. Surely this gospel evokes unconditional surrender of all that we are and all that we have to all that He is. You and I desperately need to consider whether we have ever truly, authentically trusted in Christ for our salvation. According to Jesus (*Matthew 7:22-23*) one day, not just a few, but many will be shocked – eternally shocked – to find that they were not in the kingdom of God after all. The danger of spiritual deception is real. As a pastor, I shudder at the thought and lie awake at night when I consider the possibility that scores of people who sit before me on a Sunday morning might think they are saved, when they are not. Scores of people who have positioned their lives on a religious road that makes grandiose promises at minimal cost. We have been told all that is required is a one-time decision, maybe even mere intellectual assent to Jesus, but after that we need not worry about His commands, His standards, or His glory. We have a ticket to Heaven, and we can live however we want on earth. Our sin will be tolerated along the way. Much of modern evangelism today is built on leading people down this road and crowds flock to it, but in the end, it is a road built on sinking sand, and it risks disillusioning millions of souls."[224]

The first and most important step in coming to know Jesus is recognizing we need Jesus. Unless one recognizes and understands he needs a savior – someone to save him from something terrible – a savior cannot help. In other words, if I can't swim and accidentally fall into the water and the lifeguard runs up with a life-preserver and says, "here, take hold," or extends his hand and says, "here, take my hand," and I refuse, convinced I do not need saving, that lifeguard cannot do anything for my salvation. In addition, if the lifeguard keeps coming to my aid and I keep saying, "no, I can handle it," how many times will he keep coming before he finally says, "I've had enough; I'm through." The Savior's patience also appears to have its limits. *2 Thessalonians 2:10-12 – "They perish because they refused to love the truth and so be saved. For this reason, God sends them a powerful delusion so that they will believe the lie and so that all will be condemned who have not believed the truth but have delighted in wickedness."* Many believe Paul is confirming there is indeed a limit to God's patience with the sinner – a point where He says, "enough is enough," and moves on. One can stand on the verge of salvation – asking for more time, more proof, more signs, but at some point, God says you have had enough evidence and He shuts the door; hence Pauls' warning to the Corinthian church – *"I tell you, now is the time of God's favor, now is the day of salvation" (2 Corinthians 6:2)*. Get it right now before it is eternally too late!

Noah was an interesting man of God. He lived in a day when people had never experienced rain. He was a man of righteousness and lived for God in a sinful generation among wicked people whose every thought was always evil – "*The Lord saw how great the wickedness of the human race had become on the earth, and that every inclination of the thoughts of the human heart was only evil all the time*" (*Genesis 6:5*). Because he found favor with God, He was called to construct an ark in preparation for a great flood of destruction that was coming. Imagine the scoffing, jeers and harassment he endured for 150 years while he constructed the ark in preparation for a flood, when no drop of rain had previously fallen. Peter noted (*2 Peter 2:5 – "...if He did not spare the ancient world when He brought the flood on its ungodly people, but protected Noah, a preacher of righteousness, and seven others..."*) during the time it took Noah to construct the ark, when he wasn't building, he was "*preaching*" – proclaiming – witnessing to a Godless people, bearing the brunt of their scornful wrath the entire time.

When the first drop of rain fell from the heavens, people likely began to marvel; when the rains became heavier, they began to be concerned; when the rains flooded the landscape, they became frightened and realized, maybe Noah wasn't the lunatic they had accused him of being; when the floodwaters reached waist-deep they fled to the ark and begged forgiveness; when the waters reached neck-deep, there was utter pandemonium – "let us in, let us in, let us in!" Being a compassionate soul, as a man of God should be, Noah would likely have opened the doors and let them in. But *Genesis 7:16* notes, "*The animals going in were male and female of every living thing, as God had commanded Noah. Then the Lord shut him in*." The Lord Himself had sealed the door! If Noah had attempted to open the door, he could not! It could not be opened from inside or out! As it was eternally too late for them, it too will be eternally too late for us if we ignore His plea and ignore His warning! God's patience and our death are limitations after which, it is eternally too late – neither of which we have insight as to the point of occurrence. Only God knows how long the opportunity exists for each person.

Basing one's salvation on denominational tenets loosely presented with a sprinkling of Biblical principles is dangerous. Being intentionally redundant, this is our individual salvation as noted by Paul in *Philippians 2:12 – "work out your own salvation with fear and trembling*." How do we do this? On our knees and in the Word. When we trust the words of men, we are risking our eternity on religious teaching based on human intuition – be especially wary of the teachings of men! As John warned and bears repeating – *"Dear friends, do not believe every spirit, but test the spirits to see whether they are from God, because many false prophets have gone out into the world" (1 John 4:1)*. When we stand before the Lord on the day of judgment, perhaps the worst defense we can offer is – "But my pastor, my Sunday School Teacher, my mother, my father, my uncle, my friend – all told me." There is no issue with seeking encouragement and exhortation from a believer in Christ, but remember, each of us will stand before our Lord Jesus. Salvation is between Him and us!

A pastor friend of mine who was recently called to a new church, suggested the membership be purged. As is typical in most churches, only 30% of the total membership could be accounted for; most of the inactive members were unknown by some who had been members of the church since childhood. A firestorm of response erupted as folks began to come out of the woodwork demanding their name remain on the church roll – "how dare you threaten to remove my name from membership!" Why would a person who has not set foot in the church in years be concerned or upset because they were being purged from the membership of a body they were not supporting in any way, shape, fashion, or form? There is only one answer – some believe church membership saves or will offer them some form of consolation before God. If the confidence of our salvation rests solely on being a "church" member and the result of our "profession" is to camp out inside those four walls and do nothing on behalf of Jesus Christ, we may be in for a rude, eternal awakening.

Certain theologians note there are over eighty-four verses in Scripture dealing with salvation.[225] Since we have already established the Bible as our source of truth, understanding the Gospel requires the establishment of some important Biblical precepts:

    a. *The Gospel is a gift*. It is a love-gift from God. It is offered to us by His grace (loving kindness). A gift is offered by the giver but must be received by the one to whom it is offered. The receiver has the choice of rejecting or receiving the gift. (*Ephesians 2:8a – "For it is by grace you have been saved..."*).

b. *It is received in faith.* None of us have physically seen God. So how can we trust what He is offering is true and factual? (*Ephesians 2:8* – *"For it is by grace you have been saved, through faith..."*) It is called faith. What is faith? It is believing and trusting in someone or something we have never physically seen, heard, or touched but we believe exists. (*Hebrews 11:1* – *"Now faith is confidence in what we hope for and assurance about what we do not see."*).

c. *This gift cannot be earned; it is completely unmerited.* The Gospel cannot be bought or earned in any way or by any intentional action on my part. A gift is a gift; you do not earn a gift. (*Ephesians 2:8b-9* – *"...and this is not from yourselves, it is the gift of God – not by works, so that no one can boast."*) Evangelist J. Vernon McGee presents a true "attention-getter:" "God has two ways in which men can come to Him today. The first is that you can come to Him by works. Yes, if you can present perfection in your works, God will accept you – but so far nobody has been able to make it. The only other way is by faith through Jesus Christ."[226]

d. *None of us deserve this gift.* A just and Holy God cannot look upon sin. We are all sinners – *Romans 3:23* – *"For all have sinned and fall short of the glory of God."* Sin was inherited from my Great, Great, Great, etc., Grandfather Adam (*Romans 5:12* – *"Therefore, just as sin entered the world through one man..."*). Walk into a kitchen where a three-year old is standing over spilled milk and ask the child, "who did this?" The most likely answer – "not me." Who taught a two-year old how to lie? It is natural – human instinct inherited from Adam. Nothing sinful will enter the gates of heaven (*Revelation 21:27* – *"Nothing impure will ever enter it, nor will anyone who does what is shameful or deceitful, but only those whose names are written in the Lamb's book of life."*).

e. *Unforgiven sin results in eternal damnation.* (*Romans 6:23* – *"For the wages of sin is death..."*).

f. *Are we hopelessly doomed?* Yes, we are, UNLESS we receive the gift God has offered (*Romans 6:23b* – *"For the wages of sin is death, but the gift of God is eternal life in Christ Jesus our Lord."*).

g. *Jesus took my place.* Since we are sinners and nothing sinful can enter heaven and sin results in eternal death and punishment away from God, Jesus voluntarily took the penalty of my sin upon Himself, and through His death on the cross, took upon Himself the wrath of God I deserve and as a result, I am declared "not guilty" before a righteous God. *"But God demonstrates His own love for us in this: While we were still sinners, Christ died for us"* – Romans 5:8. Sin is the breaking of God's law (*1 John 3:4 – "Everyone who sins breaks the law; in fact, sin is lawlessness."*); and *"the one who sins is the one who will die" (Ezekiel 18:4)*; and since we are all sinners, we all deserve death (*Romans 3:23; 6:23*).

Jesus committed no crime (*Luke 23:13-15 – "Pilate called together the chief priests, the rulers and the people, and said to them, 'You brought me this man as one who was inciting the people to rebellion. I have examined Him in your presence and have found no basis for your charges against Him. Neither has Herod, for he sent him back to us; as you can see, He has done nothing to deserve death."*) but died a sinner's death. He did not deserve to die but did anyway. Why did He do that? It is called love – *"agape"* love – the love that comes only from God – Jesus, His Son, took our death sentence upon Himself so that by receiving His gift, we might have eternal life. (*"For God so loved the world, He gave His one and only Son, that whoever believes in Him, shall not perish but have eternal life"* – John 3:16; *"Therefore there is now no condemnation for those who are in Christ Jesus, because through Christ Jesus the law of the Spirit who give life has set you free from the law of sin and death"* – Romans 8:1-2; *"When you were dead in your sins and in the uncircumcision of your flesh, God made you alive with Christ. He forgave us all our sins, having canceled the charge of our legal indebtedness, which stood against us and condemned us; He has taken it away, nailing it to the cross"* – Colossians 2:13-14; *"Greater love has no one than this: to lay one's life down for one's friends"* – John 15:13; *"For if, while we were God's enemies, we were reconciled to Him through the death of His Son, how much more, having been reconciled, shall we be saved through His life!"* – Romans 5:10).

"Ok – I understand I am a sinner and realize I cannot save myself. I understand Jesus is the way to eternal life – how do I "accept this gift?" Four words stand out in Scripture regarding accepting the gift of salvation: *"Confession, Belief, Repentance, and Baptism:"'*

a. *Confession* – When Scripture mentions "confession," it references three distinct applications depending on usage: confession of one's sins, confession of one's need for a savior, and confession of the Gospel through verbal testimony. Let us examine each usage:

"Confession" is the most theologically debatable step in the salvation process. Some question if it is even necessary since they consider "belief" alone is enough. Those that believe that confession of sin is a part of becoming a believer, tend to use *1 John 1:9,* as their basis – *"If we confess our sins, He is faithful and just and will forgive us our sins and purify us from all unrighteousness."* The question that arises is, if we have genuine belief – mind and heart–and have repented – and have been spiritually reborn, and God has forgiven us of our sins, (*Psalm 103:11-12* – *"For as high as the heavens are above the earth, so great is His love for those who fear Him; as far as the east is from the west, so far has He removed our transgressions from us."*), and those sins have been wiped from our slate, us being declared "justified" or not guilty in His sight, then why would He require us to "confess" our sins? If He has forgiven and forgotten my sins, then why shouldn't I?

There are numerous, differing theological views on sin confession. Some, such as Dr John MacArthur, believe there are two types of sin confession – judicial and parental. According to Dr. MacArthur, "judicial" is God's divine forgiveness He gives to us as a result of our repentance; "parental" is God's forgiveness He renders when we sin in our daily lives."[227] Some believe when we are saved, sin is behind us and we sin no more. If that is the case, I personally have missed the boat because I sin every day. As I understand Dr. MacArthur's contention, "judicial" forgiveness is God's forgiving of my past sins when I accept His gift; "parental" forgiveness is God's forgiveness of my every-day sins I commit, providing I freely "confess" them to Him.

"Sin confession" is not something that occurs in a confessional booth with a priest or at an altar with a "preacher" where I present a laundry list of all my sins. There are some religions that believe you are obligated to "confess" your sins, "one-by-one," in a "confessional room" with a priest stationed there to hear your "confessions." These "confessionals" are based on *James 5:16 – "Therefore, confess your sins to each other and pray for each other so that you may be healed."* Theologians disagree over the meaning of this verse and taken out of context, can be misleading. *Verses 13-15*, James questions Jewish believers, asking if they are in *"trouble"* or *"sick."* If so, they should pray. But he warns them, unconfessed sin will result in unanswered prayer. *"Confess"* (*"exomologeisthe"*), as used here in the Greek, means to, "agree or admit;" *"sins"* (*"amartias"*), means "failures or transgression." *"To one another"* (*"allelois, allelon"*), means "against each other." Jesus says in His "Sermon on the Mount" message, *"For if you forgive other people when they sin against you, your heavenly Father will also forgive you. But if you do not forgive others their sins, your Father will not forgive your sins" (Matthew 6:14-15)*. James appears to be confirming the message of Jesus, that if you have a grudge or issue against another person and you have not rectified this issue by confronting the individual with a forgiving heart, then do not expect your prayers for forgiveness to be heard by Him. Sin confession does not require an aisle, an audience, a "preacher," priest or a confessional. There is no human being empowered to "forgive" or pass judgment on sin. There is only One who possesses that power.

Secondly, one's "confession" or realization of his need for a savior is absolutely necessary for salvation. If a person's physical life is in danger – let's say our neighbor's house is on fire; we see the smoke and flames and rush to the front door to make sure no one is in the house. We beat on the door and scream out, "Fire, Fire, Fire." The neighbor yells back, "Go away! I am fine! I don't need your help!" He perishes in the fire. For one to be saved, he/she must recognize they need to be saved. If the one in the burning house cannot or will not see his house is burning and does not feel the impending need for someone to save him, then it matters not if the neighbor beats the door to pulp. One has no need of a savior if one does not recognize he needs a savior. This "confession" is of the heart – between myself and Jesus Christ—and involves my realization and admittance that I am indeed a sinner, I cannot save myself, I am spiritually wretched, and in need of salvation. It is to that extent I bow to my knees and "confess" before a loving, caring God – "I need YOU! I know you do not need me, but I need YOU! I am a sinner in need of your mercy and your saving grace! Oh Lord, save me!"

Per their website, "Alcoholics Anonymous" "is an international fellowship of men and women who have a drinking problem. Membership is open to anyone who wants to do something about that problem."[228] The key phrase in the mission state-ment is, "who wants to." I have never had the need to attend an "AA" meeting but understand for one to be helped by this organization, they must "confess" or admit before a group of peers, "I am an alcoholic." Once they realize they have a drinking problem and are able to face up to the fact they need help, then and only then is the fellowship able to be of assis-tance. It is the same with becoming a follower of Jesus Christ. Recognizing my unrighteousness and accepting the fact I truly have a need for salvation and no amount of effort on my part will offer me that salvation, is the first step. If we cannot get past step one, we need to stop there.

Perhaps the best Scriptural example of true "confession" and realization of one's need of a savior, is found in a parable (analogy) Jesus shared in *Luke 18:9-14 – "To some who were confident of their own righteousness and looked down on everyone else, Jesus told this parable: 'Two men went up to the temple to pray, one a Pharisee and the other a tax collector. The Pharisee stood by himself and prayed: 'God, I thank you that I am not like other people-robbers, evildoers, adulterers-or even like this tax collector. I fast twice a week and give a tenth of all I get.' But the tax collector stood at a distance. He would not even look up to heaven, but beat his breast and said, 'God, have mercy on me, a sinner.' I tell you that this man, rather than the other, went home justified before God. For all those who exalt themselves will be humbled, and those who humble themselves will be exalted'."* In the eyes of the Jew, tax collectors were the worst of sinners; Pharisees were the "respected of the respected" or the "holiest of the holy" before men, simply because of their position in the religious hierarchy. Tax collectors were cheats; their job was to collect taxes but they made their living by cheating the taxpayers – whatever monies they collected over and above the required tax, they were allowed to pocket; they also collected taxes on behalf of their Roman oppressors, which made them hated even more. Therefore, among their Jewish peers, they were worse than Gentiles – foreigners and pagans–and were literally ostracized from Jewish society. Yet, here is a prime example of one who rests on his laurels – his works – as his means to salvation– and the other, understanding his righteousness was like "filthy rags," and he could not save himself. He placed himself at the mercy of a loving redeemer. He is the one who received the gift of salvation, while the Pharisee walked away in his apostasy – having heard the Gospel believing in his mind he was in good standing for eternity but lost and due the worst punishment hell can offer.

There are some denominations who purport when one has made this heart-felt change and commitment in his life, he/she is required a step-out from a pew, walk down an aisle, grab the hand of a "preacher" and by doing so, has publicly *confessed* before his peers fulfilling his obligation of "confession." I do not believe when Jesus and the Apostles were speaking of "confession" they were envisioning the aisle of a modern-day "church." This "confession" is not owed to any man. Some say the steeple is the greatest inhibitor of salvation; if true, the aisle may be second on the list. There is no verse of Scripture found to substantiate the fact walking an aisle is Biblical "confession." It might signify one's potential commitment and his/her desire to make that decision public, but in reality, has nothing to do with confession. If so, to whom is the individual confessing? It is certainly not owed to one's peers. Not meaning to be humorous, but aisles did not exist in New Testament House Churches. We must be careful in emphasizing "Pharisaic" and denominational formalities and regulations – those "man-made" additions to Scripture that are not found in Scripture itself – as affirmation of salvation. Does this mean that one cannot be saved in this manner? Absolutely not – some have. But once again – we must be wary of trusting tradition and its inherent rules we assume to be Biblical. "Confess" to Him!

The final form of "confession" found in Scripture is our "confession" of the Gospel we have received to others; to those who are just as we were – lost or spiritually blind. We made a hole-in-one; we have a new grandchild; we received a promotion at work; we obtained our college degree; we aced the quiz; we bought a new home – all items of good news we want to share! We have just received the greatest news we will ever receive! We have received the Gospel of Jesus Christ – the gift of salvation through His blood! Good news begs to be shared! Why then do the majority who sit in the pews of today's church professing salvation, not lift a finger on behalf of the Gospel but are convinced they are saved? Truth is, they are not. This is spiritual deception at its worst! And many denominations keep preaching from the pulpit – "you are fine; you are okay; you are sealed and delivered; don't worry." *"Not everyone who says to Me, 'Lord, Lord,' will enter the kingdom of heaven, but only the one who does the will of my Father who is in heaven" (Matthew 7:21)*. How eternally horrible to hear the words of Jesus Christ on that "day" – *"Then I will tell them plainly, 'I never knew you. Away from Me, you evildoers'!" (Matthew 7:23)*.

The Apostle Paul wrote his Letter to the Romans around 57 A.D. He had an innate desire to visit Rome and witness to Caesar himself, but at the time of its writing, he had not set foot there. The church in Rome was heavily influenced by Jews who had no doubt fled there after Stephen's martyrdom in Jerusalem and the persecution that had arisen as a result, but the fellowship likely consisted of a substantial number of Gentiles (non-Jews). One of his purposes for writing the Epistle was to go into deeper detail regarding the Gospel. Admittedly, Paul goes into such detail, the Letter becomes a challenge for the most seasoned of Biblical scholars. His description of the Gospel message and our obligation to "confess" this message in *Romans 10*, is undeniably the most explicit in the Scriptures. Let us look at it:

Verse 8: "But what does it say? 'The word is near you; it in in your mouth and in your heart, that is, the message concerning faith that we proclaim':" Paul references the *"word"* twice in this verse. The first reference (*"The word is near you"*) is a reference to the Old Testament (*Deuteronomy 30:11-14 – "Now what I am commanding you today is not too difficult for you or beyond your reach. It is not up in heaven, so that you have to ask, 'Who will ascend into heaven to get it and proclaim it to us so we may obey it?' Nor is it beyond the sea, so that you have to ask, 'Who will cross the sea to get it and proclaim it to us so we may obey it?' No, the word is very near you; it in in your mouth and in your heart so you may obey it"*) and it references the Old Testament laws given by God. The second reference (*"the word of faith we are proclaiming"*) is the Gospel of Jesus Christ!

Verse 9–"If you declare with your mouth, 'Jesus is Lord,' and believe in your heart that God raised Him from the dead, you will be saved." We will examine in detail shortly, but Paul shares once again – salvation is a two-fold process – both mind and heart. He confirms mind belief by itself is not enough! James adds – *James 2:20,24,26 – "You, foolish person, do you want evidence that faith without deeds is useless? You see that a person is considered righteous by what they do and not by faith alone. As the body without the spirit is dead, so faith without deeds is dead."* Works will not save us, but once saved, they prove we ARE saved.

The Greek word for *"confession"* as used here (*Romans 10:9*), is the Greek, *"homologeses,"* which means, *"homo"* – same, and *"logo"* – speak; a more precise definition – "to profess; to speak the same message openly and publicly."[229] Paul says belief in Jesus starts with intellectual belief – of the mind- but culminates with confession by mouth – *"Jesus is Lord"*–which is the evidence of "heart belief." Jesus calls this confession of the Gospel "fruit-bearing" – witnessing – sharing His Gospel! Believers are commanded to "confess" their salvation to others – it is not optional.

We are called to be His lips, mouths, feet, and legs (*1 Corinthians 12:27 – "Now you are the body of Christ, and each one of you is a part of it."*); all who are genuinely saved are equipped with His Holy Spirit since He will never ask of us anything without providing us the means for attainment (*Acts 1:8; John 6:27; 14:15-21; 16:5-11; 1 John 3:24*); and all who refuse are warned! (*"Every tree that does not bear good fruit is cut down and thrown into the fire" – Matthew 7:19. Ezekiel 3:18-19 – "When I say to a wicked person, 'You will surely die,' and you do not warn them or speak out to dissuade them from their evil ways in order to save their life, that wicked man will die for their sin, and I will hold you accountable for their blood, But if you do warn the wicked person and they do not turn from their wickedness or from their evil ways, they will die for their sin; but you will have saved yourself." 1 John 2:3-4 – "We know that we have come to know Him if we keep His commands. Whoever says, 'I know Him,' but does not do what He commands is a liar, and the truth is not in that person." John 15:1-2 – "I am the true vine, and my Father is the gardener. He cuts off every branch in Me that bears no fruit, while every branch that does bear fruit, He prunes so that it will be even more fruitful." John 15:6 – "If you do not remain in me, you are like a branch that is thrown away and withers; such branches are picked up, thrown into the fire and burned." Matthew 7:26-27 – "But everyone who hears these words of mine and does not put them into practice is like a foolish man who built his house on sand. The rain came down, the streams rose, and the winds blew and beat against that house, and it fell with a great crash."*)

Romans 10:11-14, Paul poses a question to all true believers – mind and heart – *"As the Scripture says, 'Anyone who believes in Him will never be put to shame.' For there is no difference between Jew and Gentile – the same Lord is Lord of all and richly blesses all who call on Him, for, 'Everyone who calls on the name of the Lord will be saved.' How, then, can they call on the one they have not believed in? AND HOW CAN THEY BELIEVE IN THE ONE OF WHOM THEY HAVE NOT HEARD? AND HOW CAN THEY HEAR WITHOUT SOMEONE PROCLAIMING TO THEM?* Believers are obligated to "confess" His Gospel.

Once again, *Mark 4:14* confirms our obligation to the Gospel – *"The farmer sows the seed."* We are the *"farmer;"* the *"seed"* is the Gospel; we are not responsible for the results; the results lie in the hands of the Father. However, Jesus is crystal clear – believers are to sow – if we do not understand our responsibility, we need to re-examine ourselves to make sure we have experienced true salvation. *"Don't you understand this parable? How then will you understand any parable?" (Verse 13)*. In other words, if you don't understand the calling that has been placed on your life as a result of your salvation, don't go any further – stop here – you have not grasped the full meaning of salvation and it would be useless to pursue His teachings any further since you fail to understand the teaching on which all others are based. Sadly, this is where most members of today's "church" are at present. They have the mistaken impression one can claim salvation, do nothing for the cause of Christ and yet consider themselves saved.

The apostle Paul left us an inspiring example of confessing the Gospel – *Romans 1:16* – *"For I am not ashamed of the gospel, because it is the power of God that brings salvation to everyone who believes: first to the Jew, then for the Gentile."* And once again, *Ephesians 6:19-20* – a heartful prayer from the greatest missionary who walked the earth – *"Pray also for me, that whenever I speak, words may be given me so that I will fearlessly make known the mystery of the gospel, for which I am an ambassador in chains. Pray that I may declare it fearlessly, as I should."* As a true believer, shouldn't that be our prayer also?

b. *"Believe"* – there are almost 150 verses in Scripture that include the word "believe" and its derivatives. Perhaps the more prominent of these verses as relates to believer's salvation – *Acts 16:31* – *"Believe in the Lord Jesus, and you will be saved;"* and *"For God so loved the world, He gave His one and only Son, that whoever believes in Him, shall not perish but have eternal life"* – *John 3:16*. So, how does one "believe" or trust in something or someone he/she has never seen, heard or touched? Once again, it is called "faith" (*Hebrews 11:1* – *"Now faith is confidence in what we hope for and assurance about what we do not see."*).

Historians and theologians tell us of all the disciples and apostles, only one died a natural death – John. He was, however, exiled to a desolate island for his involvement with the Gospel. All the others were martyred – beheaded, crucified, beaten, scourged, gouged, etc. Why would they willingly give their lives in such a horrible, gruesome manner, undergoing pain and suffering unlike anything we will hopefully ever endure, based on the words of a man they knew for only a short time and for a place they had never seen but He promised? It is called "faith" – "hope for and assurance about what we do not see." It is the basis for this "belief."

"Belief" as we previously noted, is divided into two parts – mind and heart. One must possess both to be saved. One cannot possess mind or intellectual knowledge only and equate it to salvation. Unfortunately, most do per *Matthew 7:14* – *"But small is the gate and narrow the road that leads to life, and only a few find it"*. Most know about Jesus – thereby believing they are saved; few are committed to Him personally which they must do to be saved:

1. *Mind belief* – "intellectual knowledge." The author of the Hebrews is unknown, but most attribute to Paul. It is written to Jews, but its spiritual truths apply to us. Dr. John MacArthur notes the Jews to whom the Epistle is addressed, were in one of three stages of spirituality:[230] true believers – both mind and heart; Jewish non-Christians who were intellectually convinced of the Gospel, but not heart convinced; and non-believers or the lost.

   John 12:42-43 describes those who possessed intellectual belief without heart commitment – *"Yet at the same time many, even among the leaders believed in Him. But because of the Pharisees, they would not openly acknowledge their faith for fear they would be put out of the synagogue; for they loved human praise more than praise from God."*

   Salvation is not "horse-shoes" – if one is 99% saved, he is 100% lost. Because "mind" believers have no heart commitment, they choose to do nothing on His behalf and based on denominational teaching or tenet, they are convinced they are saved. This is deception straight from Hell and as David Platt notes, "it is the Gospel of today and millions are flocking to it."[231] Our churches are full of these who rest their laurels on this premise.

Just as there are degrees of reward for believers in Heaven, so there appear to be degrees of punishment in hell – *Luke 12:47-48 – "The servant who knows the master's will and does not get ready or does not do what the master wants will be beaten with many blows. But the one who does not know and does things deserving punishment will be beaten with few blows. From everyone who has been given much, much will be demanded; and from the one who has been entrusted with much, much more will be asked."*

The danger of "mind belief," as the author of Hebrews warns, is "apostasy." If a man is totally convinced that Jesus Christ is who He claims to be, then refuses to believe – both mind and heart – this man is without hope or excuse. There is nothing else God can do. *This is man's greatest sin and results in the greatest degree of punishment in hell.* For one to hear the Gospel, accept it to some degree, become involved or associated with it in a limited way, but turn and walk away from it without heart application, is apostasy. How many in our churches of today are unknowingly in this category? *Ezekiel 33:11 ("Say to them, 'As surely as I live, declares the Sovereign Lord, I take no pleasure in the death of the wicked, but rather that they turn from their ways and live. Turn! Turn from your evil ways! Why will you die, people of Israel'?")*

God takes no pleasure in the eternal damnation of the wicked; in fact, *2 Peter 3:9* affirms God's patience in holding off His coming so one more soul might be saved (*"The Lord is not slow in keeping His promise, as some understand slowness. Instead He is patient with you, not wanting anyone to perish, but everyone to come to repentance."*). Knowing the truth intellectually, but not loving the truth or committing oneself to it is not enough.

In *Hebrews 3*, the writer appeals to Jews on their own grounds of understanding, using a story very familiar to them – the Exodus of their peoples from Egypt and their wanderings in the wilderness for 40 years – *"That is why I* (God) *was angry with that generation; I said, 'Their hearts are always going astray, and they have not known My ways.' So, I declared on oath in My anger, 'They shall never enter My rest'" (Verses 10-11).* God is clear – "their hearts went astray"–not their minds. They crossed the Red Sea, they had seen the manna fall from heaven, the water from the rock, etc. – their minds could not help but believe based on the signs they had seen and experienced; but they were far from Him with only an intellectual belief. Knowing, professing and experiencing the blessings of God may not be enough; the faith to fully commit oneself to the Lord's work is required. Salvation is more than intellectual knowledge alone.

2. *Heart belief* – the culmination of genuine salvation – always manifests itself in action. In *Acts 4*, Peter and John had been brought before the Sanhedrin for their healing of a cripple. The court desired to inflict punishment of a public kind, but realized it might stir the masses, which could result in discord and violence. They decided instead to implore them to discontinue their proclamation of the Gospel and quietly fade away. Their reply in *Verses 19-20 – "But Peter and John replied, 'Which is right in God's eyes: to listen to you, or to Him? You be the judges! As for us, we cannot help speaking about what we have seen and heard.'"* If one is truly saved – both mind and heart – one cannot help but serve Him.

   In *Romans 10:8-10* , Paul lays it all out – *"'The word* (Gospel) *is near you; it is in your mouth and in your heart', that is, the message concerning faith that we proclaim: if you declare with your mouth, 'Jesus is Lord,' and believe in your heart that God raised Him from the dead, you will be saved. For it is with your heart that you believe and are justified, and it is with your mouth that you profess your faith and are saved."*

   Salvation is not the result of works; but once saved – mind and heart – it is all about works – the work of sharing the Gospel.

"How, then, can they call on the one they have not believed in? And how can they believe in the one of whom they have not heard? And how can they hear without someone preaching (witnessing, proclaiming) *to them? And how can anyone preach* (witness) *unless they are sent? As it is written: 'How beautiful are the feet of those who bring good news* (Gospel)*'!" (Romans 10:14-15).* The Gospel is commanded to be shared. Those who possess a mind or intellectual belief in Jesus Christ believe they are saved because religion tells them they are–their belief resting on their knowledge of Him alone. They may be signed, sealed and delivered – but not to Heaven!

Mark 4:21-23 – "He said to them, 'Do you bring a lamp (Gospel light) *to be put under a bowl or a bed* (kept to one's self)*? Instead, don't you put it on its stand* (for all to see and hear)*? For whatever is hidden is meant to be disclosed, and whatever is concealed is meant to be brought out into the open* (the Gospel has been revealed to you; it's not a secret). *If anyone has ears to hear, let them hear'* (believers have an obligation to proclaim the truth; listen and obey)." Our duty is proclamation–"*But you are a chosen people, a royal priesthood, a holy nation, God's special possession, that you my declare* (proclaim) *the praises of Him who called you out of darkness into His wonderful light"* – *1 Peter 2:9*. True belief – "mind and heart" – always results in "confession" of the Gospel – "*As for us, we cannot help speaking about what we have seen and heard"* – *Acts 4:20.*

c. *"Repent"* – one of the best human definitions of "repentance" I have heard came from Doctor Don Wilton (First Baptist Church, Spartanburg, S.C.) during a message he presented on-line on April 26, 2020 – "Repentance is God's summons to a personal, absolute, and ultimate unconditional surrender to God as sovereign in all, overall and through all." The Greek for repentance is "*metanoia*" – "*meta*" – meaning "change;" "*noeo*" – meaning "thinking;" literally, "a change of mind."[232] As used in *Matthew 3:2* by John the Baptist and by Jesus Himself in *Matthew 4:17* (*"Repent, for the kingdom of heaven has come near"*), it implies "a total alteration of the mind; a change in judgment, disposition and affections; consider your ways and change your mind – thinking anew."[233]

Surprisingly, there is little written about repentance in Scripture, even though the word itself is found thirty-four times in the New Testament.[234] There is theological controversy surrounding the word, some believing it is arguably one of the most misunderstood words in the Bible. Whatever the actual meaning of the word might be, Christ commanded us to "repent." In *John 3*, in his discourse with Nicodemus, Christ used a deeper train of thought – *"be born again;"* literally, not just a change of mind, but a complete change of heart, mind, body and soul.

Mark 6:7-11, Jesus commissioned the Twelve to pair up, go out and proclaim the Gospel message. This was a teaching moment for Jesus since His time on earth was ending and the urgency to share the Gospel message and training the Twelve was critical. Their message is detailed in *Verse 12 – "They went out and preached* (proclaimed; witnessed) *that people should repent."* *"Metanoia"* is used here and confirms a change of heart was required. It indicates one's present way of living is wrong. This was especially difficult for the Jews, who were and are arguably, the most religious people in the world and were being told their religion, along with its rules, regulations, obligations, and traditions, was not going to save them. It remains difficult for some today who believe their salvation is similarly based on church membership, church service, sporadic attendance, and monetary contributions. Repentance requires that one understand his present way of living is wrong and a change is required. It literally implies a change of direction in one's life. It is a change that must be manifested in action and one that can be seen by others.

d.   *Baptism* – Baptism is considered a "sacrament" in the "church of man." The word itself – "sacrament" – is not found in Scripture, but is defined as, "a religious ceremony or ritual regarded as imparting divine grace;"[235] or "a Christian rite that is believed to have been ordained by Christ and is held to be a means or a sign of spiritual reality."[236]

Some religions note as many as seven sacraments in Scripture; most Protestant denominations limit them to two – baptism and the Eucharist – Communion or the Lord's Supper. Whether one, two, or seven, is theologically debatable, but the two fore-most, at least in Protestant circles, are baptism and communion. Both were ordained by Christ and commanded to be observed.

The Lord's Supper was first celebrated by Jesus and His disci-ples during the Passover celebration on the eve of His death. *1 Corinthians 11:23-26 – "For I received from the Lord what I also passed on to you: The Lord Jesus, on the night He was betrayed, took bread, and when He had given thanks, He broke it and said, 'This is my body, which is for you; do this in remembrance of Me.' In the same way, after supper He took the cup, saying, 'This cup is the new covenant in my blood; do this, whenever you drink it, in remembrance of Me.' For whenever you eat this bread and drink the cup, you proclaim the Lord's death until He comes."* We commemorate this event as a reminder of His death and resurrection – the bread, representing His body that was beaten and scourged for us, and the wine, representing His blood shed for us on the cross. It is a time of reflection and internal examination for the believer. It was a regular obser-vance in the New Testament church – *Acts 2:42*–and should be with us.

The word, "baptism," is referenced two ways in Scripture – "baptism" by water (*1 Peter 3:21*) and "baptism" of the Holy Spirit (*1 Corinthians 12:13*). We will discuss baptism of the Holy Spirit – our seal of salvation and spiritual empowerment – in depth in a later chapter. For the sake of discussion as regards the salvation process, we will direct our attention here to "bap-tism" by water.

Mark 1, introduces us to a man by the name of John the Baptist. Since there were numerous individuals named "John," this man was differentiated from the others by the designation, "the Baptist" or the "Baptizer." John the Baptist was a proclaimer, proclaiming the coming of the Messiah – God's Son – Jesus Christ. Both his message and his style were radical and revolu-tionary. He proclaimed in the remotest of areas – the "wilder-ness"–and both his wardrobe (clothes of animal hair) and his diet were radical (wild honey and locusts). His message was direct as he proclaimed in the style of a "town crier," who's responsibility was to alert the masses of the coming of an important dignitary; he also fulfilled Old Testament prophesy regarding his calling – *Isaiah 40:3; Malachi 3:1*. His message was – "get ready; the one prophesied by the Old Testament prophets is coming!"

Per *Mark 1:4-6*, John the Baptist was also proclaiming a "baptism of repentance." "Repentance," as has already been addressed, means a change of heart; a reversal; a complete life-style change. "Repentance" results from "confession" – an acknowledgement one needs a Savior; and then "belief" – both mind and heart. With "repentance" comes rebirth – a completely changed, fruit bearing, child of God. *Matthew 3:8-9* notes this "baptism" by water is an outward showing this change has taken place.

Jews were and still are, some of the most religious peoples in the world. John's message was to Jews. They were familiar with the ritual body washings of certain body parts as required by Old Testament Law (*Leviticus 11-15*), in addition to the rules and regulations added by the Pharisees. When a Gentile – a non-Jew – converted to Judaism, he had to be circumcised, a sacrifice made and a complete baptism or full body wash. John's baptism was especially difficult for Jews since they were being asked to admit or confess to being unclean like a Gentile – a sinner–and submit to a "baptism" or body wash only Gentiles were required to observe. John's baptism was a one-time event, not a ceremonial repetition. *Mark 1*, we find several Greek variations of the word "baptism" or "baptize." "*Baptisma*"– is found 112 times in the New Testament in various forms. Viewing several Greek lexicons, all agree, "*baptizo*," and its various forms, reference a complete immersion, or total "body wash."[237]

Per *Mark 1:8*, John the Baptist proclaimed both uses of "baptism" – water and spirit – in one statement – "*I baptized you with water, but He will baptize you with the Holy Spirit.*" His message was, "I can only baptize you with water on the outside signifying your confession, belief and repentance, but He will cleanse you on the inside and confirm your salvation by

His Holy Spirit." *Verses 9-11*, Jesus came to John the Baptist, fulfilling John's proclamation of His coming, but His request of John literally took him aback–"baptize Me."

Scripture does not record the childhood of Jesus prior to His debate with the temple religious elite at the age of twelve (*Luke 2:41-52*). Based on His brothers' early non-belief in His Messianic claim (*John 7:5*), we know He lived a sinless, but normal human life up to this moment with John the Baptist. Why then would the sinless Son of Man, Jesus Christ, ask John the Baptist to baptize Him? There are several parallels from these verses that shed insight on this question and relate to our own baptism experience:

1. It was public. *Luke 3:21 – "When all the people were being baptized, Jesus was baptized too." John 1:32 – "Then John gave this testimony: 'I saw the Spirit come down from heaven as a dove and remain on Him'."* His entire baptism experience, including the voice of the Father, was witnessed by all. Ours should be also.

2. It inaugurated His ministry. It is also the inauguration of our ministry of fruit-bearing and sharing of the Gospel.

3. It was His moment of equipping for ministry by the Holy Spirit. His power came from the Father – *"...the Spirit descending upon Him like a dove" – Mark 1:10-11*; ours does also. *John 14:15-17 – "If you love Me, keep my commands. And I will ask the Father, and He will give you another advocate to help you and be with you forever – the Spirit of truth."* The personal presence of the Holy Spirit is bestowed upon us as our seal of salvation and serves as our Counselor, Teacher and Equipper, to carry out His command – *"But you will receive power when the Holy Spirit comes on you; and you will be my witnesses..."* – *Acts 1:8*. If the experience of Jesus serves as our template, then we can assume this moment of our equipping occurs at our baptism.

4. It was His moment of laying aside His divinity for our salvation – *Philippians 2:6-7 – "Who being in the very nature God,*

did not consider equality with God something to be used to His own advantage, rather He made Himself nothing by taking the very nature of a servant , being made in human likeness." As with Him, so it is with us – it is our moment of *"throwing off everything that hinders and the sin that so easily entangles. And let us run with perseverance the race marked out for us..." (Hebrews 12:1).*

Why should we be baptized? Because it is commanded to us: *Matthew 28:19-20; Acts 10:48; Acts 22:16; Acts 2:38*. Perhaps Peter put it most succinctly – *"...this water symbolizes baptism that now saves you also – not the removal of dirt from the body but the pledge of a clear conscience toward God. It saves you by the resurrection of Jesus Christ, who has gone into heaven and is at God's right hand – with angels, authorities and powers in submission to Him" (1 Peter 3:21-22)*. Does baptism save us? No – without our salvation – belief (mind and heart), confession, and repentance – baptism has no meaning or power to save anyone. Baptism is an outward symbolic gesture of the change that has taken place in our life – *"not the removal of dirt from the body, but the pledge of a clear conscience toward God" (1 Peter 3:21)*. Baptism confirms our commitment to Him. The baptism of those who by age, have no spiritual ability to understand or decide his/her spiritual commitment, has no Biblical basis. Be baptized because Jesus commanded you to do so. A command from the Son of God Himself leaves no other options.

At the beginning of this chapter we noted the Apostle John's first of three references in his Gospel to Nicodemus, the Jewish ruler who sought Jesus by night regarding salvation. *John 3:1-21* records this Gospel dialog between Jesus and Nicodemus. However, we are not told, at least in this passage, if Nicodemus accepted God's gift as relayed through Jesus. In *John 7:50-52* he is mentioned the second time where he stands before his Pharisaic peers arguing for fair treatment of Jesus who they were threatening to arrest. In *John 19:38-42* he is mentioned for the final time, where he and Joseph of Arimathea prepared the body of Jesus for burial after His crucifixion – *"Later, Joseph of Arimathea asked Pilate for the body of Jesus. Now Joseph was a disciple of Jesus, but secretly because he feared the Jewish leaders. With Pilate's permission, he came and took the body away. He was accompanied by*

Nicodemus, the man who earlier had visited Jesus at night. Nicodemus brought a mixture of myrrh and aloes, about seventy-five pounds. Taking Jesus body, the two of them wrapped it, with the spices, in strips of linen. This was in accordance with Jewish burial customs. At the place where Jesus was crucified there was a garden, and in the garden a new tomb, in which no one had ever been laid. Because it was the Jewish day of Preparation and since the tomb was nearby, they laid Jesus there." I believe we can safely surmise Nicodemus found salvation by his acceptance of God's gift through His Son Jesus Christ! This same Savior awaits us with the same open arms, and we are invited to come in like manner! There indeed is no other way!

SALVATION SUMMARY

W ithout question, this is the most important chapter contained in this book. Much has been written and as previously noted, "salvation" can be confusing – not because God meant it to be – but because "man" has made it that way. In summary – what does the Bible say about how to be saved?

a. God is the almighty creator. *"In the beginning, God created the heavens and the earth" (Genesis 1:1).*

b. He created the world in perfection. *"God saw all that He had made, and it was very good" (Genesis 1:31).*

c. Sin came into the world from Satan, through Adam. *"Therefore, just as sin entered the world through one man, and death through sin, and in this way death came to all people, because all sinned" (Romans 5:12).*

d. A sinless God cannot look upon or accept sin. *"Your eyes are too pure to look on evil; you cannot tolerate wrongdoing" (Habakkuk 1:13).* If He hates the sin, then He hates the sinner.

e. All of us are sinners. *"All have sinned and fall short of the glory of God" (Romans 3:23).*

f. There is absolutely nothing we can do on our own to save our-selves from His wrath of sin. *"I will expose your righteousness and your works, and they will not benefit you" (Isaiah 57:12).*

g. God's punishment for sin is death. Both physical death – *"To Adam He said, 'By the sweat of your brow you will eat your food until you return to the ground, since from it you were taken; for dust you are and to dust you will return'" (Genesis 3:17,19);* and spiritual death are a result of sin – spiritual death being eternity away from God in a place called 'hell' – *"They will be punished* with everlasting destruction and shut out from the presence of the Lord and the glory of His might" (2 Thessalonians 1:9); "...and throw them into the blazing furnace, where there will be weeping and gnashing of teeth" (Matthew 13:50); "For the wages of sin is death" (Romans 6:23).

h. There is no escaping His wrath – He hates sin and we are all sinners. "Because of your stubbornness and your unrepentant heart, you are storing up wrath against yourself for the day of God's wrath, when His righteous judgment will be revealed. God will repay each person according to what they have done. But for those who are self-seeking and who reject the truth and follow evil, there will be wrath and anger. There will be trouble and distress for every human being who does evil: first, for the Jew, then for the Gentile. For God does not show favoritism" (Romans 2:5-6, 8-9, 11).

i. Old Testament Law required a blood sacrifice (animal) must be made to atone for one's sins. Since all were sinners and continued to sin, many sacrifices were continuously offered, but none could offer permanent forgiveness. "Day after day, every priest stands and performs his religious duties; again and again he offers the same sacrifices, which can never take away sins" (Hebrews 10:11).

j. What am I to do? Am I doomed? "What a wretched man I am! Who will rescue me from the body that is subject to death?" (Romans 7:24). God, in His infinite love, provided a way of escape! "For God so loved the world, that He gave His one and only Son, that whoever believes in Him, shall not perish, but have eternal life" (John 3:16); "...the punishment that brought us peace was on Him, and by His wounds we are healed" (Isaiah 53:5).

k. Rather than endless animal sacrifices that could never atone for my sins in His sight, He offered one true sacrifice that could give me permanent forgiveness. "It can never, by the same sacrifices repeated endlessly year after year, make perfect those who draw near to worship. Otherwise would they not have stopped being offered? For the worshipers would have been cleansed, once for all, and would no longer have felt guilty for their sins. Since that time, He waits for His enemies to be made His footstool. For by one sacrifice He has made perfect forever those who are being made holy" (Hebrews 10:1-2, 13).

l. God's salvation plan, through the blood sacrifice of His Son on the cross, is a gift to any who would receive it; it cannot be earned by our efforts. *"For it is by grace you have been saved, through faith-and this not from yourselves. It is the gift of God-not by works, so that no one can boast" (Ephesians 2:8-9).*

m. To receive or not to receive the gift is a choice – our choice – He gives us the freedom to decide. *"Here I am! I stand at the door and knock. If anyone hears My voice and opens the door, I will come in and eat with that person, and they with Me" (Revelation 3:20).*

n. If we choose NOT to receive the gift, WE – not HE – have destined ourselves to hell as our eternal destination. *"'Do I take any pleasure in the death of the wicked'?, declares the Sovereign Lord. 'Rather, am I not pleased when they turn from their ways and live? For I take no pleasure in the death of anyone,' declares the Sovereign Lord. 'So, turn and live! Say to them, 'As surely as I live,' declares the Sovereign Lord, 'I take no pleasure in the death of the wicked, but rather that they turn from their ways and live. Turn! Turn from your evil ways! Why will you die, people of Israel'?" (Ezekiel 18:23,32; 33:11).*

o. How can we accept and trust in something or someone we have never seen? It is called faith. *"For it is by grace* (His goodness and unmerited favor) *you have been saved, through faith"* (Ephesians 2:8); *"Now faith is confidence in what we hope for and assurance about what we do not see" (Hebrews 11:1); "Though you have not seen Him, you love Him; and even though you do not see Him now, you believe in Him and are filled with an inexpressible and glorious joy, for you are receiving the end result of your faith, the salvation of your souls" (1 Peter 1:8-9).*

p. Where do I begin? Salvation begins with confession – our realization we cannot save ourselves and we truly need saving. If we do not realize the need for salvation, then a Savior is of no benefit. *"For all those who exalt themselves will be humbled, and those who humble themselves will be exalted'" (Luke 18:9-14).*

q. I must believe. This involves two types of belief – mind or intellectual–and heart – full committal. *"The word is near you; it is in your mouth and in your heart, that is, the message concerning faith that we proclaim: 'If you declare with your mouth, 'Jesus is Lord,' and believe in your heart that God raised Him from the dead, you will be saved'" (Romans 10:8-9).*

r.   I must repent. There must be a complete change in my life; a rebirth, so to speak. A different *"me"* that can be seen by all. *"'The time has come,' He said. 'The kingdom of God has come near. Repent and believe the good news'!" (Mark 1:15)*; *"Repent, then, and turn to God, so that your sins may be wiped out, that times of refreshing may come from the Lord" (Acts 3:19)*.

s.   I must be baptized. Baptism does not save but is a symbolic gesture to show this change has taken place in my life. *"Peter replied, 'Repent and be baptized, every one of you, in the name of Jesus Christ for the forgiveness of your sins'" (Acts 2:38)*.

t.   Receiving of the Holy Spirit. The Holy Spirit is our proof of salvation; His personal presence in our life as our Teacher and Equipper; equipping us to be His arms, hands, feet and lips to share the Gospel. He promised to *"not leave us as orphans"* and through His Holy Spirit, lived up to that promise. *"If you love me, keep My commands. And I will ask the Father, and He will give you another advocate to be with you forever – the Spirit of truth" (John 14:15-16)*; *"But you will receive power when the Holy Spirit comes on you; and you will be my witnesses in Jerusalem, and in all Judea, and Samaria, and to the ends of the earth" (Acts 1:8)*; *"Peter replied, 'Repent and be baptized, every one of you, in the name of Jesus Christ for the forgiveness of your sins. And you will receive the gift of the Holy Spirit. The promise is for you and your children and for all who are far off – for all whom the Lord our God will call'" (Acts 2:38-39)*.

u.   Once saved, our "work" begins – sharing the Good News with others. *"Produce fruit in keeping with repentance" (Matthew 3:8)*.

v.   One who claims salvation but refuses to share the Good News, needs to re-examine himself; he may not be saved at all. It is impossible to possess the Holy Spirit and ignore His commands. *"As for us, we cannot help speaking about what we have seen and heard" (Acts 4:20)*.

w.   Be sure of your salvation. Many filling pews today believe they are saved but by their lack of fruit-bearing, prove they are not. *"By their fruit you will recognize them" (Matthew 7:16)*; *"Not everyone who says to Me, 'Lord, Lord,' will enter the kingdom of heaven, but only he who does the will of My Father who is in heaven" (Matthew 7:21)*; *"Therefore, my brothers and sisters, make every effort to confirm you calling and election. For if you do these things, you will never stumble, and you will receive a rich welcome into the eternal kingdom of our Lord and Savior Jesus Christ" (2 Peter 1:10-11); "Examine yourselves to see whether you are in the faith; test yourselves. Do you not realize that Christ Jesus is in you – unless, of course, you fail the test" (2 Corinthians 13:5).*

x. It is our salvation – between us and Jesus Christ. Trust no man, no religion, no creed, no tradition, no denomination – Trust Jesus! *"Continue to work out your salvation with fear and trembling, for it is God who works in you to will and to act in order to fulfill His good purpose" (Philippians 2:12-13).*

y. Become involved in a believer's fellowship. Two reasons – first – "encouragement" – we will face trials and tribulations now that we have become His follower; there will be joy and happiness knowing our eternal future but pressures from the world will not disappear, but rather increase. We need the fellowship of other believers – *"And let us consider how we may spur one another on toward love and good deeds, not giving up meeting together, as some are in the habit of doing, but encouraging one another – and all the more as you see the Day approaching" (Hebrews 10:24-25).*

Secondly – our spiritual growth – there is much to learn about His kingdom – *"Like newborn babies, crave pure spiritual milk, so that by it you may grow up in your salvation, now that you have tasted that the Lord is good" (1 Peter 2:2).* Can we find this in a "traditional church of man?" Yes – we can. Is it likely? No, it is not. When entertainment values become the focus rather than the Gospel and its outreach, we are in the wrong place. When money to fund the complex and its leadership becomes the primary focus, we are in the wrong place. When all is centered around a "one-man show," programing us to be a passive listener, we are in the wrong place. When we are muzzled, with no way to question or discuss the teaching, we become stagnated and are in the wrong place. When formality and "worship" structure become more important than His commands, we are in the wrong place. Can it be done? Yes it can, but the odds of it happening are small, and time is short!

Get involved – but involve yourself in a believer's fellowship – one where the Word of God is the foundation and the sharing of the Gospel is paramount and you have the freedom to question, discuss, and act upon it. Keep in mind, the New Testament church was small in numbers but active and focused—"together as one" regarding the Gospel message – *"Do not merely listen to the word, and so deceive yourselves. Do what it says. Anyone who listens to the word but does not do what it says is like someone who looks at his face in a mirror and, after looking at himself, goes away and immediately forgets what he looks like. But whoever looks intently into the perfect law that gives freedom and continues in it—not forgetting what they have heard but doing it – they will be blessed in what they do"—James 1:22-25*. Be a *"doer"* of the *"Word"* – not a hearer only! Jesus Himself confirmed – there are many *"hearers,"* but few *"doers"* – *"The harvest is plentiful, but the workers are few"* – *Matthew 9:37*. *"Hearers"* and *"doers"* bear fruit.

Chapter 13

WHY QUESTION IT?

"It is true that we need to make a one-time decision to follow Jesus. But a true one-time decision is followed by the everyday decision to follow Jesus" – Mike McKinley.[238]

S atan is known by many names in the New Testament – *"Beelzebub prince of demons" (Matthew 12:24); "the evil one" (Matthew 13:19); "the enemy" (Matthew 13:39); "murderer" (John 8:44); "liar" (John 8:44); "prince of this world" (John 12:31; 14:30); "god of this age" (2 Corinthians 4:4); "ruler of the kingdom of the air" (Ephesians 2:2); "ruler of darkness" (Ephesians 6:12); "tempter" (1 Thessalonians 3:5); "holder of the power of death" (Hebrews 2:14); "roaring lion (1 Peter 5:8); "enemy" (1 Peter 5:8); "angel of the abyss" (Revelation 9:11); "Abaddon – Destroyer" –* Hebrew *(Revelation 9:11); "Apollyon – Destroyer"-* Greek *(Revelation 9:11); "dragon" (Revelation 12:7); "accuser" (Revelation 12:10); "ancient serpent" (Revelation 20:2);* and perhaps the most notable – *"deceiver" (Revelation 20:10).* Throughout the entirety of Scripture he has been predominantly referenced by the adjectives: *"accuser"* and *"deceiver."*

The name Satan or Adversary is referenced over fifty times in the New Testament. Since the Garden of Eden his deceiving efforts have centered on the distortion of God's Word and questioning His promises. He targets those who are lost – spiritually blind – with the deceiving message Jesus is not the Christ nor the Way to eternal life – *"Many deceivers, who do not acknowledge Jesus Christ as coming in the flesh, have gone out into the world. Any such person is the deceiver and the antichrist"* – *2 John 7*; to those who are "professed" believers – mind only – his deceiving message is serve religion and all is well – *"Do not be deceived: God cannot be mocked. A man reaps what he sows"* – *Galatians 6:7*; and to those who are saved, both mind and heart committed to Jesus as Savior and Lord, he says your past sins will find you out and as a result, your testimony on His behalf is worthless. He seeks to convince believers assurance of salvation is not possible and to claim such is the height of hypocrisy. If we have Jesus – both mind and heart–we have life – not just for this world, but for eternity – *"If you declare with your mouth, 'Jesus is Lord,' and believe in your heart that God raised him from the dead, you will be saved"* – *Romans 10:9*. The key is to know we are saved and not just believe we are based on a religious or denominational mandate. This assurance comes from the author of salvation Himself–Jesus Christ–and can be found in His Word and through consistent communication with Him. Basing one's assurance of salvation on religious tenets and dogmas may be Satan's greatest deception.

Deception destroys relationships since it undermines preconceived notions resulting in a loss of confidence, confusion, and misdirection, taking one away from his/her mission. It is seriously destructive when it comes from someone we have placed our trust, especially when it comes from and through religious outlets. The problem is spiritual deception results in eternal consequences. Trusting religion based on its human intuition and wisdom is dangerous – eternally dangerous.

As newlyweds during the late seventies, close friends similar in marital age and former members of our fellowship, invited us to dinner. We were told the dinner would be intimate and the sharing of "something special." During this time there were several pyramid schemes being offered primarily targeting young couples. In the most direct but tactful way possible, we let them know we were delighted, but if the "something special" involved a pyramid opportunity, we would not be interested. We were assured it was not and would be a quiet time of socialization over dinner. Upon arrival we immediately recognized the intimacy was non-existent since six other couples were in attendance. In addition, the "something special" was indeed a pyramid scheme and the promised intimacy turned into intense pressure resulting in a very uncomfortable atmosphere. Needless to say we were upset, hurt and offended because we had been blatantly deceived, and it destroyed a close relationship.

Peter wrote two Letters or Epistles, to Jewish and Gentile believers scattered throughout Asia Minor. Some reciprocates were likely in attendance when he spoke on the Day of Pentecost in Jerusalem. Peter's message was directed to individuals who believed they were saved and in good standing for an eternity with Christ simply because of their family lineage and adherence to religion and its practices – *"Therefore, my brothers and sisters, make every effort to confirm your calling and election. For if you do these things, you will never stumble, and you will receive a rich welcome into the eternal kingdom of our Lord and Savior Jesus Christ" (2 Peter 1:10-11).*

Misled peoples are a result of misled leadership; and misled leadership are the result of Satan's deceiving influence – *"Do not trust in deceptive words and say, 'This is the temple of the Lord, the temple of the Lord, the temple of the Lord'! You are trusting in deceptive words that are worthless. I did not send these prophets, yet they have run with their message; I did not speak to them, yet they have prophesied" (Jeremiah 7:4,8; 23:21).* Satan's deceiving influence is alive and well today, especially among "professed" believers who expend their efforts on things that do not contribute to the mission of the Gospel, all the time believing they are doing it for Him. Then when he convinces us our misdirected efforts are successful, he is assured we will not change and will continue doing the same thing. We must be prepared to learn from history and grow from our own misgivings and failures. Since it is our salvation, it is eternally imperative we get it right!

Satan deceives individuals and he deceives churches (*"But I am afraid that just as Eve was deceived by the serpent's cunning, your minds will somehow be led astray from your sincere and pure devotion to Christ" – 2 Corinthians 11:3; "The great dragon was hurled down, that ancient serpent called the devil, or Satan, who leads the whole world astray" – Revelation 12:9*). He knows the Bible – at the temptation of Christ (*Luke 4:9-11*), he bolstered his arguments by quoting Scripture – *"it is written."* Paul warns he can even disguise himself as a leader of religion – *"For such people are false apostles, deceitful workers, masquerading as apostles of Christ. And no wonder, for Satan himself masquerades as an angel of light. It is not surprising, then, if his servants also masquerade as servants of righteousness. Their end will be what their actions deserve" (2 Corinthians 11:13-15).* Thirty plus times in the New Testament we are warned by Jesus and the Apostle writers to, *"not be deceived."*

Satan attacks our spirituality and attempts to destroy our ministry. When we adhere to the message proclaimed by religious leadership – "just keep going through the motions and all will be okay" – he has succeeded. The "church" is living in a state of spiritual deception when this message is proclaimed. Jesus prophesied it in *Revelation 3:14-18. Hebrews 12:27 – ('The words 'once more' indicate the removing of what can be shaken – that is, created things – so that what cannot be shaken may remain')* – warns one had better be careful what he or she builds their lives upon and make sure their foundation is on the solid rock of Jesus Christ and not on the sinking sand of religion or denomination. The one who puts his faith in denominational edicts might be sadly and eternally shocked upon meeting Jesus to find they had contracted the disease of spiritual deception. Be warned it is contagious!

"Webster" defines "covenant" as, "an agreement or contract."[239] The Old Testament contains numerous covenants authored by God and verbally agreed to by man. They were meant to cement our partnership and relationship with Him. A covenant begins with words from the authoring party – "I will, if you will." There were four Old Testament Covenants – one with Noah, one with Abraham, one with the Israelites, and one with David. All of these were presented to the other party or parties by God and agreed upon by both groups. Unfortunately, the agreeing party never lived up to their end of the covenant, while God remained true and continues to be true to His promises. We can be assured He will never break any promise He has made – *"God is not human, that He should lie, not a human being, that He should change His mind. Does He speak and then not act? Does He promise and not fulfill?" (Numbers 23:19).*

Throughout the Old Testament, the prophets prophesied of a day when God would create a "New Covenant" replacing all the old broken covenants. This "New Covenant" was ushered into the world through Jesus Christ – *"For if there had been nothing wrong with that first covenant, no place would have been sought for another. But God found fault with the people and said, 'The days are coming, declares the Lord, when I will make a new covenant with the people of Israel and with the people of Judah. It will not be like the covenant I made with their ancestors when I took them by the hand to lead them out of Egypt, because they did not remain faithful to my covenant, and I turned away from them, declares the Lord.' By calling this new covenant 'new', He has made the first one obsolete. For this reason Christ is the mediator of a new covenant, that those who are called may receive the promised eternal inheritance – now that He has died as a ransom to set them free from the sins committed under the first covenant"* (Hebrews 8:7-9,13; 9:15). Under the New Covenant, the wording of agreement has changed – "I did – Will you accept?"

Many professed believers choose the Apostle John's first Epistle (*1 John*), as an assurance of their salvation – "to know, that they know, that they know, they are saved." It is true this short, but meaty Letter, was written so we can know what being a child of Christ truly means. "*Know*" – is found forty-four times in this Letter; "*love*" – is found forty-one times; but it is important to note – the preposition "*IF*" – is found over twenty times. This Letter confirms God's love for us, and we can know our salvation is genuine, but it also notes there is a cost for salvation, and it may be greater than we have been led to believe and are willing to pay. John lists seventeen ways under the New Covenant of Jesus Christ, one can know he/she has genuine (not "professed") salvation – '*IF*':

1. *(1:6)* – "*If we claim to have fellowship with Him yet walk in the darkness, we lie and do not live out the truth.*" "Light" in scripture is always used to symbolize Christ from whence comes all spiritual illumination (*John 1:4-5* – "*In Him was life, and that life was the light of all mankind. The light shines in the darkness, and the darkness has not overcome it.*"). One cannot claim salvation and live for religion or self. To do so is evidence we have never truly repented. Adherence to religion's tenets, doctrines, and mandates, all the while ignoring the needs of a lost world, is no guarantee of salvation. We should not be deceived into believing we can claim salvation and continue doing or not doing what we choose and are "okay" because man's religion says so. Sorry, but John says it does not work that way. Beware of those who tell you otherwise.

2. *(1:8) – "If we claim to be without sin, we deceive ourselves and the truth is not in us."* If we are without sin, why would we need Jesus? We *ARE* sinners which is why we need a Savior! John is likely referencing Gnostic philosophical teaching of that day that God does not punish sin. The belief echoed by the Gnostics was that sin was instinctive and since God made us, we cannot help but sin, therefore God will overlook it. Paul, in a possible effort to refute the Gnostics, spoke in *Romans 3:23 – "...for all have sinned and fall short of the glory of God."*

3. *(2:3-4) – "We know that we have come to know Him if we obey His commands. Whoever says, 'I know Him,' but does not do what He commands is a liar, and the truth is not in that person'."* The work of "fruit-bearing" begins at salvation. It is evidence of one's salvation – *"Thus by their fruit you will recognize them" – Matthew 7:20.* There are no other options, regardless what organized religion says. Obeying His commands does not include spinning one's wheels inside the four walls of a building. That person who says he cares but by his actions or lack thereof, proves he does not, is still lost in his sin – apostate – and will never see the gates of Heaven.

4. *(2:6) – "Whoever claims to live in Him must live as Jesus did."* What did Jesus do and how did He "walk?"

   a. He proclaimed repentance (*Matthew 4:17 – "From that time on Jesus began to preach, 'Repent, for the kingdom of heaven has come near'."*).
   b. He taught and discipled *(Matthew 4:23 – "Jesus went throughout Galilee, teaching in their synagogues, preaching the good news of the kingdom..."*).
   c. He prayed (*Matthew 26:36, 39 – "Then Jesus went with His disciples to a place called Gethsemane, and He said to them, 'Sit here while I go over there and pray.' Going a little farther, He fell with His face to the ground and prayed."*).
   d. He ministered (*Matthew 4:24 – "News about him spread all over Syria, and people brought to Him all who were ill with various diseases, those suffering severe pain, the demon-possessed, those having seizures, and the paralyzed; and He healed them."*).
   e. He was compassionate (*Matthew 9:35-36 – "Jesus went through all the towns and villages, teaching in their synagogues,*

proclaiming the good news of the kingdom and healing every disease and sickness. When He saw the crowds, He had compassion on them, because they were harassed and helpless, like sheep without a shepherd."). He had a heart for the lost.

f. He was gentle and humble (*Matthew 11:29 – "Take my yoke upon you and learn from me, for I am gentle and humble in heart..."*).

g. He met needs – both the physical as well as spiritual (*Matthew 14:14-16 – "When Jesus landed and saw a large crowd, He had compassion on them and healed their sick. As evening approached, the disciples came to Him, and said, 'This is a remote place, and it's already getting late. Send the crowds away, so they can go to the villages and buy themselves some food.' Jesus replied, 'They do not need to go away. You give them something to eat'."*).

h. He didn't seek fame or fortune (*Matthew 13:57 – "But Jesus said to them, 'A prophet is not without honor except in his own town and in his own home'." John 7:3-5 – "Jesus brothers said to Him, 'Leave Galilee and go to Judea, so that your disciples there may see the works you do. No one who wants to become a public figure acts in secret. Since you are doing these things, show yourself to the world.' For even his own brothers did not believe in Him."*).

i. He condemned and eschewed religion – (*Matthew 21:12-13 – "Jesus entered the temple courts and drove out all who were buying and selling there. He overturned the tables of the money changers and the benches of those selling doves. 'It is written,' He said to them, 'My house will be called a house of prayer, but you are making it a den of robbers'."*)

j. He loved – to the point of giving his life freely for others (*Matthew 27:31 – "After they had mocked Him, they took off the robe and put his own clothes on Him. Then they led him away to crucify Him."*)

k. He wanted all to be saved – (*Matthew 28:19-20 – "Therefore go and make disciples of all nations, baptizing them in the name of the Father, and of the Son and of the Holy Spirit, and teaching them to obey everything I have commanded you. And surely I am with you always, to the very end of the age."*).

5. *(2:9)* – *"Anyone who claims to be in the light but hates a brother or sister is still in the darkness."* "Brother" is a reference to fellow Christians. The love of God will express itself in our actions. How can one manifest His love to others if he does not manifest it among his own brothers and sisters in Christ?

6. *(2:15-16)* – *"Do not love the world or anything in the world. If anyone loves the world, love for the Father is not in them. For everything in the world – the lust of the flesh, the lust of the eyes, and the pride of life– comes not from the Father but from the world."* It is impossible to love and crave the "things" of the world and serve God at the same time. This message holds true for today's "church."

7. *(2:23)* – *"No one who denies the Son has the Father; whoever acknowl-edges the Son has the Father also."* Gnostics of that day and New Agers of today would have us believe there are other ways to the Father than through Jesus, all religions being conduits to God; if we are sincere in what we believe we can earn heavenly entry based on our works alone. (*John 14:6* – *"I am the way and the truth and the life. No one comes to the Father except through me."*). He – Jesus – is the only Way!

8. *(3:6)* – *"No one who lives in Him keeps on sinning. No one who continues to sin has either seen Him or known Him."* Salvation is not a "license to sin," regardless what denominational doctrine might teach. "Signed and forever sealed" is no confirmation of that "license." (*Ephesians 5:5-6a* – *"For of this you can be sure: No immoral, impure or greedy person – such a person is an idolater – has any inheritance in the kingdom of Christ and of God. Let no one deceive you with empty words..."*).

9. *(3:15)* – *"Anyone who hates a brother or sister is a murderer, and you know that no murderer has eternal life residing in Him."* He has already discussed our relationship with our *"brothers and sisters"* in Christ. One claiming salvation and refusing to confess the Gospel message to those outside the body is a murderer. He has shown his/her hatred for their fellowman by lack of compassion, love and concern and has destined his lost brother, sister, parent, child, neighbor, to eternal damnation because of his/her lack of obedience to His command. In *Verses 12-13*, John notes Christians are to the world as Abel was to Cain. When a lost

soul dies without Christ because of our intentional lack of testimony, we are guilty of first-degree murder.

10. *(3:17-19)* – *"If anyone has material possessions and sees a brother or sister in need but has no pity on them, how can the love of God be in that person? Dear children, let us not love with words or speech but with actions and in truth. This then is how we know that we belong to the truth and how we set our hearts at rest in His presence."* Our faith may or may not require us to lay our life down for our fellow brother or sister in Christ, but it does require us to show our love in our actions. Love that is not active is not true and one who does not love in Christ does not have the love of God in his heart. Missions breeds ministry. We cannot have one without the other.

11. *(3:24)* – *"The one who keeps God's commands lives in Him, and He in them. And this is how we know that He lives in us: We know it by the Spirit He gave us."* One's seal of salvation is the Holy Spirit; without the Holy Spirit one is not saved – regardless what religion tells them – *"And if anyone does not have the Spirit of Christ, they do not belong to Christ"* – *Romans 8:9; "And you also were included in Christ when you heard the message of truth, the gospel of your salvation. When you believed, you were marked in Him with a seal, the promised Holy Spirit, who is a deposit guaranteeing our inheritance until the redemption of those who are Gods possession – to the praise of His glory"* – *Ephesians 1:13-14*. Christians know God will not make a demand on their lives without providing a way. The "demand" has been made to every born again believer (*Matthew 28:19-20*) and the way has been provided through the power of the Holy Spirit (*John 15:26-27* – *"When the Advocate comes whom I will send to you from the Father, the Spirit of truth who goes out from the Father, he will testify about Me. And you also must testify…"*).

12. *(4:4-6)* – *"You, dear children, are from God and have overcome them because the one who is in you is greater than the one who is in the world. They are from the world and therefore speak from the viewpoint of the world, and the world listens to them. We are from God and whoever knows God listens to us; but whoever is not from God does not listen to us. This is how we recognize the Spirit of truth and the spirit of falsehood."* People reject Jesus because they enjoy their sin and detest having it confronted and exposed. Those who are of God are the agents of that exposure through their testimony for Him through

His living Word and as a result, should expect denial, condemnation, ostracization and rejection – *"If the world hates you, keep in mind that it hated Me first. If you belonged to the world, it would love you as its own. As it is, you do not belong to the world, but I have chosen you out of the world. That is why the world hates you"* – John 15:18-19. Since we are empowered by the Holy Spirit, those who buckle to the world and choose the way of comfort rather than the work of salvation, may need to reexamine their spiritual status. *"For I am not ashamed of the gospel, because it is the power of God that brings salvation to everyone who believes: first to the Jew, then to the Gentile"* – Romans 1:16.

13. *(4:7-8)* – *"Dear friends, let us love one another, for love comes from God. Everyone who loves has been born of God and knows God. Whoever does not love does not know God, because God is love."* John has already made clear to fellow Christians they are to love their brothers in Christ. Here he re-emphasizes the love of Jesus goes beyond the limits of Christians loving Christians. He notes in *(4:9-10)*, Christ showed his love for us by His coming as a man and willingly sacrificing Himself for our salvation. He challenges us to *"love one another"* in the same way. But what about those who are of the world and lost? We are challenged to sacrifice ourselves and what greater sacrifice can we render than that of leading a lost soul to Jesus Christ? *"Those who sow with tears will reap with songs of joy. Those who go out weeping, carrying seed to sow, will return with songs of joy, carrying sheaves with him"* – Psalm 126:5-6.

14. *(4:13-15)* – *"This is how we know that we live in Him and He in us: He has given us of His Spirit. And we have seen and testify that the Father has sent His Son to be the Savior of the world. If anyone acknowledges that Jesus is the Son of God, God lives in them and they in God."* Three key words in these verses are: *"seen"* (been saved), *"testify"* (witnessed, shared what we have 'seen'), and *"acknowledges"* (we "acknowledge" by sharing). Many claim "intellectual belief" by giving a token of their time and allegiance to religion, refusing to "acknowledge" or "confess" Him before others. Is this enough??? Once again—James 2:26 – *"As the body without the spirit is dead, so faith without deeds is dead."*

15. *(4:16-17)* – *"And so we know and rely on the love God has for us. God is love. Whoever lives in love lives in God, and God in them. This is how love is made complete among us so that we will have confidence*

on the day of judgment: In this world we are like Jesus." Simple formula – if we love God and have a genuine walk with Jesus Christ, we will make every effort to live as He lived; if we love God, we love each other (our brothers in Christ); if we love God, we love those who do not know Him, which proves our manifestation of His Spirit and equals confidence of our salvation. The word *"love"* is used 43 times in this letter; 32 times it is found here in *(4:7-21)*.

16. *(5:1)* – *"Everyone who believes that Jesus is the Christ is born of God, and everyone who loves the Father loves His child as well."* Another added emphasis to *(2:23)* – Faith in Jesus as the Messiah is salvation; there is none other or no other way. Throughout this Letter, John uses the family to illustrate the relationship between Jesus and His children and the Christian and his brothers in Christ. The Gnostics of the day taught there was a division between Jesus the Messiah and Jesus the man. Based on their teaching, Jesus was only a man. John emphasizes, to be born of God we must believe that Jesus is the Christ. We must believe that He came to earth; that He was both God and man. We must believe that Jesus the Christ died for us. But death was not the end. Jesus Christ rose from death to life, achieving what he came to do. He rose from the dead to prove death is not the end.

17. *(5:5)* – *"Who is it that overcomes the world? Only the one who believes that Jesus is the Son of God."* Since John heard these words from the mouth of the Savior Himself, this verse appears to be an extension of *John 14:6* – *"I am the way and the truth and the life. No one comes to the Father except through me."* Pretty direct and self-explanatory.

The New Covenant was ushered into the world through Jesus Christ (*"I did – will you accept?"*). Once we accept it, we have an obligation – *"Therefore everyone who hears these words of mine and puts them into practice is like a wise man who built his house on the rock. But everyone who hears these words of mine and does not put them into practice is like a foolish man who built his house on sand"* – *Matthew 7:24,26.* Otherwise our end of the covenant agreement remains "tingling cymbals and sounding brass."

Chapter 14

WHY THE HOLY SPIRIT?

"Will God ever ask you to do something you are not able to do? The answer is yes — all the time! It must be that way, for God's glory and kingdom. If we function according to our ability alone, we get the glory; if we function according to the power of the Holy Spirit within us, God gets the glory. He wants to reveal Himself to a watching world" – Henry Blackaby.[240]

R on McDonald (not related to the fast food mascot) had just received the news he had been waiting for. A man of twenty-eight years of age, Ron had climbed the ladder of success with his company and it had finally paid off! He was being offered a promotion fulfilling his life-long dream of acquiring a management role with a successful company, opening the doors to eventually owning his own business. He called his wife Sara and could not wait to get home to celebrate with the family. He knew she would be excited about the opportunity and impending challenge. The kids, Barney and Joanna, could not help but get caught up in the elation, but Ron was fully aware due to their ages – Barney, eight and Joanna, six and one-half – the full impact of the news would take a while to fully register. Sara suggested they call their parents and share the news.

After a special night out on the town – a pizza buffet and movie that was catered to the kids, Ron's family returned home and prepared for bed. The excitement was still fresh on his mind and sleep was going to be a challenge. As was typical, all prepared for bed and met in the den for the nightly family devotion and prayer. Ron and Sara jointly led the devotion time, but tonight Ron shared from *Hebrews 11:8*, and the story of Abraham. *"By faith Abraham, when called to go to a place he would later receive as his inheritance, obeyed and went, even though he did not know where he was going."* The kids especially seemed to grasp the story and how it related to Ron's job change and the challenges of moving to a new town and meeting new people. Even though the family knew where they were to relocate, they all realized this meant the start of a new life and new opportunities of service to the Lord. As Ron related, they were being called to a new mission field.

The next few weeks went by like a blur. It was early Summer, so locating a top-notch school for the kids was important, but not an immediate priority. Finding a reasonably priced house in a nice, middle-class neighborhood certainly was. Luckily, one of Ron's work partners knew of a friend of a friend who owned a real estate business. Call it divine guidance or luck, the very first house he introduced to them was love at first sight. It was an 1800 square foot, two-level Chesapeake with dormer windows; three bedrooms and 2-1/2 baths, so it was ideal for the kids to have upstairs rooms and the adults could maintain some sense of privacy utilizing the downstairs. It was a nice community – middle class, with an accredited school within four blocks. Even the next-door neighbor stopped by during their initial visit with the realtor – either out of curiosity or a genuine heartfelt desire to see the McDonalds' buy the house. At any rate, the wheels were in motion for the purchase of a new home and with Ron's company committed to buying his former house, that hurdle was now behind them.

The next step was to find a church. Ron and the family had been active in their former church and leaving the fellowship was going to be difficult. Finding a replacement would be even tougher. Ron's church was not a mega church, but a non-denominational fellowship which was less than ten years old. It had started as a "church plant" from a larger church in a nearby community. Growing up in a traditional church setting and adjusting to the format of a non-denominational fellowship had been a challenge. Ron never assumed any leadership position in the fellowship or anything resembling responsibility, but he did consider himself a compassionate believer who had a heart for lost people. He led a visitation group on Tuesday evenings where a group of six or so would meet for prayer at 7:00 pm and then depart into the community, canvasing the neighborhood with flyers and invites to the church. Even though Ron considered himself a champion for the Gospel, realistically there was little opportunity to share it in this setting. Most folk, though appearing not to be bothered, looked at him with an intent stare and a silent message – "say what you need to say and get the heck off my porch." Seldom was he invited into the home.

The services at Ron's church were not spiritually challenging to say the least. He had a special appreciation for the pastor and loved him dearly, but what really attracted him to the church was the fellowship. Sara had grown close to several of the ladies and was enamored with the attention given to the children, especially since one of her best friends headed that department. The preaching was adequate at best. The presentation aspect was acceptable for Ron, but there was hardly any doctrine ever covered in the messages. The sermons were usually dry and had all the appearances of a seminary class presentation – a subject, three to four points peppered with a little Scripture and an invitation. If no one came forward, as they seldom did, it was trimmed to two verses.

As Ron considered the impending move to a new fellowship, he could not help but critique his spiritual growth as a result of being a part of his present fellowship for some eight years. The results of his critique were less than stellar. He had to honestly question whether he had truly grown as a Christian and had to admit his knowledge of God's Word was severely limited. He had no one to blame but himself but was inwardly angry the tutelage from the pulpit had been less than conducive to spiritual growth. Luckily, Ron's peer partner from the new office, Jim, was eager to provide him with a list of several churches to begin visiting. A major question arose when Jim mentioned "spirit-filled" churches would only be included on his list of potential visits.

Ron was puzzled – what did Jim mean by a "spirit-filled" church? He knew the basics of Biblical doctrine – the Father, Son and the Holy Spirit – but what does that really mean? Ron pondered, "The Father – oh that's God, Father of the Son; the Son – that's Jesus Christ, the begotten Son of the Father; but who is the Holy Ghost? I have never been taught that aspect of the Trinity. Oh well, guess when I visit Jim's three "spirit-filled" churches I will find out soon enough."

The following week the family moved into their new home. By the end of the week they were semi-settled, and Ron suggested they begin on the upcoming Sunday visiting the first of the three churches on Jim's list of "spirit-filled" churches. On Sunday morning the family put on their 'Sunday-go-to-meeting' duds and headed out.

The church on the list they chose for this first Sunday sampling was First Church. It was a large denominational church with an impressive complex of buildings. Luckily, there were parking staff who helped guide the family into a parking spot reserved for – you guessed it – first-time guests. Ron could not help but wonder how long the walk would be from the parking area if they decided to join and were forced to park with the regular members. At any rate, they parked and entered the building.

The entryway or vestibule was impressive. At the main entrance was a large kiosk that contained a coffee station that rivaled the Starbucks located next to Ron's office. They even served cinnamon buns that were to die for. Time was pressing so coffee was out of the question, especially with this being the first visit. The family entered the sanctuary and found a pew that would accommodate the entire family without splitting the clan. The prelude from the orchestra began with a wonderful rendition of religious sounding music designed to put one in the mood for worship. Things seemed to be going well until Ron noticed a semi-elderly lady standing adjacent to him at the end of the pew. Ron looked up – smiled and nodded a greeting, which the lady responded accordingly. It was at that point the lady motioned to the pew and, in what Ron deemed as a tone of arrogance said, "You're in my seat. I have been a member of this church going on fifty-five years and for the bulk of those fifty-five years, this has been my seat. I hate to be rude, but I'm not interested in breaking my string and would appreciate if you could please relocate." With that note of greeting, Ron motioned to Sara and the kids and prodded them to move to the opposite end of the pew.

The service finally began. Ron noticed it was not totally different from his former church, but much more ritual. There was a lot of sitting, standing, recitals, singing – mainly congregational – an offering, special music and then the sermon. Pretty cut and dried, Ron pondered, for most traditional churches. Ron wondered if the members were so accustomed, they could perform the formalities blindfolded and from memory and without the bulletin. He brushed it off since he was anxious to hear the pastor.

Frustrated and disappointed, Ron saw the sermon as dreadfully boring – difficult to listen to and remain attentive. The pastor rambled on and on about the church and its many ministries, noting the recent $3.5 million expansion project to the educational building and how God, under his direction, had so blessed the fellowship and he expected the church to be debt free within ten years as long as the members kept up their "financial commitment." Afterwards, Ron could honestly not remember if there was a Scripture reference used or not. It reminded him of his college days and those classroom lectures during a 3:30 pm class on a Friday afternoon.

The pastor eventually began to wind down. One verse of an "invitational hymn" was played instrumentally without singing. Ron was puzzled a hymn of invitation was even offered since there was nothing that remotely resembled a Gospel message in the sermon. No one came forward, but why should they? He couldn't help but mentally compare the pastor to a seasoned radio disc jockey who smoothly transitions his listening audience into a commercial, since in the same way the pastor moved the congregation straight into a business meeting to discuss the new budget for the coming year. It became clear to Ron the reason behind the 'pro-church' sermon.

Ron and the family had no interest in the budget and considered slipping out the back door, but since they had been relegated to the end of the pew and were over half-way down the auditorium, he decided against at the risk of drawing attention. He could not help but pick up a Bible that was placed in the Hymnal rack of each pew. As he began to flip pages to pass the time, his fingers inadvertently took him to *1 Corinthians 1:23* – Paul speaking – *"we preach Christ crucified."* "Wow", Ron thought. "I have always wondered what it would have been like to sit and hear a message preached by the apostle Paul and wondered what he would preach? Gee – now I know. He preached the same message – and it never got old – he preached the Gospel!" He looked back at *Verse 20 – "Where is the wise person? Where is the teacher of the law? Where is the philosopher of this age? Has not God made foolish the wisdom of the world? For since in the wisdom of God the world through its wisdom did not know Him, God was pleased through the foolishness of what was preached to save those who believe."* Ron could not help but ponder, based on what he had just sat through, "what – in the so-called sermon that was just presented this morning – could it possibly have to do with sharing the Gospel message? God forbid that any lost person be here this morning that needed to hear the Gospel and was subjected to a praise directed to man and man only. God have mercy!" The good news was the kids were sound asleep along with half of the remaining congregation.

Then came the dreaded budget. Ron could not help but glance at the numbers (copies had been pre-placed in the bulletin) since he too was an accountant. "Wow!" he thought. "A $1.5 million budget! This is more than my new company's budget." In fact, Ron was amazed at the resemblances. The church accountant was earning $80,000 annually, which was $20,000 more than he made prior to his job transfer. The staff payroll exceeded 41% of the entire budget! Ron could not help but surmise how his business, or any business for that matter, could survive with labor costs of that amount.

Another number that stood out was the coffee kiosk he had seen upon entering the sanctuary–$35,000 annually to operate! Again – "wow!" "That's a lot of coffee," he thought. On and on, he could not help but critique – literature – 20% of the budget; capital needs 20%; utilities, insurance another 20%. And then there was missions – 5% of the total budget – most of which was reserved for a denominational fund called "United Ministries", where member churches were encouraged to contribute a certain percentage of their budgets to support denominational "mission efforts," per a footnoted addendum. "A whopping 5%," Ron surmised. $75,000 seems like a lot of money and it is, but Ron could not help but ask himself – "How could this church – any church for that matter – spend 95% of its budget on itself and justify only 5% on something outside the front door?" He could not help but recall one of his recent family devotions – *Matthew 18:12-14 – "What do you think? If a man owns a hundred sheep, and one of them wanders away, will he not leave the ninety-nine on the hills and go to look for the one that wandered off? And if he finds it, truly I tell you he is happier about that one sheep than about the ninety-nine that did not wander off. In the same way your Father in heaven is not willing that any of these little ones should perish."* Ron surmised to this fellowship, ministering to the ninety-nine was definitely more important than reaching the one.

Then came the pledge card he had surprisingly failed to notice, since it was conveniently placed in plain view in front of the Bible in the hymnal rack. The pastor made sure to call attention and urged each member to pledge a certain amount to help meet the budget. Once again, Ron was mystified. He wondered if that strategy might be doable in his own business – if he could find a way to get his customers to complete a pledge card and commit to a certain amount of business for the coming year. Boy, that would be a Godsend and certainly make his new job a lot easier. As quickly as that thought entered his mind, it vanished.

Finally, the service ended. The ride home was quiet and uneventful. He did not need to ask Sara or the kids their thoughts about the service; he could surmise their opinion was the same as his. He could not help but feel relief, but at the same time concern, not only for the fellowship, but for his own family's spiritual well-being and growth. "How could Jim have listed this church in his top three "spirit-filled" churches? What about this church was "spirit-filled?" In fact, Ron could not help but wonder more than ever, "what exactly is the Holy Spirit? Where do we find a church possessed by this 'Holy Spirit?' And for that matter, what does a 'Spirit-filled' church even look like?"

The week passed by in a flash and the following Sunday came quickly. The next church on Jim's list of "spirit-filled" churches was Antioch Church of the Holy Spirit. Based on the name alone, Ron was sure it would fit the bill. The services started thirty minutes earlier than First Church, but they decided to make the effort. Upon arrival, the family quickly realized this was a much smaller fellowship and more "traditional." There was nothing fancy about the campus, no coffee kiosks and the buildings appeared to be from the 1950's or before. There was no parking attendant and it was first come first serve. Ron noticed the railing on the steps entering the sanctuary to be rusty and loose, but he reckoned if they had sufficed that long, they could safely handle him. Upon entering the small vestibule, he was greeted and given a one-page bulletin, consisting of announcements and order of service. The family took their seat at about the same location in the sanctuary as they did in First Church, but this time they were not prodded to move by a concerned member.

The service was very traditional; the hymns recognizable with no "7-11 choruses" as Ron's dad used to call them – "tunes that have seven words and you sing them eleven-times." The service did not turn Ron off, but what did was a small sign adjacent to the pulpit that provided information, which in Ron's eyes, summarized the outreach of the church or in this case, the lack thereof. Included on the sign were such statistics as total membership, today's Sunday School or Bible Study attendance, last Sunday's offering and weekly budget needs, today's sermon topic, and baptisms year-to-date. The irony was blatant; the sermon topic – "The Power of the Holy Spirit;" secondly, membership – 150 members; thirdly, Bible Study attendance – 38; fourthly, and glaringly – baptisms. It was early August – past mid- year and the church had zero baptisms! Zero! Ron could not help but wonder how a business could survive with only 20% of its employees active and using the same analogy, how a church could survive accordingly, and secondly, how could a church considering itself "spirit-filled," baptize zero persons? He could not help but ponder, "this sermon is going to be really interesting."

The pastor was fiery – nothing wrong with that, Ron thought. The kids looked a little mystified and somewhat fearful, but a "hell-fire and brimstone" sermon was afoot, and Ron felt it might possibly benefit him. He had not heard a sermon like that since he was a child. The congregation was charismatic – nothing wrong with that either, provided no one got physically hurt. What was concerning was the message. The crux of the message was the power of the Holy Spirit and "its" manifestation through the work of the church. "Huh?" Ron began scratching his head. "What did I miss?", he thought. "Can you feel it?" the pastor screamed. "Can you feel it?" he repeated several times. The congregation responded with a chorus of, "amens" and "preach it brother." Ron was confused – he had always noted the Scripture's reference to the "Person" of the Holy Spirit. If this is true, how can the pastor refer to the Holy Spirit as, "it," and not as "He?"

Several men and ladies began to gyrate in the aisle. One man ran to the pulpit and knelt before the pastor and implored him to "anoint" him with the Holy Spirit. The pastor urged him to rise and touching his head, blew a strong gust of breath in the man's face and he immediately fainted and fell backwards, where two ushers stationed at the pulpit caught him and eased him to the floor. Eight-year-old Barney pulled on his dad's arm and asked if the pastor had bad breath that had caused the man to faint. Ron could not help but chuckle. He also could not recall ever reading any Scripture referencing any human being blowing in the face of another and by doing so, "bestowing" the Holy Spirit. Even if he could, what would give this man the authority to "anoint" or "bestow" the Holy Spirit on anyone?

Ron was fascinated by the lady dancers, focusing on one in particular who appeared to have hurt herself physically. She did not want the other members to notice, but she had an obvious hitch in her step when she returned to her seat. The pastor rambled on, talking about how the church was "spirit-filled" and on fire with the power of the Holy Spirit. Again, Ron could not help but wonder, "if this church is so "spirit-filled," how in the world could they have zero baptisms?" The last straw was when a dear lady sitting beside Joanna rose abruptly and jumped the pew in front of her and began uttering words that were completely incoherent. Ron took two languages in college, in addition to Latin, but could not decipher what the lady was uttering. Little Joanna was frightened to tears, prompting the family to abruptly exit the service. Their leaving did not affect the party atmosphere or the physical work-out. In fact, Ron was positive they were so consumed with themselves, not a single person noticed their exit.

Ron was again confused – now more than ever. Is this raucous environment a typical result of the outpouring of the Holy Spirit in one's life? Where in Scripture is it shown that these are attributes of one possessed by the Holy Spirit? The confusion was not only evident with Ron, but Sara and the kids began to question also, to the point the kids were questioning their own salvation. That was it! Ron had had enough.

The following Sunday came and went, and Ron awoke on Monday morning determined to confront Jim about his two experiences. Surprisingly, Jim responded with a smile and urged Ron to be patient. Jim vehemently encouraged Ron to consider visiting the third church on his list. It was Jim's church. Ron reluctantly agreed to consider but wanted to know more about the church before committing and more importantly, subject his family to more religious humiliation. Jim proposed he buy Ron lunch and promised to answer all Ron's questions regarding his church. He jokingly, but with a devious sincerity, shared with Ron he had saved the best for last.

The following week was unlike the first two as it seemed to drag by. Ron was not sure if it was because of the reality of a new job and the hassles of the move had finally set in, or if it was because of the family's frustrations over finding a new church. He had convinced himself it was the latter. The kids were totally disgruntled with church; six-year old Joanna was severely scolded by her mom when she made the statement that she was "tired of church." Both Ron and Sara knew to take this with a grain of salt coming from a child, but Ron secretly could not help but feel the same way. Saturday rolled around and both the parents made a joint decision to skip this Sunday's church search and perhaps try again the following week. Ron knew this was dangerous, as missing church can easily become habit forming. It was a pretty easy decision though and the kids had no objection. He telephoned Jim to break the news.

Jim vehemently objected. "Ron," he implored, "you promised to visit my fellowship and by golly, I'm holding you to it. In fact, I will throw in a free family pizza dinner afterwards. I'll seduce you anyway I can, but you absolutely must go." Ron would have probably stayed true to his decision not to attend, but Jim's wife Betty began to call Sara. She let Sara know she worked with the kids and had already shared with everyone to expect guests. At the family meal on Saturday evening, Ron and Sara informed the kids there had been a change in plans and they would be attending church with Betty and Jim – a decision that met with less than stellar approval.

As Sunday afternoon approached, the family was more shocked than surprised since they were not driving up to a sprawling campus or "traditional" steepled building, but rather the public library. The kids were excited since they expected a day with the "story lady." "Jim", Ron prodded as they met in the parking lot, "I believe you have your wires crossed. We are not checking out books or perusing the latest periodicals – this is not a church. It's the library, for Pete's sake." "Just sit tight", Jim answered. "You'll see in due time." Into the library they trudged. The lady at the check-out nodded politely but quietly and by her nod, Ron assumed she was directing them to a room located directly behind her and down the hall. His assumption was correct, and the family followed Jim and Betty down the hall into a spacious, but strangely intimate, room.

Upon entering they were welcomed by a sweet elderly couple. "Welcome to our fellowship," the man said. "You are my brother and sister in Christ, and we are glad you have chosen to be a part of God's family and participate in our fellowship meeting." At that point, another gentleman walked up and was introduced by Jim as Briscoe Barton, the "elder" or "overseer" of the fellowship. Ron could not help but chuckle under his breath at the name – Briscoe. He almost laughed out-loud when he thought of a character from his favorite TV show – "Andy Griffith" – by the name of Briscoe Darling, the family patriarch of a backwoods mountain clan blessed with the talent of blue grass music. In fact, Pastor Barton reminded him in both looks and mannerisms of Briscoe Darling.[241]

Sara and Betty continued conversing with the elderly lady greeter. Ron reached out to Sara to introduce her to brother Barton. "Sara," Ron said, "Allow me to introduce Preacher Briscoe Barton." "Whoa," brother Barton replied. "I appreciate the title of respect, but that is exactly what it is – a title and you will not find that here. We are all one body – working together in service to Jesus Christ." Brother Barton opened his Bible to *Hebrews 7:25* (it was as if he knew this question might arise as he turned directly to the verse without flipping a single page) and began to read – *"For the law appoints as high priests men in all their weakness; but the oath, which came after the law, appointed the Son, who has been made perfect forever."*

"You see Ron", brother Barton noted, "we have no need for a 'preacher' or 'mediator.' Our High Priest is seated at the right hand of the throne of God and He is our mediator." Ron could not help but ask, "But what about seminary or special training – surely you have been formally educated in the Word – haven't you?" "No son, I have not," brother Barton replied. "If seminary education was a requirement for the study of God's Holy Word, then we have been grossly misled. You see, as children of God, we serve the same Savior and are taught by the same Holy Spirit." Once again, he turned almost directly to another verse – *Philippians 2:12* – *"Continue to work out your salvation with fear and trembling, for it is God who works in you to will and to act in order to ful-fill his good purpose."* "God has a plan designed specifically for you and it's through you He desires for that plan to be accomplished; He equips you to accomplish that plan – and never forget – it's your salvation – not your wife's, not the kids, not Jim or Betty's, your parents or even Briscoe

Barton. Work it out on your knees and in His Word – see for yourself; you are the one who will stand before the Almighty in judgment. What you will find here is exhortation, encouragement and learning through mutual dialog and study of the Word. If you are a believer, the Holy Spirit you possess is your Teacher, Counselor, and Equipper, and was trained in Heaven by the Father Himself!" "Wow!" Ron blurted. "I have attended two churches over the past three weeks and sat through an hour and forty-five minutes of sermons and I must say, that is the most dynamic message I have heard, and all in less than five minutes!" Ron could not help but ponder to himself – "There was that word again – Holy Spirit. I want to know more; I need to know more."

"If you don't mind me asking, is it ok if I call you Pastor?" Brother Barton laughed, "I guess technically, I would be considered an 'elder,' as described by Paul in *1 Timothy 5:17*; most people equate Pastors to 'elders.' I am, for lack of a better term, a 'shepherd' over the many fellowships that meet in our area and as an 'elder,' use my spiritual gifts accordingly. Not that I'm blessed with any special abilities over any other, but I utilize the spiritual gifts I believe God has blessed me with and one of those is to use my many years in the Word to help others understand and disciple them off the milk and onto the meat of the Word. No seminary degree is required to understand one's spiritual gift and how to use it." "Pastor," Ron implored, "I want to know more, especially about the Holy Spirit. Can you help me?" "Later, my son. There is much to discuss, and the service is about to begin."

The kids went with Mrs. Betty to an adjacent room. Ron, Sara, and Jim sat on the second row of chairs from the podium. It was not an elaborate pulpit with fancy furnishings–no table for offering plates or large chair for the "preacher." The podium was a simple piece of furniture, designed more for holding papers rather than for "pounding." Ron could not help but wonder should things get exciting, as it had in the previous church they visited, it could easily tip over. "What a scene that would make!"

Ron whispered to Jim, "That Preacher, I mean Pastor Barton, is pretty smart and knows the Bible. You must have to pay him a bundle." "Actually," Jim chuckled, "we don't pay him a penny. He is a volunteer; as he told you, he holds no special title or office; much less a paid position." "Well, how about the building", Ron asked, "the library must be charging you a bundle for this room." Jim once again chuckled – loud enough this time for the folks behind them to hear – "Ron, the library is a public building – there is no charge for using the room and we have a standing reservation for one Sunday afternoon per month at 4:00 pm. We have no budget – there is no need for one. We have no staff, no building to pay for, no office supplies or capital equipment to invest, no literature since the only literature we utilize is the Holy Bible. In fact, we take no offering – we meet needs. There is no one in this fellowship that has a physical or spiritual need that is not met. Note, I said need, not want. We also reach outside the fellowship to address needs in the community. These are researched carefully and addressed. Meeting the physical need is accompanied with meeting the spiritual need. This fellowship is patterned as close and as prayerfully possible to the fellowship or *'ekklesia'* of the New Testament Church as detailed in *Acts 2:42-47*." With that, before Ron could respond with more questioning, the service began.

Interesting to Ron how simple the service was. There was no formality; no offering; no recitals; no responsive utterances; just each person sharing as they felt led – testimonies, insight on certain Scripture passages that generated intense conversation, and several individual music arias. Just as Jim noted, there was no preaching. With Elder Barton presiding, the group celebrated Communion. Never had Ron experienced such intimacy and closeness. At his former church it seemed more a formality than a remembrance, being more interested in making sure the kids did not spill the juice or drop the bread.

Two ladies shared a song. One did a beautiful rendition of "Blessed Assurance." And then it was testimony time – each person shared a personal testimony or commentary on Scripture they had read during their Bible study time the previous week. Because Ron and Sara were visitors, they were not pressured to participate, but Ron wanted to be a part. He could not help but testify regarding the experiences he had encountered at his home church, being busily involved, but as he described – "running wide open in neutral." He did not sense growing or maturing as a Christian. Then he shared about the family's experience at First Church (he refused to call the church by name), the 95% inwardly-based budget and accompanying messages and then the "lively" experience at Antioch Church of the Holy Spirit – where Ron's limited knowledge of the Holy Spirit was severely questioned and clouded. He began to share with the group his desire to learn and understand more about the power of the Holy Spirit and what role He plays in his life. "As a matter of fact," Ron added, "I'm deeply concerned and questioning myself if the Holy Spirit is even a part of my life."

The lady who performed the rendition of "Blessed Assurance" introduced herself as Thelma Jones. Ms. Jones informed Ron and Sara the Sunday meetings were monthly sessions, but on each Tuesday evening at 7:30 pm, the fellowship splits up into seven "house churches" or "small group Bible studies." She gave Ron the address (only two streets over from the McDonald home) and a verbal invitation to the service at her home the upcoming Tuesday evening. She promised coffee and maybe a sip of soft drink, but plenty of spiritual food, prayer and fellowship. With that, the meeting was called to a close and each person knelt at their station in prayer. Ron could not remember the last time, if ever, he prayed kneeling. He could also not believe how quickly time elapsed and looked twice at his watch to confirm an hour had gone by. Ron had been in church for what seemed like forever, but he had never experienced such sweet, sincere closeness and fellowship. Pleasantries were shared with the rest of the group, then grabbing the kids, they headed to the pizza parlor. Jim was true to his word and covered the tab for the entire group over Ron's objections. "It is I that should be paying your tab", Ron beamed. "Great day and wonderful fellowship. Great to be in God's house, even if it was in the public library."

Returning home, everyone prepared for bed but before retiring for the evening, Ron called a brief family meeting in the den. Sara and the kids knew family meetings, especially ones called by Ron, were serious business. Ron promised to make it quick since Monday morning meant work. "I want to hear your opinions about your experiences today; and I'm not talking about the pizza." Everyone got the drift. Surprisingly, little Joanna was the first to speak.

"I had fun with Mrs. Betty; she is a great teacher." "What did you learn?" quipped Sara. "Well," Joanna responded. "It was more of a lesson than a story." "What do you mean?" Ron asked. "Well, it was about Noah's Ark. I knew this story from my pre-school days, but Mrs. Betty shared it in a different way. First, she gave us the Bible verse, and asked us to find it in our Bibles. She helped those of us who had problems. Then she explained the true meaning of the ark – how it was a "figure" or a "shadow" of Jesus Christ – how He is our ark and how He loves and protects us. But the sad thing she shared was from *Genesis 7:16* – once Noah and his family along with the animals entered the ark, the Bible says – *'then the Lord shut him in.'* She asked us, why did God Himself shut and seal the door. Dad, do you know why?" "No honey, I really don't", Ron replied. "Didn't Mrs. Betty tell you?" "Yes, she did, dad. She explained there is a time in our life when it is too late. In fact, she said the words, 'too late,' are the two saddest words in our language. I am too late for school; I am too late for the game; I am too late for piano practice. In fact, Mrs. Betty said anything you can say using those two words means sadness. And what was so sad, it took Noah over 150 years to build the ark and people walked by every day, laughing at him. I bet he was sad! But imagine when the rains came and the water became ankle deep, knee deep, waist deep, and eventually, neck deep, how many people were banging on the ark's door, begging for Noah to let them in – they were sorry – but God said, 'it's too late' – and even though Noah wanted to open the door, he could not because God had shut them in."

"Wow, what a lesson," Sara thought, and could not believe her ears. Most of the time when she asked the children what their Bible lesson was about on Sunday morning, she always received the same SOP answer – "sin or Jesus." Strange how that was the same lesson every Sunday. Ron too was enamored, but what Joanna said next really pierced his heart. "Mrs. Betty told us because there comes a time when it's 'too late,' it is very important for us who are saved to allow the Holy Spirit to work in our lives to reach out to lost people and make sure they find Jesus." Ron's antenna went up – there it was again – the Holy Spirit. He could not help but wonder, "does the Holy Spirit do that?" He absolutely needed to know. With that, the family prayed together and hit the sack.

Tuesday evening could not come quickly enough. Ron, Sara and the kids, walked to the home of Mrs. Jones for the "house-church" Bible study. It was a small home – quaint – but spacious enough for her since she was a widow. Surprisingly, and to his great excitement, Pastor Barton was also in attendance. Even though the seating arrangements were somewhat snug, they were circularly arranged with each participant able to see the face of the others. Ron counted about fifteen adults and maybe five to six kids – early teens and under. The fellowship began on time and in this setting, the kids remained with the adults. There were no interruptions from any of the children other than one diaper change before the service began. There was no constant "in and out" interruptions from kids and their parents headed to the bathroom or water fountain as was common in Ron's former church. He could not help but smile when he thought of how many boring sermons he had sat through and came close to thinking an interruption might do him some good.

The content of the meeting was akin to the library fellowship but more intimate. The meeting began with prayer – on their knees–and continued with testimonies. All testified of something they believed to have been divinely inspired that had occurred during the past week, especially witnessing opportunities. Several shared a song or a hymn. Ron was quick to note, most of the singers were extremely talented and could have participated in any large, mega-church choir. Then there was Bible study – the "Apostles Teaching," as Mrs. Jones called it. There was no preaching since there was no preacher and what really caught Ron's attention – there was no offering. The Bible study was just that – a group study of God's Word. The group had begun a verse-by-verse study in the *Gospel of Mark* several weeks ago. Ron could not help but wish he had been in the study from the beginning. Everyone participated – even the kids – especially the older ones – with comments and questions. There was no pressure on anyone to be an active part, but all chose to do so.

Ron had never spent much time in the *Gospel of Mark*, but this evening was different and kept his attention and brought the Scriptures alive for the first time in his life. He had never felt this from any pew. It also reminded him of Paul's admonition to the "house-churches" of Corinth – *1 Corinthians 14:26* – *"What then shall we say, brothers and sisters? When you come together, each of you has a hymn, or a word of instruction, a revelation, a tongue, or an interpretation. Everything must be done so that the church may be built up."* From this initial experience, Ron saw all had been orderly and was truly catered to the individual's spiritual growth in the Word. He could not help but ponder, "this is not what I am accustomed to as 'church;' not the same 'church' I was brought up, but for the first time in my life, I feel like I have been to 'church'."

For the first time in his "church" life, Ron felt the urge to participate. He was quick to share his desire to know and learn more about the purpose of the Holy Spirit. Pastor Barton spoke up – "Ron, I would love to talk with you and would prefer to do it on an individual basis if you are willing. I have a small hardware store at the corner of Main and Elm and we are closed tomorrow afternoon – in fact, every Wednesday afternoon – if you can take some time from work and could stop by, we can talk." Ron looked at Jim and no verbal confirmation was needed – a simple nod from Jim, and Ron knew he could be spared for the afternoon, so he quickly agreed. "Bring your Bible", Pastor Barton said, "you will need it."

With that, the meeting closed in prayer, but prior, a middle-aged man by the name of Ben Simmons stood and noted his thankfulness for the attendance. He announced that he and his wife Peggy would be opening their home on the following Tuesday evening for a new "house-church" in an effort to continue the outreach. There was applause and "amens." But then came the clincher – Pastor Barton broke out into a big smile and announced, from the seven "house-churches" he "oversees" there had been fifteen salvations in the past two weeks, prompting the Simmons' to graciously open up their home for the new fellowship. A baptism would be held at the next library meeting. Ron quickly recalled another verse – from *Acts 2:47* – *"And the Lord added to their number daily those who were being saved."*

Barton's Hardware was easy to find since it was located directly across the street from the pizza parlor where the family had dined with Jim and Betty the previous Sunday evening after the library fellowship. The store had a "closed" sign on the door but after several knocks, the lights flickered, lighting up the show room and the door swung open. Pastor Barton greeted Ron with a hug. "Hope you're hungry", he said. "Picked up some deli sandwiches from the pizza parlor across the street and grabbed some sodas from the canteen. Step into my home away from home." Both men went into Pastor Barton's office. It was small and looked as if it had been a storage closet at one time. It was, however, large enough to accommodate the two men comfortably, along with their dining supplies.

Ron jumped quickly to his subject of concern, "Reverend Barton, I want to sincerely thank you for taking this time to help me understand the

Scriptures, especially as they relate to the Holy Spirit." "Ron," quipped Pastor Barton, "It is not necessary for you to call me 'preacher' or 'reverend.' As I told you at the fellowship, there is no laic/cleric distinction at our fellowship and titles are not only obsolete, but also non-Biblical, at least in my eyes. Please call me BB; that is what my wife has called me for 38 years and my closest friends have picked up on it also. As a friend and a brother in Christ, I would expect you to do the same." "That's a deal, Pastor – I mean BB," said Ron. Anxious to change the subject, Ron asked BB if they could get started.

"Absolutely," said BB. "Let's go. Without question you are not alone. The Holy Spirit is the most misunderstood person of the Trinity. And you are correct, the Holy Spirit is a person. You will never find the Holy Spirit referenced in Scripture using the pronoun, 'it.' The foundation for the Holy Spirit is laid in *Matthew 28: 19-20*." "Wait a minute, Pastor – I mean BB," Ron interrupted. "I know those verses – that is the Great Commission." "Right you are Ron," answered BB. "This is the preparation for the coming of the Holy Spirit. I am truly not a profound individual, but one thing I can tell you, based on experience, God will never make a demand on your life without providing a means of accomplishing that demand. God has made a demand on your life as a Christian – it is found here: *'Therefore go and make disciples of all nations, baptizing them in the name of the Father and of the Son and of the Holy Spirit, and teaching them to obey everything I have commanded you. And surely I am with you always, to the very end of the age.'* Ron, what does that passage mean to you?" Ron thought for a moment and shot back, "It means as a Christian I have a job to do. I am obligated to share the Gospel to the lost." "Right you are again my friend," confirmed BB. "But look closely at that last phrase – *'and surely I am with you always, to the very end of the age.'* What does that mean to you?" "Well", Ron pondered for a moment, "if what you say is true about God never making a demand on your life without providing a way, I would think it means, He will provide a way for me to accomplish His purpose, which is for me to share the Gospel. But how can He do that?"

"You are once again correct," B.B. replied. "Where is Jesus at present?" "I'm not sure I understand the question", Ron answered. Pastor Barton explained, "in *Acts 1:9-11*, Jesus shared His final words with His disciples before being Transfigured or 'taken up,' as the Scripture describes. *'After He said this, He was taken up before their very eyes, and a cloud* hid Him from their sight. They were looking intently up into the sky as He was going, when suddenly two men dressed in white stood beside them. 'Men of Galilee,' they said, 'why do you stand here looking into the sky? This same Jesus, who has been taken from you into Heaven, will come back in the same way you have seen Him go into Heaven.'" "So, I ask you again – where is Jesus presently?" Ron pondered again – "would the answer be – Heaven?" "'Correct my friend – at the right hand of the Father as detailed in *Hebrews 8:1-2* – 'We do have such a high priest, who sat down at the right hand of the throne of the Majesty in Heaven, and who serves in the sanctuary, the true tabernacle set up by the Lord, not by a mere human being.' At the right hand of the Father denotes He sits in a position of authority serving both God and man as Intercessor on our behalf." "I understand and I absolutely believe it," Ron replied, "but if He is in Heaven, how can He do anything for me here on earth to help me accomplish His will of sharing the Gospel?" "Glad you asked my brother." And with that, B.B. began to deepen his dialogue.

"*Acts 1,* is the second stage of preparation for the coming of Holy Spirit to New Testament man. Jesus was with his followers for a period of forty days after his resurrection. On one occasion He was dining with them and He gave them this command: *Verse 4 – 'Do not leave Jerusalem, but wait for the gift my Father promised, which you have heard Me speak about. For John baptized with water, but in a few days, you will be baptized with the Holy Spirit.'* Now look at *Verse 8 – 'But you will receive power when the Holy Spirit comes on you; and you will be My witnesses in Jerusalem, and in all Judea and Samaria, and to the ends of the earth.'* The purpose of the Holy Spirit is to equip you to be that witness for the Lord Jesus Christ. We see this same "equipping" and subsequent results in *Acts 4:31 – 'After they prayed, the place where they were meeting was shaken. And they were all filled with the Holy Spirit and spoke the word of God boldly'.*" "But Pastor, I mean BB," asked Ron, "where and when in Scripture did Jesus ever promise the coming of the Holy Spirit to those who follow Him?"

"Perhaps this will answer your question, Ron. Look at *John 14:15 – 'If you love me, you will obey what I command.'* What Ron, did Jesus command?" "He has commanded I share the Gospel." "Exactly," shouted BB. He continued, "*And I will ask the Father and He will give you another advocate to help you and be with you forever – the Spirit of truth. The world cannot accept Him because it neither sees him nor knows him. But you know him for he lives with you and will be in you. I will not leave you as orphans; I will come to you. Before long, the world will not see me anymore, but you will see me. Because I live, you also will live. On that day you will realize that I am in my Father and you are in me, and I am in you. Whoever has my commands and keeps them, he is the one who loves me.*" "Wow", said Ron, "there's a lot of meat in that passage." "You are right", said BB. "Let's analyze the meat."

"*Verses 15-16* confirms Christ's demand for believers to witness and the means for carrying it out – the Holy Spirit. 'Truth,' Ron, in Scripture is whom?" "That one I know," Ron answered, "*John 14:6*, Christ says *'I am the way and the truth and the life. No man comes to the Father except through me.'* 'Truth' is Jesus Christ." "Exactly", said BB, "you're on the right track." "Ron, do you know what a spirit or ghost is?" "You are kidding, aren't you?" Ron asked, concerned BB had lost his marbles. "I guess it's something that runs around covered in a sheet scaring folks like me." "That's a pretty good description," B.B. said, "but let's consider Scripturally. A ghost or spirit is an entity that cannot be seen or related to in a physical sense. Believe it or not, Scripture, especially the Old Testament, references ghosts, and spirits. Paul himself, in *Ephesians 6*, speaks of a spirit world of which we are not familiar. In the case of *John 14,* the Apostle is speaking of a *'Holy'* Spirit – a good and perfect 'spirit' (or 'ghost'), that is set apart. That Spirit is Jesus Christ Himself. Yes, He is in Heaven at the right hand of the Father, but His Holy Spirit resides on earth – in you – if you are truly saved! In fact, the Holy Spirit is your seal or proof you are indeed saved! Without the Holy Spirit in your life you have no salvation – no matter how many church services you have attended or how many aisles you have walked!"

"Ron, look closely at *Verse 17,*" B.B. continued. "It states, '*The world cannot accept him, because it neither sees him nor knows him. But you know him, for he lives with you and will be in you.*' Paul also confirms in *1 Corinthians 2:14* – '*The person without the Spirit does not accept the things that come from the Spirit of God, but considers them fool-ishness, and cannot understand them because they are discerned only through the Spirit.*' What good would it be for a lost person to possess the Holy Spirit when he is totally clueless as to whom Jesus Christ truly is? The proof of the seal is found in *Romans 8:9* – '*You, however, are not in the realm of the flesh but are in the realm of the Spirit, if indeed the Spirit of God lives in you. And if anyone does not have the Spirit of Christ, they do not belong to Christ;' in 1 John 3:24 – 'And this is how we know that He lives in us: we know it by the Spirit he gave us;' and in Ephesians 1:13-14 – 'When you believed, you were marked in Him with a seal, the promised Holy Spirit, who is a deposit guaranteeing our inheritance until the redemption of those who are God's possession – to the praise of His glory'."*

"Ron," B.B. implored, "I know this is a lot to digest. But hear me out. Christ made a demand – for His children to witness and share the Gospel; He fulfilled His promise of, *'And surely I am with you always, to the very end of the age,'* by *'not leaving us as orphans,'* and He provided the equipping and the way for us to share the Gospel through the power of the Holy Spirit. Any of this making sense?", BB asked. "Yes, absolutely," Ron gleamed! "I think I understand. It is like Christ has called me to be his witness and He is telling me I am to be his arms, hands, feet and mouth; my job is to 'go' – make myself available. He will do all the talking through me; He is looking for a willing vessel; He will accomplish His ministry through me. All I need to do is to answer as Isaiah did in *Isaiah 6:8 – 'Here am I, send me!'* He will accomplish it all through little old me – I just need to understand my ability is not my own but through His power working through me through His Holy Spirit." "Exactly," BB replied. "He's standing at your heart's door knocking – pleading – make yourself available – you go, but I'll do the rest. I will speak through you. It may be your tongue flapping, but it will be My words rolling off that flapping tongue!"

B.B. was quick to expound on Ron's understanding, "One of my favorite Bible expositors is Brother J Vernon McGee. In his commentary on the Hebrews he made a pretty straightforward statement regarding *Hebrews 13:15-16* (*"Through Jesus, therefore, let us continually offer to God a sacrifice of praise – the fruit of lips that openly confess His name. And do not forget to do good and to share with others, for with such sacrifices God is pleased."*), which relates completely to our discussion – "if Christianity does not walk in shoe leather it is no good at all. The Lord Jesus is up yonder, at the right hand of God – that is where He is, as head of the church – but His feet are down here, right where the rubber meets the road. He wants Christianity to be in shoe leather, and He would like to walk in your shoes."[242]

"So why the frown?" asked BB. For the first time, Ron looked really puzzled – "Well, if so many people claim Christianity and Christ has outlined His plan for sharing the Gospel and He has equipped us through the power of the Holy Spirit – His spiritual presence in our lives – this means we can literally accomplish anything He pleases or calls us to do in this life. Correct"? Before B.B. could respond, Ron continued, "It gives new meaning to Paul's testimony to the believers at Philippi in *Philippians 4:13* – '*I can do all this through Christ who give me strength.*' I guess my problem is – if I'm supposed to be His 'shoe leather,' and He has done all this to prepare me to carry out His will of sharing the Gospel, and His Holy Spirit is my seal of salvation and my empowerment, then why are so many churches dying on the vine and the vast majority of their members doing absolutely nothing to further His Gospel? It makes me wonder if sharing the Gospel doesn't need to start with witnessing to those in the pew. This is frightening." "You are correct again my friend", said BB. "You are sadly correct. You see, Christ Himself says in *Matthew 7: 21-23* – '*Not everyone who says to me, "Lord, Lord," will enter the kingdom of heaven, but only he who does the will of my Father who is in heaven. Many will say to me on that day, "Lord, Lord, did we not prophesy in your name, and in your name drive out demons and perform many miracles?" Then I will tell them plainly, "Away from me, you evildoers*"!' It's sad but true, Ron, eternally true." And with that, BB began to weep. Thinking of his own father, not since Ron's grandfather passed away, had he seen a grown man weep.

"Ron," B.B. added, between tears, "I am reminded of a testimony from the book, '*Radical*'." Picking up a worn paper-back book, B.B. continued his dialogue. "David Platt, who led a mega church in Birmingham, Alabama, shared: 'Three weeks after my third trip to underground house churches in Asia, I began my first Sunday as the pastor of a church in America. The scene was much different. Dimly lit rooms were replaced by an auditorium with theater-style lights. Instead of traveling for miles by foot or bike to worship, we had arrived in millions of dollars-worth of vehicles. Please do not misunderstand this scene. It was filled with wonderful, well-meaning, Bible-believing professed Christians, who wanted to welcome me, and enjoy one another. People like you, and people like me, who simply desire community, who want to be involved, and believe God is important in their lives. But as a new pastor, comparing the images around me that day, with the pictures, still fresh in my mind, of brothers and sisters, on the other side of the world, I could not help but think, that somewhere along the way, we had missed what is radical about our faith, and replaced it with what is comfortable. We were settling for a 'Christianity,' that revolves around ourselves, when the central message of Christianity, is about abandoning ourselves. The danger of spiritual deception is real. As a pastor, I shudder at the thought, and lie awake at night, when I consider the possibility, that scores of people, who sit before me on a Sunday morning, might think they are saved, when they are not. Scores of people, who have positioned their lives, on a religious road, that makes grandiose promises, at minimal cost. We have been told, all that is required, is a one-time decision, maybe, even mere intellectual assent to Jesus, but after that, we need not worry about his commands, his standard, or his glory. We have a ticket to Heaven, and we can live however we want on earth. Our sin will be tolerated along the way. Much of modern evangelism today is built on leading people down this road, and crowds flock to it, but in the end, it is a road built on sinking sand, and it risks disillusioning millions of souls'."[243]

"Wow", Ron thought, as his mind went back to First Church, and even back to his home church prior to his move. "Pew-warmers really won't make it, will they brother BB?" "I'm afraid you are sadly correct once again my brother," BB replied, almost wailing. "James renders sad confirmation in *James 2: 14, 26 – 'What good is it, my brothers and sisters, if a man claims to have faith but has no deeds? Can such faith save them? As the body without the spirit is dead, so faith without deeds is dead'*. No, it appears there will be no pew-warmers in Heaven and sadly, Jesus confirms in *Matthew 7:13-14,21-23*, the vast majority in our churches fall into this category."

"Brother BB, this has been especially enlightening, but I have a major concern," Ron shared. "I worry about my own life. I honestly believe in the presence and the power of the Holy Spirit within the believer's life and how He works through me, but I feel so inadequate – so inept. I guess my faith is weak." "Your concern is legit, my son" brother BB interjected. "That is where faith, prayer, study and meditation in the Word and encouragement from fellow believers comes into play. As a matter of fact, I myself have questioned many times how a mighty, all knowing, all powerful God could use a spiritual runt like me. Hear me once more Ron and let me give you two Scriptural testimonies that might help."

Ron was all ears as B.B. opened his Bible once again. "Let us consider Peter. I think you would agree, old Peter was a feisty boaster, maybe even border-line hypocrite whose antics were probably sometimes unappreciated by his peers. He certainly felt his faith was much stronger than what it truly was. He was certainly not alone since this is true many times in our lives today. Jesus obviously recognized this and rather than reprimand and discourage him, He sought to discipline and teach him." At this point, it appeared to Ron, BB began to digress slightly.

"Ron, let me give you some Briscoe Barton theology, if I may. I believe God uses the family relationship in Scripture for many important reasons. We are called His children because we belong to Him and He loves us as a Father loves a child; we can relate to that as parents. He is our Father; we are brothers and sisters in Christ. We are His family. Because we belong to Him, the devil cannot touch us, unless God allows him. We see this in Job's experience where Satan had to ask permission from God to inflict his hand upon him. This does not keep Satan from tempting or seducing us to the dark side, but as God's children, we belong to Him and no one can discipline or lay a hand on His children but He Himself, just as you would be totally unjustified attempting to discipline my children knowing you would have to deal with me first." With that statement, BB's expression changed from a stern, stoic expression, to a brief chuckle. "My premise for this is found in *1 John 5:18-19* – *'We know that anyone born of God does not continue to sin; the One who was born of God keeps him safe, and the evil one cannot harm them. We know that we are children of God, and that the whole world is under the control of the evil one.'* I belong to God."

"Now – back to Peter. Turn with me in your Bible to *Luke 22:31-34*." As Ron began to turn the pages, BB was already there. Once again, it was as if he had twenty fingers and each one was strategically placed at exactly the correct page of the Scripture he wanted to reference. "Let us examine this closely, Ron. '*Simon, Simon, Satan has asked to sift all of you as wheat. But I have prayed for you, Simon, that your faith may not fail. And when you have turned back, strengthen your brothers." "But" he replied, "Lord, I am ready to go with you to prison and to death." Jesus answered, "I tell you Peter, before the rooster crows today, you will deny three times that you know Me"*.' Notice Ron, Satan asked permission from Jesus to 'sift' or grab hold of Peter for a time. Jesus obviously allowed him to do just that, as He interceded (before the Father) for

Peter, praying that he would bear up under the temptation and would become a better Christian as a result. You know the rest of the story – from the same chapter – *Verses 54-62* – where prior to the crucifixion in the courtyard of the High Priest, in the presence of a young servant girl and again in the face of a man's accusations, he vehemently denied He even knew Jesus! Look then at *Verses 60-62 – 'Just as he was speaking, the rooster crowed. The Lord turned and looked straight at Peter. Then Peter remembered the word the Lord had spoken to him: "Before the rooster crows today, you will disown Me three times." And he went outside and wept bitterly'.*" "Wow – and double wow", Ron repeated. "Talk about being taken down a notch or two; Jesus really put him in his place. Guess he found out the hard way his faith was not near as strong as what he had boasted." "You are correct, Ron." Ron could tell all of this was leading to a dramatic finish and BB did not disappoint.

"Now – look over into *Acts.* We have already read in *Chapter 1,* the blessing and purpose of the Holy Spirit. But look at *Chapter 2* – the Day of Pentecost. Thousands – literally thousands, were in attendance for the celebration. Jews from every nation speaking over fifteen different languages. But look especially at *Verse 14 – 'Then Peter stood up with the eleven and raised his voice and addressed the crowd'.*" "Wow, and triple wow!", Ron blurted. "Maybe this guy wasn't such a 'braggadocious' wimp after all." "Good surmise", BB responded. "This wimp as you call him, proclaimed one of the greatest messages on the Gospel from the lips of a human being and speaking in the 'tongues' or languages understood by all the different peoples that were present that day. But the question I have for you is, what changed in the two months since he denied Christ and rode off into the sunset in his cowardness? What happened?" "Ron," B.B. went to his knees and clasped both Ron's hands, "Something dramatic had to have happened during this time to have taken that wimp of a man from the precipice of spiritual collapse to being able to step out on a stage before thousands of his countrymen and deliver perhaps the greatest Gospel proclamation by man ever presented? Think Ron – what changed that man?" "Well", Ron said pondering, "the only thing that comes to mind is the Holy Spirit – he was empowered by the Holy Spirit! His mouth and jaws were flapping on that stage in front of all those people, but it was not him speaking at all – it was Jesus speaking through him!!! I think I understand!" "And Ron, that is not all. Look at *Verse 41 – 'Those who accepted his message were baptized, and about three thousand were added to their number that day'.*" "Wow, wow, and quadruple Wow!" Ron was almost in a fever pitch. "This is unbelievable – I mean hard to wrap my hands around – that same power and that same ability that Peter possessed on that day is in me if I truly belong to Him! I truly am equipped to do all things through Christ from whence cometh my strength!"

"But that is not all, Ron. Let me give you another quick example how through the Holy Spirit God uses ordinary people like you and me. Look with me to one of my favorite passages in all of Scripture – *Acts 4.* Peter and John had been sharing the Gospel at Solomon's Colonnade, a porch along the wall of the Temple. They were sharing regarding the resurrection and had performed a miracle, by healing a cripple. The priests and captain of the temple guard and the Sadducees, who did not believe in the resurrection of the dead, seized them and put them in jail. Many, according to Luke, had heard their testimony and Scripture says 5,000 men were saved! The next day, the teachers of the law, along with the rulers and elders, met to discuss the situation. They had Peter and John brought before them and began to question them. '*By what power or what name did you do this?*' Then Peter, filled with the Holy Spirit, began to testify before them sharing the Gospel. The key here is *Verse 13 – 'When they* (the Sanhedrin) *saw the courage of Peter and John and realized that they were unschooled, ordinary men, they were astonished, and they took note that these men had been with Jesus'.*" "Unbelievable" yelled Ron. "Proof God can take an ordinary person like you and me and use us for the advancement of His kingdom!" "Also," he said with a sarcastic smile, "means one does not need a college or seminary education to be used by Jesus." "Remember Ron, let me share with you another statement from Rev. David Platt in his book '*Radical'* that I can relate to wholeheartedly – "A church or body of believers can have the least gifted people, the least talented people, the fewest leaders, and the least money, and this church under the power of the Holy Spirit could still shake the nations for His glory."[244]

"One last comment", BB noted. "Look down to *Verses 18-20–'Then they called them in again and commanded them not to speak or teach at all in the name of Jesus. But Peter and John replied, "Which is right in God's eyes: to listen to you, or to Him? You be the judges! As for us, we cannot help speaking about what we have seen and heard.'* This is an important statement and a good place to close our discussion for today. What happens, Ron, when you pour liquid into a glass and the glass is full to the rim – if you continue to add the liquid?" "Finally, you ask me a question that even I can answer – it overflows." "Exactly," BB replied. "It is full, and it overflows. This is exactly what happens when one is 'full of the Holy Ghost,' as Scripture confirms – when one is filled with the Holy Spirit, He – Jesus Christ – has to flow out – He has nowhere else to go." "So what Peter is saying," Ron replied, "is he is so filled with the Holy Spirit, he cannot help but let Him spill out and share Him with others! He is literally saying, 'I cannot hold Him in'!" "Exactly", BB smiled, confirming. But then a grimace appeared on Ron's face. "Did I say something wrong Ron; something you don't understand?" "No, I understand it ok", Ron answered. "What bothers me is what I shared earlier in our conversation – pretty much answers the question regarding dying churches – preachers, teachers, and pew sitters – not sharing the Gospel, which would mean they aren't Spirit-filled and if the Holy Spirit is our seal of salvation – well – we have our churches filled with folks – leaders and laity alike – who think they are saved but they are nowhere close." "Once again, you are sadly and painfully correct, my friend", BB said in a low moaning reply.

Ron glanced at the old Stanley Tool wall clock behind BB – it must be broken because the hands were showing 4:15 pm. "That old clock looks like an antique", Ron noted. "Looks like it has seen better days." "No", BB replied, "it's in perfect working order." Ron's mouth dropped – he absolutely could not believe they had been in conversation for over three hours. "I absolutely must go, but I do have one last question, actually two, brother BB." "If I possess the same Holy Spirit that Peter and John possessed, does that mean I am equipped to heal and per-form miracles just as they? And lastly, what about the second church we visited – Antioch Church of the Holy Spirit – all that huffing and puffing – hand gestures, yelling, screaming in unrecognizable languages, blowing on folks and causing them to faint, all claiming they have been endowed by the Holy Spirit – I am a child of Jesus Christ and as a result, a possessor of the Holy Spirit – but I certainly don't feel the need to participate in Olympic games in worship. Can you comment?"

"Well, Ron", BB interjected, "those are good questions. I guess, once again, I need to rely on Briscoe Barton Theology. Yes, you do possess the same Holy Spirit as Peter and John. Paul provided a list of spiri-tual gifts that the Holy Spirit bestows on believers in his Letters to the Romans, Corinthians and Ephesians. I am sure you are familiar with these." Ron nodded his assent. B.B. continued, "I personally, however, believe there were certain gifts that were bestowed and reserved only for the apostles – healing being one of those gifts. Jesus Christ is our Great Physician and we have direct access. As to the antics at Antioch Church, I can find no Scriptural evidence that any of these 'activities,' if that is what you want to call them, are a by-product of Spiritual possession – at least the Holy Spirit. What about the man or woman full of the Holy Spirit, evidenced by the fruit they bear through carrying out the Great Commission, sitting on a pew quietly, reverently, meditating on the Word – because they are not participating outwardly in the 'antics' some attribute to the Holy Spirit, does this mean they are not 'Spirit-filled?' I think not. Seems to me – once again, Barton's Theology – many get caught up in the emotional and psychological aspects of the moment and want to attribute it to 'spiritual possession.' I honestly do not see that in the Scriptures – not saying there is anything necessarily wrong with it, other than maybe calling attention to oneself, which is certainly not Scriptural. To Him be the glory! Jesus says in *Luke 15:7*, we are to rejoice when one enters the fold and is saved and comes to know Him through the power of the Holy Spirit working through one of His children – *'I tell you that in the same way there will be more rejoicing in heaven over one sinner who repents than over ninety-nine righteous persons who do not need to repent'*."

"While I'm sharing some Briscoe Barton Theology, let me in closing interject one other tidbit, Ron. Time is of essence – eternal essence. *2 Corinthians 6:2*, Paul says, '*I tell you now is the time of God's favor; now is the day of salvation.*' Men of God need to be at work channeling the Holy Spirit. Peter notes in *2 Peter 3:8-9, 'But do not forget this one thing, dear friends: With the Lord a day is like a thousand years, and a thousand years are like a day. The Lord is not slow in keeping His promise, as some understand slowness. Instead He is patient with you, not wanting anyone to perish, but everyone to come to repentance.'* "Do you know what that verse is saying, Ron?" "I think I do – it means God is patient – He is waiting and delaying judgment, wanting all to be saved. I know all won't be saved, since all won't repent, but it appears He is waiting on one more soul; He is holding off judgment on behalf of one more." "You are correct", BB replied. "And notice *Verses 11-12 – 'Since everything will be destroyed in this way, what kind of people ought you to be? You ought to live holy and godly lives as you look forward to the day of God and speed its coming'.*" "Ron, if you knew for a fact Christ was coming back tonight at 10:00, would that change your life? How would you spend the next five hours? Would you be calling loved ones, friends, co-workers you know are lost, or on the street corner proclaiming Christ is coming – get ready? Peter says even though we don't know when He's coming back, we need to be living with this same urgency! And finally, some real Briscoe Barton Theology – Peter says we can 'speed its coming.' I see that as meaning, God does not have a cosmic calendar with a date circled as to when He is coming back for His children. Perhaps, this may be why the angels in Heaven do not know – only the Father. We can 'speed it up' by doing what He has called, commanded and equipped us to do."

With that, BB checked the Stanley Tool clock and for the first time, he revealed today was his 38th anniversary and he had planned a special night out on the town with his bride – dinner at the pizza parlor across the street. Ron gave BB a big hug and promised to see him at the Jones' next Tuesday evening. "I can't wait!"

The story of Ron, his family and his relationship with Jim and B.B. is purely fictional, but the truths are Scriptural. It is true, the most misunderstood Person of the Trinity is the Holy Spirit and could even be argued it may be more ignorance than misunderstanding. It is sadly true, if one is saved and the seal or proof of our salvation is the Holy Spirit, and the purpose of the Holy Spirit is to equip us to carry out the Great Commission, then those that claim this salvation and are content to do nothing for the cause of the Gospel, may be as lost as the one who has never heard the salvation message. This may be why Paul once again reminded the Corinthians in *1 Corinthians 11:28*, regarding the partaking of the Lord's Supper, *"Everyone ought to examine themselves before they eat of the bread and drink from the cup."* Peter confirms in *2 Peter 1:10* – *"Therefore, my brothers and sisters, make every effort to confirm your calling and election."* Per a famous clip from a Clint Eastwood movie – "a man's got to know his limitations."[245] Both Paul and Peter seem to be saying here, "a man's got to know his salvation and be sure of it before it is eternally too late." One cannot claim salvation and do nothing for the cause of Christ and be saved – regardless of what his religion tells him. It is not possible! *"We cannot help speaking about what we have seen and heard"* – *Acts 4:20*.

Chapter 15

WHY ETERNAL SECURITY?

"If a righteous person turns from their righteousness and commits sin, they will die for it; because of the sin they have committed they will die. But if a wicked person turns away from the wickedness they have committed and does what is just and right, they will save their life" – Ezekiel 18:26-27.

The Physician Luke gives us the most accurate and beautiful picture of the early New Testament Church. He provides us with intimate details in *Acts 2:42-47*. The key verse for this discussion is *Verse 44 –* *"All the believers were together and had everything in common."* God was obviously pleased with the early church since the result of their efforts were salvations – *"those who were being saved"* – *Acts 2:47*. In Antioch, where many believers had fled due to persecution after the martyrdom of Stephen, believers continued to share the Gospel, not only to their own peoples but also to non-Jews or Gentiles, and Luke once again confirms God's blessings upon them as a result of their actions – *Acts 11:21 – "The Lord's hand was with them, and a great number of people believed and turned to the Lord."*

"Acts 1, the early church started with about a hundred and twenty believers, and by *Acts 2*, there are more than 3,000. If you do the math, that is almost 2500% growth...in a day."[246] Per the request of Barnabas,

Paul accompanied him in Antioch, assisting him in ministry to the new believers, hence the beginning of Paul's missionary efforts – *Acts 11:26* – *"So for a whole year Barnabas and Saul met with the church and taught great numbers of people. The disciples were called Christians first at Antioch."* These new believers were not called Baptists, Presbyterians, Methodists, Catholics, Freewill Baptists, Independent Baptist, Church of God, Church of Christ, Church of the Nazarene, or any of the more than 40,000 denominations or sects existing in the world today. They were simply "believers" and were called "Christians" because their salvation was through Jesus Christ – not the deceptive doctrines of men. As previously noted, today's denominations trace their beginnings to doctrinal differences, resulting in the creation of religious entities catering to human beliefs and lifestyles, thus providing peace, comfort, and confirmation of acceptable spiritual standing among their peers. Many are disillusioned themselves, but they risk disillusioning others and the consequences are eternally damning.

Some denominational differences are so dramatic, one risks being accused of heresy should he/she question the popular notion of that particular body. The doctrine of eternal security, or "once saved always saved," is one of those "heretically dangerous" subjects. The plethora of opinions is overwhelming – both pro and con – and are typically segregated along religious and denominational lines. Consider the following:

A. Doctor Charles Stanley–"The Bible clearly teaches that God's love for His people is of such magnitude, that even those who walk away from the faith, have not the slightest chance of slipping from His hand. Salvation can be compared to receiving a tattoo. Even if moments later, you regret receiving the tattoo, it cannot change the fact that you have it."[247]

B. Doctor Sam Morris–"We take the position, that a Christian's sins, do not damn his soul. The way he lives – what he says, his character, his conduct, or his attitude toward other people – have nothing, whatever, to do with the salvation of his soul. All the prayers a man may pray, all the Bibles he may read, all the churches he may belong to, all the services he may attend, all the sermons he may practice, all the debts he may pay, all the ordinances he may observe, all the laws he may keep, and all the benevolent acts he may perform will not make his soul one whit safer; and all the sins he may commit , from idolatry to murder, will not make his soul in any more danger. The way a man lives has nothing to do with the salvation of his soul."[248]

C. "Grace Evangelical Society"–"A very large segment of independent, fundamental Baptists (represented by thousands of churches and tens of thousands of members), emphasizes this approach, to such excess, that staggeringly, huge numbers of salvations and baptisms are reported each year – which, if really true, would make the Great Awakening look like a picnic. People are converted in five minutes or less – even through a rolled down window, during the duration of a stop light. One church has boasted of a million souls saved in the past 25 years, and yet, less than 500 are in attendance on any given Sunday."[249]

D. John Piper – founder, teacher, Chancellor–"A few years ago, I spoke to a high school student body on how to fight lust. One of my points was called, 'Ponder the Eternal Danger of Lust.' I quoted the words of Jesus – that it's better to go to Heaven with one eye, than to hell with two – and said to the students, their eternal destiny was at stake in what they did with their eyes, and with the thoughts of their imagination. After my message, one of the students asked – 'Are you saying that a person can lose his salvation?' This is the same response I received a few years ago, when I confronted a man in my church about the adultery in which he was living. I pled with him to return to his wife. I noted, 'You know, Jesus says that if you don't fight this sin, with the kind of seriousness that is willing to gouge out your own eye, you will go to hell.' As a professing Christian, he looked at me in disbelief, as though he had never heard anything like this in his life, and said, 'You mean I could lose my salvation?' So, I have learned again and again, from firsthand experience, that there are many professing Christians, who have a view of salvation that disconnects it from real life, and that nullifies the threats of the Bible, and puts the sinning person, who claims to be a Christian, beyond the reach of Biblical warnings. I believe this view is comforting thousands, who are on the broad way that leads to destruction (*Matthew 7: 13*)."[250]

E. Anonymous Student–"Are you telling me that if a serial killer is genuinely saved and lives for Christ for a while and decides to go back to his old ways of being a serial killer, that he is still saved? His reply was, 'that is correct.' Then I said, 'You mean he can be right in the middle of murdering someone, and cutting up their body pieces, and when the rapture takes place, that he will go up in the rapture, with all those in Christ?' His reply to me was, 'yes, that is what I am saying.' To me that is scary. *1 John 3: 15 – 'Anyone who hates a brother or sister is a murderer, and you know that no murderer hath eternal life residing in Him.'* I was completely turned off from the church."[251]

I have often cautioned fellow believers, the best word of advice I can render when sharing the Gospel is to never use the phrase, "I believe." No one is interested in what "you" or "I" believe; people want truth. Truth comes from the Word of God. With that said, there is one doctrine where that is easier said than done – the "Doctrine of Eternal Security" or "once saved, always saved." This doctrine has been the heated subject between denominations since the resurrection of Jesus Christ. Take the "wrong" side of the debate and risk excommunication from some fellowships. Granted, this question will not be answered here and likely, more questions than answers will be presented. However, it would be impossible to discuss the *"why's"* of "Churchianity" and not discuss the subject.

Once I am saved, does this mean I am saved for eternity, regardless of how I live or any sin or sins I commit, and should I intentionally decide to turn from God back to the world, I am still saved, whether I want to be or not? If this is true, the contention arises that salvation grants me a full-fledged license to sin; the other side is, should I choose the path of the world after salvation, it simply means I was never saved to start with. Either way – the results are the same – I am guilty of the worst sin of all – apostasy–and due the worst punishment hell can offer–*2 Peter 2:20-21 – "If they have escaped the corruption of the world by knowing our Lord and Savior Jesus Christ and are again entangled in it and are overcome, they are worse off at the end than they were at the beginning. It would have been better for them not to have known the way of righteousness than to have known it and then turn their backs on the sacred command that was passed on to them."*

There is a dangerous trend in today's churches used by "preachers" and teachers alike called "proof-texting." A typical textbook sermon, as we have already seen, consists of a title and three to four points, with a few Scripture verses sprinkled in. "Proof-texting" is using a verse or verses, hand-picked by the "preacher" or teacher to prove a point. Studying Scripture is not as easy as opening one's Bible and reading. One must prepare in advance. According to John Wycliffe, *"It shall greatly help thee to understand Scripture if thou mark not only what is spoken or written, but of whom and to whom, with what words, at what time, where, and to what intent, under what circumstances, considering what goeth before and what followeth."*[252]

It is critical when preparing to study the Scriptures: identify the writer – if possible; the date written; the purpose; to whom it is written; and perhaps most importantly, what was the historical context at the time it was written. For example, when reading Paul's letters to the Corinthians and his discussions on the adornment of women, hair length and head covers for men, unless one does the background study–in this case the influence of paganistic worship practices on the Corinthian believers– directives can be taken out of context and to religious extremes. In the same way, "proof-texting" can be a dangerous misuse of God's Word. An extreme but potent illustration – *Matthew 27:5* – *"So Judas threw the money into the temple and left. Then he went away and hanged himself"*; turning to *Luke 10:37* – *"Jesus told him, 'Go and do likewise'."* This is a harsh example, but one can readily see the danger of "proof-texting" and how it is misused by many church leaders to prove or disprove a doctrine.

The reason I mention, "proof-texting" in this context is one must be careful not to fall into the trap of using Scripture arbitrarily to bolster one's defense or non-defense of the doctrine of "eternal security," or any doctrine for that matter. With that said, both the supporters and the denouncers of the "eternal security" doctrine appear guilty of at least some "proof texting." The supporters of "eternal security" champion *John 10:27-30*, as one of their key verses for their contention – *"My sheep listen to My voice; I know them, and they follow me. I give them eternal life, and they shall never perish; no one will snatch them out of My hand. My Father who has given them to Me, is greater than all; no one can snatch them out of My Father's hand. I and the Father are one."* Those who oppose the doctrine cannot deny this verse since it came from the lips of Christ Himself. The message is clear, no man can snatch a person from the hands of God – all agree – Jesus Himself proclaimed it.

The opposing view is, what if one chooses on his own to remove himself from the hand of God? God did not force him/her to get saved – will God force him/her to stay saved? Once you are in the hand of God, is freedom of choice nullified? Is one saved forever whether he wants to be or not? If one finds the cost of Christianity too great after accepting God's gift and so chooses to return that gift, is that person not free to do so? To contend the person's initial acceptance of the gift was not genuine does not seem a fair assessment in all instances. It would seem naïve to assume in 2000 years, there has not been one single person who has drifted away from the faith on his own accord – one who might have been genuinely saved, but in the face of persecution, rejection, or for whatever reason, counted the cost too great to remain a follower of Jesus Christ, and jumped ship. To write him/her off as saying, "they weren't genuinely saved to start with," seems a little too easy for some tastes. We must once again be reminded – whether he/she were never genuinely saved or, whether they walked away and fell from grace, the result is the same – both are lost.

Other prominent Scripture references supporting "eternal security:" *John. 3:16 – "For God so loved the world, He gave His one and only Son, that whoever believes in Him shall not perish but have eternal life;" Romans 5:8 – "But God demonstrates His own love for us in this: While we were still sinners, Christ died for us;" Romans 8:38-39 – "For I am convinced that neither death nor life, neither angels nor demons, neither the present nor the future, nor any powers, neither height nor depth, nor anything else in all creation, will be able to separate us from the love of God that is in Christ Jesus our Lord;" and 1 John. 3:1 – "See what great love the Father has lavished on us, that we should be called children of God! And that is what we are! The reason the world does not know us is that it did not know Him."*

On the side of those opposing the doctrine, the following verses are typically used as references to champion their views. They call attention to the conditional statements in these passages: *Colossians 1: 22-23 – "But now He has reconciled you by Christ's physical body through death to present you holy in His sight, without blemish and free from accusation—IF you continue in your faith, established and firm, and do not move from the hope held out in the gospel;" 1 Corinthians 15: 2 – "By this gospel you are saved, IF you hold firmly to the word I preached to you. Otherwise you have believed in vain;" Hebrews 3: 6 – "And*

we are His house, IF indeed we hold firmly to our confidence and the
hope in which we glory;" Hebrews 3: 14 – "We have come to share in
Christ, IF indeed we hold our original conviction firmly to the very end;"
John 8: 31 – "IF you hold to My teaching, you are really My disciples;"
Mark 13: 13 – "Everyone will hate you because of Me, but the one who
stands firm to the end will be saved;" 2 Timothy 2: 12 – "IF we endure,
we will also reign with Him. IF we disown Him, He will also disown us;"
Galatians 6: 8-9 – "Whoever sows to please their flesh, from the flesh
will reap destruction; whoever sows to please the Spirit, from the Spirit
will reap eternal life;" 2 John 1: 8 – "Watch out that you do not lose
what we have worked for, but that you may be rewarded fully;" 2 Peter
1: 10 – "Make every effort to confirm your calling and election. For IF
you do these things, you will never stumble, and you will receive a rich
welcome into the eternal kingdom of our Lord and Savior Jesus Christ."
Whether a champion or foe on "eternal security," it might be eternally
dangerous for one to presume because they experienced salvation,
they have "arrived" – signed, sealed and delivered–and are outside
the bounds of Scripture's warnings.

In *Luke 15:11-31,* Jesus presents a familiar parable – the Parable of the
Lost Son. All know the story – a man had two sons; the younger one
decided to take his share of his inheritance and leave home, so the
father divided the estate. The younger son left home, squandered his
wealth on wild living and in a short period of time was broke. He hired
himself out to slopping pigs and soon came to realize his life was in
shambles and his father's servants were better kept than himself. He
returns home and begs his father's forgiveness and his father greets
and accepts him back with open arms; a wonderful parable Jesus told
to the Pharisees and the teachers of the law who were condemning
Him for eating and welcoming sinners into His presence.

It cannot be denied this son belonged to his Father – joined by blood
as a true son – but if the story ended differently – if the son decided
the life of worldly living – which he willfully chose – was what he truly
desired, and because of either his Father's restrictions, the lure of the
world, or whatever reason, willfully made the eternal decision to never
return to his Father, would he have still have received his father's blessings, even though on his own accord he intentionally removed himself
from his father's care? Or, because he is a true son, would his Father
never deny him his blessings, even though he denied his father? Would

his father intentionally have overlooked his life of sin and his lack of repentance? Again – more questions and less answers.

I have referenced John MacArthur's commentaries extensively in my Bible studies and find them especially helpful and enlightening. His commentary on the Hebrews is especially intriguing. Hebrews is an Epistle ripe for "proof texting," especially regarding the "eternal security" debate. The Letter was written by a Jew to fellow Jews. As we earlier noted, one of the premises for understanding this Epistle is to understand to whom it was written. Examining once again, Dr. MacArthur identifies the recipients as being comprised of three groups of Jews: 1. Hebrew Christians; 2. Hebrew non-Christians who possessed adequate head–knowledge regarding Jesus Christ, but no heart commitment; and 3. Hebrew non-Christians who were not convinced that Jesus Christ was who He claimed to be.[253] Types 2 and 3 would be considered lost. Sadly, the type 2 "professors" are indicative of many filling today's pews (and pulpits), as evidenced by the fruit of their labor or lack thereof.

Hebrews has been used by debaters from both sides of the "eternal security" debate attempting to prove or disprove their personal theories regarding the issue. The purpose of Hebrews was threefold: encourage Jewish Christians to remain true to the faith and persevere through persecution, rejection and the suffering they were incurring from their own peoples; encourage and warn those who possessed the knowledge of the Gospel but were considering risking it all and falling back into Judaism; and encourage those who had expressed no belief at all in Christ, seeking to prove Jesus Christ is indeed the Messiah and who He claimed to be. With the groundwork laid, let us look at several key passages from this Letter that are sometimes used to "proof-text" "eternal security." Arguably, the first and foremost passage would be *Hebrews 6:4-6.* To avoid the danger of "proof- texting," it is important to review *Verses 1-3 – "Therefore, let us move beyond the elementary teachings about Christ and be taken forward to maturity, not laying again the foundation of repentance from acts that lead to death, and of faith in God, instruction about cleansing rites, the laying on of hands, the resurrection of the dead, and eternal judgment. And God permitting, we will do so."*

Verses 1-3 have rendered many different theological translations, but the word, *"Therefore"*, in *Verse 1* is extremely important, as it links *Chapter 6* to what was previously discussed. In that context, it would appear the writer is encouraging Jews who are considering salvation through Jesus Christ – the New Covenant – to abandon the Old Covenant or Old Testament rituals associated with obedience to the Law and its regulations, including but not limited to the sacrifices and the cleansing or washing rituals–*"the laying on of hands"* being a reference to the regulation of preparing an animal for sacrifice. When an animal was brought for sacrifice, the individual was required to "lay hands" on the head of the animal to signify his identification with the sacrifice. These things were not *"elementary"* or unimportant, but the writer is encouraging them to put away those things they have been holding on to and move on to something eternally greater.

To adequately understand *Verses 4-6,* we must identify to whom these verses are addressed. It appears the writer is focusing on those Jews who knew the truth of the Gospel, had experienced the workings of the Gospel by being exposed to some degree, and had even applied some of its truths. They had even become involved with the *"ekklesia,"* and may have made some type of faith profession in Christ, yet they were seriously considering walking away. Based on *Hebrews 10:32-33,* there was intense, outward persecution – *"Remember those earlier days after you had received the light, when you endured in a great conflict full of suffering. Sometimes you were publicly exposed to insult and persecution; at other times you stood side by side with those who were so treated,"* but *12:4* notes this persecution stopped short of *"the shedding of blood"* or martyrdom which was yet to come. However, the pain of rejection from one's own family, the loss of jobs, of social status, of acceptance by the world, the enticement of tradition, the seduction of a work-based religion, etc., may have been enough to entice many of these professed believers back into Judaism. The question, debated by theologians – "did they willingly walk away, or were they not genuinely saved to begin with?" Being redundant – either way – they walked away lost and apostate.

The supporters of "eternal security" believe the Jews referenced in *Verses 4-6,* were not genuine believers. This premise is further enhanced by *1 John. 2:19* – *"They went out from us, but they did not really belong to us. For if they had belonged to us, they would have remained with us; but their going showed that none of them belonged to us."* On the opposing side, there may be a bit of "proof texting" here since many believe John is likely referencing those of the Gnostic philosophy who, even though may have professed a belief in Jesus Christ, they still clung to worldly materialism. Gnosticism in the early church was considered heresy, hence proof it had its beginnings within the body. John's contention is they were never saved.

Hebrews 6:4b, however, appears to be describing those individuals – Jews–who appear to have possessed a much deeper conviction – *"... who have shared in the Holy Spirit."* To adequately analyze these verses, let us look at them in-depth:

a. *"It is impossible"* – *"'adunatos"* – the emphatic tense of something that under no circumstance can be changed.

b. *"for those who have once been enlightened"* – *"gar tous hapax photisthentas"* – "the ones once given light" – exposed to and in complete understanding of the Gospel – not necessarily denoting acceptance.

c. *"who have tasted the heavenly gift"* – *"geusamenous tes doreas genethentas"* – "ones who have eaten of a gratuity or food that was offered to them;" some translational controversy as to what this *"gift"* may have been; some believe the writer is referencing the Holy Spirit, but others, noting he discusses the Holy Spirit in the next phrase, believe he is referencing the greatest *"gift"* of all – Jesus Christ. The conjecture is, they saw and understood the Gospel and in some way, were exposed to the love and power of Jesus Christ.

d. *"who have shared in the Holy Spirit"* – *"metochous agiou pneumatos"* – "sharers or partakers of the sacred or Holy wind or Spirit." Here is where the real controversy begins. Some expositors, John MacArthur being one, believe the Greek word, *"metochos,"* used here, means association and not possession. This conjecture confirms only a true believer can be indwelt by the Holy Spirit. The premise of Dr. MacArthur's conjecture is, all who "profess" belief in Jesus Christ are not necessarily genuine believers, but can by "association" with true believers, "share" in the benefits of the Holy Spirit.[254] In other words, they may not possess the Holy Spirit (therefore not saved), but, being a part of a "believer's fellowship," are by association exposed to the Holy Spirit through those who are genuinely possessed. Those who espouse this view believe it is quite possible to be a "sharer" of the Holy Ghost without being a "possessor." Judas Iscariot is their illustration of this view. He walked, talked and heard every Gospel message from the lips of Christ Himself, experiencing every miracle, but he was only exposed and associated with the power of Jesus Christ – he did not possess Him.

Others believe this word "*metochos*," is emphatic in describing one who was a "true partaker." In other words, they were more than exposed by association; they were indwelt which brings up another interesting question – Is it possible, once genuine believers receive the Holy Spirit, they can lose the Spirit as a result of a complete rejection or "falling away" from God's saving grace? Those espousing this translation reference *Ephesians 4:30* where Paul talks about "*grieving the Holy Spirit of God*". The Holy Spirit, being the personal presence of Jesus Christ living in and through us, to "*grieve Him,*" would likely be one's refusal to carry out His commands and living in a way that does not glorify Him. In addition, Paul admonishes us in *1 Thessalonians 5:19*–"*Do not quench the Spirit.*" "*Quench*," in Scripture, references "suppressing fire."

Based on the Holy Spirit being one's seal of genuine salvation, some expositors believe it is indeed possible for one to lose the Holy Spirit and in turn, one's salvation by willingly rejecting God's grace. This raises another question – if one "quenches" the Spirit, can the fire be "reignited?" Based on the phrase – "*it is impossible*" – those theologians believe no "reignition" is possible. Again – more questions than answers.

e. "*who have tasted the goodness of the word of God and the powers of the coming age*" – "*geusamenous kalon rema theou aionos*" – "those who have tasted or eaten of the good Word of God – or a god–and the miraculous strength or power of an age or space of time to come – most believing, "*the coming age*" to reference the second coming of Jesus Christ." Many of these teetering Jews had seen and experienced the miracles and wonders performed by the disciples. It is quite possible, some still living at the time of this writing, had even seen the miracles of Christ Himself while He walked on earth. The writer seems to be relating, what they have already seen and experienced is just a sampling of what is to come in the new Kingdom of Christ.

f. *"and who have fallen away"* – *"mellontos parapesontas"* – "to fail or move away from". The Greek root is *"parapipto"*, which when broken down means, *"para"* – "to side;" and *"pipto"* – "to fail" or "fall aside." The key word is *"fall."* If one is in danger of a fall, he must be set or established on a perch or position from where such a fall can occur. Those who espouse support for "eternal-security" remind us, a Christian has no reason at any point in his life to believe he can lose his salvation and those who *"have fallen away,"* were never genuinely saved. The opposing view notes this phrase, in addition to the previous statement regarding the *"sharing in the Holy Spirit",* are proof one can forfeit his/her salvation should he/she desire to do so. Again – either way – whether they were never genuinely saved, or they forfeited their salvation, they both end up in the same place – hell.

"Webster" defines "apostasy" as a, "desertion of one's faith, religion or principles."[255] Perhaps the two most concise definitions in Scripture are found in *Hebrews 10:26* – *"sinning willfully after receiving the knowledge of the truth…;"* and *2 Peter 2:20-21* – *"If they have escaped the corruption of the world by knowing our Lord and Savior Jesus Christ and are again entangled in it and are overcome, they are worse off at the end than they were at the beginning. It would have been better for them not to have known the way of righteousness than to have known it and then turn their backs on the sacred command that was passed on to them."* As Dr. MacArthur explains, "every apostate is an unbeliever, but not every unbeliever is an apostate."[256] Some have never heard the Gospel and as a result, are lost and unbelieving. The apostate lacks nothing – he has heard the Gospel and may have even received it to some degree. He possesses more than enough knowledge to make a commitment to Christ.

The Greek for *"knowledge"* in *Verse 26*, is *"epignosis,"* which denotes "full and complete understanding." Supporters of "eternal-security" espouse these individuals had full knowledge of the Gospel but willfully chose to revert to Judaism, therefore not genuine believers. The antithesis begins by analyzing the word *"willfully"* – *"hekousios"* – "deliberate intention; something done with forethought." For one to *"fall away"* from the faith would mean they knew the Gospel and had accepted it because they *"willfully,"* or intentionally, walked away. They did not *"fall away"* by accident – they fell away by their own accord – not because of anything God did or did not do, but by their own choice.

Whether one believes in the doctrine of "eternal-security" or not, there is eternal danger to be considered. Just as there are degrees of reward in heaven for believers, there are degrees of punishment for the unbeliever (one who has never heard the Gospel), and the one guilty of apostasy (one who has heard it, may have professed it and participated in it by "association" – but walked away from it or refused it). How can one who has never heard the Gospel be punished to the same degree as the one who has heard it, knows it and perhaps accepted it, but for whatever reason, walked away or his initial acceptance was not "genuine?" *Luke 12:44-48* notes the one guilty of apostasy is due the "worst of the worst" when it comes to eternal punishment – regardless if he never genuinely "accepted" or simply walked away from it. The one who "falls away" from the faith, or the one who walks away after being exposed (not genuinely committed) are both guilty of apostasy. *This may be the most critical of all the warnings revealed in Scripture*!

g. *"...to be brought back to repentance. To their loss, they are crucifying the Son of God all over again and subjecting Him to public disgrace."* Repeating – the definition of apostasy implies the possession of knowledge, in this case the Gospel, and willful, intentional rejection of it. This is the only use of the word in the New Testament.

Six times in the Old Testament (*Jeremiah 2:19; 3:22; 5:6; 14:7; 15:6; Ezekiel 37:23*), we find another word–*"umesubowtaik"*

– which translates out of the Hebrew into the same meaning and usage as *"parapipto"* (*"falling away"*), in the Hebrews. In the Old Testament, the Hebrew translation is "backslider" or "backsliding." There is, however, a marked difference. Numerous times in the Old Testament prophecies, God implores His people to *"repent from their backslidings"* – *Jeremiah 15:19* – *"If you repent, I will restore you that you may serve Me..."*; *Ezekiel 18:30* – *"Therefore, you Israelites, I will judge each of you according to your own ways, declares the Sovereign Lord. Repent! Turn away from all your offenses; then sin will not be your downfall"*; *Ezekiel 18:32* – *"For I take no pleasure in the death of anyone, declares the Sovereign Lord. Repent and live!"*[257]

We earlier discussed "backsliding" versus "falling away," but in this context, it bears review. Under the Old Covenant, "backsliding" could be forgiven because it was a sin of disobedience. However, the New Testament warning is *"it is impossible"* for those who have rejected the Gospel–*"having once been enlightened, to be brought back to repentance.?"* What changed?

Once again – the difference is Jesus Christ! The Old Testament saints served by faith, as outlined in *Hebrews 11*. In other words, they were not exposed to Christ since He was yet to be born. Their faith rested on the promise of His coming! And the direct result of their faith was obedience – obedience to God. *Hebrews 11:1-2* – *"Now faith is confidence in what we hope for and assurance about what we do not see. This is what the ancients were commended for."* The faith "Hall of Famers"–Abel, Enoch, Noah, Abraham, Isaac, Joseph, Moses, Rahab, Gideon, Barak, Samson, Jephtinah, David, Samuel, and the martyrs of *Hebrews 11* – they never experienced Jesus Christ in the flesh, but lived the promise and the certainty and the hope of His coming by their obedience to God. For each of these it meant serving God, even when service was not the correct thing in the eyes of the world to do. Their "faithfulness" was considered as *"righteousness"* before God. *Hebrews 11:39* – *"These were all commended for their faith, yet none of them received what had been promised, since God had planned something better for us so that only together with us would they be made perfect."*

Obedience by faith was the basis for the salvation of the Old Testament saints, but they too were sealed by the blood of Jesus at the cross – *"The blood of goats and bulls and the ashes of a heifer sprinkled on those who are ceremonially unclean sanctify them so that they are outwardly clean. How much more, then, will the blood of Christ, who through the eternal Spirit offered Himself unblemished to God, cleanse our consciences from acts that lead to death, so that we may serve the living God! For this reason, Christ is the mediator of a new covenant, that those who are called may receive the promised eternal inheritance – now that He has died as a ransom to set them free from the sins committed under the first covenant"–Hebrews 9:13-15*. The Old Testament saints lived by obedience – their faith credited to them as righteousness. Their salvation was based on what Christ would someday do; ours is based on what He did. In basic terms, they were saved on credit; awaiting the day when Christ would come and forgive the loan.[258] Their faith was forward searching; ours looking back to what has already occurred

"Blessed are those who have not seen and yet have believed" – *John 20:29. Isaiah 24:5 – "The earth is defiled by its people; they have disobeyed the laws, violated the statutes, and broken the everlasting covenant. Therefore, a curse consumes the earth; its people must bear their guilt."* As saintly as these Old Testament saints were viewed, they were imperfect people, just as we – *Romans 3:23 – "For all have sinned and fall short of the glory of God;" James 2:10 – "For whoever keeps the whole law and yet stumbles at just one point is guilty of breaking all of it."* Their sin of disobedience at the time was not covered by the blood of Jesus since He was yet to come. This disobedience was forgiven as a result of true repentance. Unfortunately, it was a never-ending cycle resulting in the slaughter of multitudes of sacrificial animals – *"Day after day every priest stands and performs his religious duties; again and again he offers the same sacrifices, which can never take away sins" – Hebrews 10:11*. These saints were not perfect, but their obedience through their faith in the promise of the coming Messiah was accounted to them righteousness in the sight of God. This righteousness in God's sight was completed with the ultimate sacrifice of Jesus Christ

– *"And by that will, we have been made holy through the sacrifice of the body of Jesus Christ once for all"* – *Hebrews 10:10*.

Once again—the difference in the *"backsliding,"* or disobedience of the Old Testament peoples and the *"falling away"* of the New Testament professors of faith, is Jesus Christ. *"'Backsliding"* or disobedience was forgivable through repentance; without repentance it was "apostasy;" *"'falling away"* is apostasy period. Why? Again – Jesus Christ – His blood sacrifice! To walk away from Jesus Christ after being exposed to His truth is equivalent to denying His crucifixion and sending Him back to the cross – *"to their loss they are crucifying the Son of God all over again and subjecting Him to public disgrace"* – *Hebrews 6:6*. He came once as a crucified servant; the next time He comes will be as a conquering King. There will be no other sacrifices on behalf of sinners; God has done all He can do.

Paul, from all indications, had nothing directly to do with establishing the *"ekklesia,"* or body of believers in Rome. Since most of his Letters were to *"ekklesias"* he had established, they typically dealt with doctrinal questions and daily issues facing new believers who were faced with serving the Lord while dealing with the pressures of worldly influence. Worldly pressures and passions in the Roman arena would have been a challenge for any Christian, much less a new believer. Hence, his Letter to the believers in Rome is more theology than correction, which arguably brings theological debate since Paul was a man of deep theological thinking. *Romans* (written c.58 AD) may have been the Letter Peter was referencing in *2 Peter 3:15-16* (written c.68 AD) – *"His letters contain some things that are hard to understand, which ignorant and unstable people distort, as they do the other Scriptures, to their own destruction."*

Upon graduation from college, my first job involved manning a telephone as an inside sales representative for a metals service center. Each sales rep was given a price book to quote numbers to potential buyers for certain steel commodities. Initially this did not appear it would be much of a challenge, but no one prepared me for the intense and sometimes confrontational negotiations that occurred on practically every phone call. Buyers were not satisfied with the quoted price, as all felt they were being over-charged and most counter-offered repeatedly. I recall on one occasion, a particularly obtrusive person accused me of having a "license to steal." Not knowing exactly what that meant, I asked my boss. Laughing, he let me know the customer felt he was being taken advantage since he was seeking an item no one else inventoried and as a result, felt he was being "ripped off."

In a similar way, Paul called attention to the Roman *"ekklesia"* that sin came to human beings through one man – Adam (*"Therefore, just as sin entered the world through one man, and death through sin, and in this way death came to all people, because all sinned" – Romans 5:12*). Salvation came to human beings through one divine man – Jesus Christ (*"For if, by the trespass of the one man, death reigned through that one man, how much more will those who receive God's abundant provision of grace and of the gift of righteousness reign in life through the one man, Jesus Christ!" – Romans 5:17*). But it is *Verses 20-21 of Chapter 5,* that create a stir among modern-day theologians (*"The law was brought in so that the trespass might increase. But where sin increased, grace increased all the more, so that, just as sin reigned in death, so also grace might reign through righteousness to bring eternal life through Jesus Christ our Lord."*). These verses set the stage for Paul's comments in *Chapter 6.*

Through His "grace" – His divine goodness and His love for us, that while we were sinners wallowing in our sins – He created a way of escape for us through the blood of His Son, Jesus Christ (*"But God demonstrates His own love for us in this: While we were still sinners, Christ died for us" – Romans 5:8*). Being "justified" in His sight – declared "not guilty" in the eyes of God – through Jesus Christ, His Son, meant our guilt from sin was removed – the sin and the penalty for that sin being removed at the moment we received His gift of salvation. Apparently there were those in the Roman fellowship, as there are in today's "church," who took salvation as a "license to sin." In other words, "we're redeemed, saved, and declared righteous in His sight, so we can live and act as we see fit and we will be just fine. Since we are saved – signed and sealed – He doesn't care how we live and will not punish us for our disobedience."

Some of this, no doubt, originated from the influence of Gnostic philosophies prevalent at that time, purporting the notion the human body was made imperfect; God made the body; since He made the body in imperfection, He will overlook our sin, since it is simply the expression of His imperfection. It worked for Satan in that day; strange how some denominations appear to be holding on to that same philosophy today. Regardless of what religion may teach today, Paul adamantly refutes the idea a believer can do as he pleases after supposedly receiving the gift of salvation ("*What shall we say, then? Shall we go on sinning so that grace may increase? By no means! We are those who have died to sin; how can we live in it any longer?*" – *Romans 6:1-2*). True mind and heart believers have a new nature. The "justified" believer cannot continue in sin and claim salvation. As J. Vernon McGee says, "He gives us freedom, but that freedom is not license."[259]

Hell is not concerned by what method people arrive there. One may be lost by unbelief; one may be lost by an ungenuine belief; one may be lost by walking away from their belief; Satan does not care – he just welcomes them all. Whether one believes in the "doctrine" of "eternal-security" or not, be ready! Jesus is coming for His own! Many who believe they are part of His "own" may be eternally and sadly surprised on that day to find out they are not. Religious or denominational tenets will not save us! Salvation is not a "license to sin!" Anyone who says otherwise is delivering a message straight from hell and the lips of the devil himself – "*Do not be deceived: God cannot be mocked. A man reaps what he sows. Whoever sows to please their flesh, from the flesh will reap destruction; whoever sows to please the Spirit, from the Spirit will reap eternal life*" – *Galatians 6:7-8*. This applies to both those who were never saved to start with and those who may have experienced the Gospel in some form but chose life without Him. As warned – more questions than answers. But have no fear

– those questions will be answered soon. Let us pray we are not eternally surprised![260]

Chapter 16

WHY REVIVAL?

"Have you noticed how much praying for revival has been going on of late – and how little revival has resulted? I believe the problem is that we have been trying to substitute praying for obeying, and it simply will not work" – A.W. Tozer.

There are five verses in Scripture – all in the Old Testament – containing the word "revive" or "revival:" *Psalm 19:7* references the *"reviving"* or *"refreshing"* of the soul (*"mesibat"* – Hebrew – "converting") through the uplifting power of God's Word; *Psalm 80:18* references *"revival"* (*"hasibenu"* – Hebrew – "restoration") with the coming of Jesus Christ; *Psalm 85:6* references *"revival"* (*"tehayyenu"* – Hebrew – "bring back") in a corporate prayer for renewal of God's mercy upon His people for what many believe is directed to the return of the Jews from exile under the leadership of Nehemiah; *Isaiah 57:15* – references *"revive"* (*"ulehahayowt"* – Hebrew – "uplift") in relation to God's righteous wrath against Israel for rebellion and His door of forgiveness that stands open; *Hosea 6:2* references *"revive"* (*"yehayyenu"* – Hebrew – uplifting restoration) in a prophetic sense regarding Israel's restoration. Oddly, the word "revival" and its offshoots are not found in the New Testament.[261]

Some reference *Acts 3:19 ("Repent, then, and turn to God, so that your sins may be wiped out, that times of refreshing may come from the Lord, and that he may send the Messiah, who has been appointed for you – even Jesus."*) as a New Testament text purporting the idea of "revival" in the sense of imploring a "believer" to return to his/her senses and move back into a "personal" relationship with the Savior he/she apparently once enjoyed. But this is strictly "proof texting" and has nothing to do with "revival" in the sense most professional orators utilize attempting to "revitalize" an apathetic church.

The emphasis is typically centered on the word *"refreshing"* (*"ana-psyxeos"* – recovery), but this passage describes an incident where Peter and John had healed a man at the temple gate called Beautiful who was crippled from birth. He had requested money, but the Apostles introduced him to someone who could offer him something much more important and everlasting – Jesus Christ. The result of this man's healing caused pandemonium among the Jewish onlookers who were left in amazement. This opened the door for testimony and the sharing of the Gospel by Peter and John. Peter's message was akin to the one he delivered at Pentecost – God's eternal plan, the coming of Jesus Christ, His ministry, His death, His resurrection and His open arms of salvation. In other words, he shared the Gospel to his own people who were lost – not to an audience of apathetic professed believers. *Verse 19* is Peter's invitation to the crowd for salvation – to repent of their sins and accept Jesus as their Lord and Savior and receive His ensuing forgiveness and *"refreshing."* This is not a message to waning Christians needing a wake-up call. In fact, I can find no such message in the New Testament.

Examining the use of "revival" in the Old Testament and its noticeable absence from the New Testament, one can assume one reason – Jesus Christ. In most Old Testament examples, "revival" is a direct or indirect reference to restoration of a disobedient, wayward peoples – the Jews. As we discussed in the previous chapter, pre-Messianic Jewish believers lived by faith, and that faith was accounted to them as righteousness – reason being – Jesus Christ had not yet come into the world. The atoning death of Jesus Christ was retroactive; they were saved same as us – by the blood of Jesus Christ. Their faith, being "credited to them as righteousness" – *"For this reason Christ is the mediator of a new covenant, that those who are called may receive the promised eternal inheritance – now that he has died as a ransom to set them free from the sins committed under the first covenant" – Hebrews 9:15* – His atoning blood retroactively covering their sins. Their "revival" was one of forgiveness and restoration as a result of disobedience. But what about us?

Throughout the Scriptures, the relationship between the believer and the Divine God is pictured as that of a family – God the Father, Jesus the Son, children of God, the bride and the bridegroom, brothers and sisters in Christ, etc. Perhaps the most loving of these is found in three New Testament passages: *Romans 8:15, Mark 14:36; and Galatians 4:6.* It is in these passages we find the term, *"Abba Father,"* spoken by both Paul and Jesus Christ. *"Abba"* is an Aramaic word that means "Father," or as some translate, "Daddy." It signifies the close relationship of a father and his child, as well as the childlike trust that a young child puts in his "daddy."[262] Based on the earthly scenario, what child in his right mind and living in a loving relationship with a caring, compassionate father, would go to him and say–"Dad, I am so sorry, but I just do not love you as much as I once did; my feelings for you have become strained and I have lost my enthusiasm and do not have the interest or feel the desire to serve you as in the past? Can you do something to 'revive' me and bring me back into the right relationship we once enjoyed?" First of all, no child who loves his father would ever approach him with that hurtful message; secondly, most caring fathers have unique ways of "reviving" or "revitalizing" wayward and apathetic children and it is normally never pleasant. In the same way, it might be dangerous for "professed" believers to approach their Heavenly Father with the same condescending message of spiritual lethargy and in the same breath, ask to be "revived." We may not get what we expect.

Based on what we profess to believe – mind and heart – regarding the supreme sacrifice of Jesus Christ for us on the cross, how is it people who supposedly belong to Him, can somehow lose or allow their love for Him to wane to the point they need to be "revived?" After all – *"For Christ's love compels* (drives) *us, because we are convinced that one died for all, and therefore all died"* – *2 Corinthians 5:14.* If Christ's love that we profess drives us, why would a Christian ever need "revival?" Clamoring for "revival" might be an "SOS" call for salvation from people who have been convinced by religion they are believers but are not. The New Testament apostles knew nothing of the need for "revival" since they were "compelled" (driven, prodded) by His love, thus allowing it to grow stronger day by day. Why does ours need to be continually "revived?"

In 1964 a Rhythm and Blues duo by the name of The Righteous Brothers released a hit song entitled "You've Lost That Loving Feeling."[263] The refrain goes – "You lost that lovin' feeling'; Whoa, that lovin' feeling'; You lost that lovin' feeling'; Now it's gone, gone, gone, woe." Expounding on romance, especially as teenagers, how many times did we fall in love and confirm that love over and over with "love notes" or letters plastered with – "I will always love you and will never stop! Me and you forever!" We gave "Promise Rings" with the intent of sealing this love that would never cease. Most of the time it did despite the promises. We outwardly professed an eternal love, but be it immaturity or insincerity, it seldom lasted. In the moment we were convinced of a lifetime commitment, but time and circumstance usually won out. We thought we were in love, but truth be known, we never knew its meaning.

The second refrain to the song is, "Bring back that lovin' feeling;' Whoa, that lovin' feeling;' Bring back that lovin' feeling;' Cause it's gone, gone, gone." In a remote way, some see spirituality as similar. We fall in love with Jesus, promising to love and obey Him forever, then for whatever reason, we become apathetic and lethargic, drift away and sometimes find a new love. Then at some point in time we decide to return and want Him to rekindle that love that *we* intentionally lost. How can this happen among people who profess a personal relationship with Him, especially with the ultimate sacrifice He made on our behalf? How can people professed to be His followers forsake His love for another? We never see any indication of this happening with the apostles – in fact, quite the opposite. Is it possible those whose love for Him wanes, never possessed it to begin with? Is it possible, once that love is gone, we can never get it back? Many points to ponder.

The word "revival" means "an improvement in the condition or strength of something; returning something to life that ceased to exist or was dead. Synonyms include, improvement, rallying, betterment, resurrection, etc."[264] The definition of "revival" in a Biblical context is, "an awakening of interest in and care for matters relating to personal religion."[265] "Preachers" are notorious when they feel the "spiritual vitality" of their fellowship is stagnant, to dig back in their files and round up a sermon on "revival." Sometimes they call in a visiting preacher from another church to conduct a series of meetings, usually lasting from three to five evenings, to "revive" the masses. It's usually fiery messages culminating with the clamor of – "Lord, send a great revival amongst our midst! Revive us again!" It is equivalent to a football coach prepping his team in a pre-game challenge speech; then when the team returns to the locker room at half-time, having fallen behind on the scoreboard, the coach once again tries to rally or revive the team with a motivational challenge. They return to the field fired up and ready to play, only to find when hit in the face by an opposing player, the fire ebbs away once again.

When a "preacher" clamors for revival, he may be self-incriminating himself by confessing his own personal need for an awakening, in more ways than one. A body of professed believers asleep at their posts, are the result of the captain being asleep at the wheel. When this occurs, people become apathetic – indifferent, unenthusiastic, lethargic, unalert and oblivious to the iceberg dead ahead. In business, apathy from management does not lead to stagnation, rather to regression and if not stemmed, to bankruptcy and closure. In the spiritual world, the results are the same, but at a much greater cost.

What causes spiritual apathy and what are the results? How can believers become apathetic?

1. Spiritual apathy among "professed" believers is typically the result of an insincere commitment to the Gospel. Be warned of those "preaching" otherwise – "*Do not trust in deceptive words and say, 'This is the temple of the Lord, the temple of the Lord, the temple of the Lord! You are trusting in deceptive words that are worthless. And Then come and stand before Me in this house, which bears My Name, and say, 'We are safe'– safe to do all these detestable things? Has this house, which bears my Name, become a den of robbers to you? But I have been watching', declares the Lord*" (Jeremiah 7:4, 8, 10-11).

2. The "Parable of the Sower" found in *Mark 4*, once again gives us insight as to why "most" are asleep at the wheel. When "spiritual sleep" occurs, the result is always the same – "bare trees" with no fruit resulting in no Gospel outreach. Repeating – "*The farmer* (the believer) *sows the word* (Gospel). Spiritual lethargy results from unconcerned farmers who have no desire to sow seeds, and if no seed is sown, no harvest is reaped.

When the preacher clamors for "revival," maybe he needs to be sharing the Gospel – starting among his own parishioners.

3. *"To the angel of the church of Ephesus write: 'These are the words of him who holds the seven stars in his right hand and walks among the seven golden lampstands: I know your deeds, your hard work, and your perseverance. I know that you cannot tolerate wicked men, that you have tested those who claim to be apostles but are not and have found them false. You have persevered and have endured hardships for My name and have not grown weary. Yet I hold this against you: You have forsaken the love you had at first. Consider how far you have fallen! Repent and do the things you did at first. If you do not repent, I will come to you and remove your lampstand from its place'"* – Revelation 2:1-5.

    The Ephesian fellowship had busied itself with "deeds and hard work" – committees, programs, meetings, service – to each other. The sin of this fellowship was not their zeal, but rather their neglect of "holy" love for Jesus Christ and the external service that accompanies that love. Jesus confirms, if this love is not exercised and channeled, it will be lost. This fellowship was doctrinally correct, but while their efforts appeared committed to Him, their hearts were far from Him. In other words, they knew what they were called to be to the world, but their zeal was all inwardly based. They were in danger of losing their *"lampstand"* – their spiritual influence. Once an individual or a fellowship loses his/her spiritual influence, they become useless and worthless for His service.

The disciples of Jesus – His most intimate followers – had seen every miracle, heard every sermon, experienced every healing, listened to every teaching – yet they still did not understand His mission. They believed He was the redeemer sent from God, but believed His redemptive purpose was to free the Jews from Roman oppression. In *Luke 24,* after His resurrection and during His disguised walk with two of His followers on the road to Emmaus, He questioned them regarding their understanding as to the Messiah's purpose. *"He asked them, 'What are you discussing together as you walk along'?" (Verse 17);* their reply, *(Verses 19-21)* – *"'About Jesus of Nazareth', they replied. 'He was a* prophet, powerful in word and deed before God and all the people. The chief priests and our rulers handed Him over to be sentenced to death, and they crucified Him; but we had hoped that He was the one who was going to redeem Israel'" (from Roman rule). It was not until His dining with them In Emmaus and His prayer of thanksgiving, they recognized Him. It was at this same time they finally realized who He truly was! It was here they finally understood His mission — "Then He opened their minds so they could understand the Scriptures. He told them, 'This is what is written: The Messiah will suffer and rise from the dead on the third day, and repentance and forgiveness of sins will be preached in His name to all nations, beginning first at Jerusalem. You are witnesses of these things. I am going to send you what my Father has promised; but stay in the city until you have been clothed with power from on high'" (Verses 45-49).

During his final plea in *Acts 7:48-51*, delivering the Gospel message to his own people before his martyrdom, Stephen made clear this Holy Spirit — this personal presence of Jesus Christ — resides in the true believer — not in a building built by man. Paul echoes when he notes: *"Don't you know that you yourselves are God's temple and that God's Spirit dwells in your midst?" "For we are the temple of the living God. As God has said: 'I will live with them and walk among them, and I will be their God, and they will by my people'" (1 Corinthians 3:16; 2 Corinthians 6:16)*. It is not within the church building where His mission will be accomplished; it is through the believer's action He will manifest Himself through the sealing of His Holy Spirit. This cannot be accomplished through spiritually lifeless people who think they need "revival," when in truth, they need salvation!

In his Letters to the believers at Ephesus and Thessalonica, Paul issues two warnings regarding the Holy Spirit — *"And do not grieve the Holy Spirit of God, with whom you were sealed for the day of redemption"* — *Ephesians 4:30; "Do not quench the Spirit"*–*1 Thessalonians 5:19*. As previously discussed, there is much theological debate regarding these verses. Part of the debate is the difference between *"grieving"* and *"quenching."* It would appear when Paul warns the Ephesians to *"not grieve the Holy Spirit of God,"* he is not equating *"grieving"* with the believer's potential loss of the Spirit since he once again confirms the Holy Spirit as our seal of salvation. The real theological debate focuses on the Thessalonian passage – "*quenching*" – "*sbennyte*" – "extinguishing" – what is it that "quenches" the Holy Spirit?

Paul makes a stern warning in a previous verse–*1 Thessalonians 5:14* – *"And we urge you brothers and sisters, warn those who are idle, and disruptive, encourage the disheartened, help the weak, be patient with everyone."* Is it possible, Paul's charge to believers ("*brothers*") to "*warn those who are idle,*" sets the tone for the "*quenching of the Holy Spirit?*" In other words, is it possible, "*idleness*" – "*ataktous–*"disorderly by being slack in performance of duty" – can cause one to "*quench the Spirit's fire?*" If so, this may give new meaning to *Hebrews 10:24-25* – *"And let us consider how we may spur one another on toward love and good deeds, not giving up meeting together, as some are in the habit of doing, but encouraging one another – and all the more as you see the Day approaching."* If it is indeed possible there exist genuine believers within a body of Christ who have in some way become lackadaisical to His commands, "*encouragement*" and warning, instead of "revival," should be directed to these "lukewarm idlers" who may be in danger of "*quenching the Spirit's fire.*"[266]

Peter warns us regarding the "last days" – that period of time between His resurrection and His second coming – *"The Lord is not slow in keeping His promise, as some understand slowness. Instead, He is patient with you, not wanting anyone to perish, but everyone to come to repentance" (2 Peter 3:9).* True believers indwelt by the Holy Spirit are His hands, feet, arms, legs, tongues, mouths, ears – channels of the Gospel. It is impossible for a believer to be "full" of the Holy Spirit and sit idly by and do nothing on God's behalf. The "*YOU*" here could be the "lost" – that one additional soul He is waiting; but since "lost" people shun Him along with His message and His Word, "*YOU*" may mean "professed" believers – those He is patiently waiting to take the Gospel message to those that are "lost." If this is the case, "*He is patient with you* (us)," means He is waiting on us to wake up from our deep sleep and do what we have been commanded to do – share the Gospel. A working believer on his/her mission from the Master, "*compelled by His love, because we are convinced that one died for all, and therefore all died" (2 Corinthians 5:14),* has no fear of spiritual apathy or lethargy. "Revival" is not in their vocabulary.

William P. Mackay (1839-1888) was a Scottish Presbyterian pastor. He wrote one of the most famous Protestant hymns that still rings out in our churches today – "Revive Us Again."[267] The lyrics go: "We praise Thee O God! For the Son of Thy love, For Jesus who died, and is now gone above. We praise Thee, O God! For Thy Spirit of light. Who hath shown us our Savior and scattered our night. All glory and praise to the Lamb that was slain. Who hath bourn all our sins, and hath cleansed every stain. All glory and praise to the God of all grace, who hast brought us and sought us and guided our ways. Revive us again, fill each heart with Thy love, may each soul be rekindled with fire from above." The refrain: "Hallelujah! Thine the glory. Hallelujah! Amen. Hallelujah! Thine the glory. Revive us again." This is a wonderful hymn I recall singing from my childhood; it is an uplifting hymn of praise. However, this hymn has always stirred a heartfelt question. It praises God for His Son Jesus, who's shed blood bought us, and His Spirit of light – the Holy Spirit – indwelling us, yet in the same breath, it seems to be asking Him to do it all over again because for some reason, our hearts have grown cold, passive and apathetic and we need "reviving." Does this not seem hypocritical on our part since we appear to be blaming God for our spiritual lethargy and imploring Him to fix it? Christians are not immune from the trials and tribulations of life and we absolutely need encouragement and exhortation from our brothers and sisters in the faith. But how can we lose our passion for the One who sacrificed His life in the most brutal way possible and in the same breath, ask Him to basically do it all over again and "revive" us once more?

An old seasoned pastor stood in the pulpit one Sunday morning preaching fire and brimstone of impending judgment (we can ascertain he was old since this type preaching is a rarity today). He began to implore God to send the fire down from Heaven and revive his church so they would once again rise up and take up arms in the spiritual battle against Satan. For three months he pounded this message into his pulpit and hopefully into the mind of his parishioners. He called upon his deacons each Sunday morning to lead the congregational prayer with the theme – "send a great revival; send the fire from heaven!" Truth is, if the fire did come, it would likely empty his church, but only to the foxhole and not to the battlefield. If "preachers" continue to scream for "revival," from whence do they expect it to come? "Revival" came into the world through Jesus Christ. Those that are sealed with the Holy Spirit, thus guaranteeing their salvation, and understand their calling and mission, do not need "revival" in the sense today's church defines it. They possess "revival." They have already been "revived" through a personal relationship with the "Reviver." Those "professing" salvation – have a mind belief only – sit idly praying for this "revival" to lift them off the pew, but it will never come. "Revival" will not fall from heaven like manna. God, through Jesus Christ, "revived" us once through His Son's death, resurrection and promise of eternal life; why should He do it again? Truth is – He will not.

Prayer is a wonderful thing to a committed Christian. It is our open line to God the Father Himself. The blood of Jesus Christ granted us that direct access. God wants us to communicate with Him – He desires it – "The Lord detests the sacrifice of the wicked, but the prayer of the upright pleases Him" (Proverbs 15:8). But He also demands our action. It is not God's will for His children to spend all their time on their knees and none on their feet. I am reminded of a statement I heard on one occasion, "Prayer will not do our work for us; but it will prepare us for the work that is set before us." In other words, we can pray till the "dogs come home" and spend all our time on our knees, but at some point, we must rise up and be body parts – His arms, legs, mouths, feet – that He called us to be! Dr. William Barclay says, "There is a type of religion which is fonder of committees than it is of housework, which is more set on quiet times than it is on human service. It prides itself on serving the Church and spending itself in devotion – but in God's eyes it has got things the wrong way around."[268]

There are numerous occasions in the Gospels where Jesus and the Apostles prayed, but impending action immediately followed:

a. He prayed before His baptism (Luke 3:21-22) – then He was baptized.
b. He prayed in the morning before going to Galilee (Mark 1:35-36) – then He went to Galilee.
c. He prayed before He healed people (Luke 5:16) – then He healed them.
d. He prayed before calling the Twelve (Luke 6:12-13) – then He called them.
e. He prayed before feeding the 5000 (John 6:11) – then He fed them.

f. He prayed before walking on the water (*Matthew 14:23*) – then He treaded water.

g. He prayed at the Transfiguration (*Luke 9:28-29*) – then He was transfigured.

h. He prayed before teaching the Twelve the Lord's Prayer (*Luke 11:1*) – then He taught them.

i. He prayed before raising Lazarus (*John 11:41-42*) – then He raised him.

j. He prayed at the Lord's Supper (*Matthew 26:26*) – then He ate.

k. He prayed in the Garden before His betrayal (*Matthew 26:36-46*) – then He faced betrayal.

l. He prayed on the cross (*Luke 23:34*) – then He was crucified.

m. He prayed before He died (*Luke 23:46*) – then He died.

n. He prayed before His ascension (*Luke 24:50-53*) – then He ascended.[269]

Yes, Jesus prayed! But that prayer prepared Him for the ensuing action. His prayers prepared Him for the work, but they did not perform or replace that work. The work and the action were His responsibility to the Father. In the same way, only through our actions can our prayers truly be realized, since it is through our actions we see His hand. Regardless of how much we implore Him, He will not do our work for us – but He will prepare us and walk with us as we do the work He has set before us.

"Revival" came in the form of a willing servant, who gave His life freely that we may inherit eternal life. It will not come that way again. The next time He comes, He will come as a King and a conqueror. "Revival" began with God and nothing has changed. But for us to ask for Him to "revive" us over and over again, will not happen. To ask to be "revived" insinuates resurrecting something that has died or is dead; if we need to be "revived," perhaps we need rebirth.

In my studies of the New Testament, I have yet to find one verse that describes any of the Apostles becoming apathetic or lethargic to the Gospel. Peter and John, once again before the Sanhedrin – "*But Peter and John replied, 'Which is right in God's eyes: to listen to you, or to Him? You be the judges! As for us, we cannot help speaking about what we have seen and heard'*" – Acts 4:19-20. How could they lose their zeal for the One they had experienced a personal, physical, and spiritual relationship? How does one lose his zeal for the Gospel and service to Christ – unless he never possessed it to begin with? There is no Biblical evidence of a true believer losing his/her zeal for the Gospel and needing to be "revived."

The Greek word for "encouragement" is, "*parakalountes,*" which means, "to personally, closely, intimately call or summon one to action."[270] "Encouragement," for the believer, comes from time spent in the Word and on our knees, but it can also come from other believers, hence the mandate in *Hebrews 10:25* – "*And let us consider how we may spur one another on toward love and good deeds, not giving up meeting together, as some are in the habit of doing, but encouraging one another – and all the more as you see the Day approaching.*" As constantly noted throughout this book, one should seek this fellowship within a body of true believers – "*By their fruit you will recognize them*" – *Matthew 7:16.* Time is short – we should spend our fellowship time wisely!

"*We want each of you to show this same diligence to the very end, so that what you hope for may be fully realized. We do not want you to become lazy, but to imitate those who through faith and patience inherit what has been promised*" – *Hebrews 6:11-12.* Renewal or "revival" from spiritual apathy, laziness or lethargy, comes from within. These traits are not of God, therefore, to seek Him for restoration would seem blasphemous – imploring Him to "revive" me from something He did not generate or intend – blaming Him for my issue. Being redundant, if we have a problem staying "revived," then it is our problem and the issue may be deeper than spiritual apathy or passivity. It could be we never experienced His "revival of salvation," even though we may have convinced ourselves we have based on a religious teaching or what we have been told. Instead of sitting within the four walls of the church praying for "revival" to "rain" down, maybe we should pray as Paul – "*Pray that I may declare the Gospel fearlessly as I should*" – *Ephesians 6:20.* Don't wait for the "rain" – take the "seed" and get up and GO! His "rain" will fall once the "seed" is planted. "Action" is the antithesis of "apathy." He will not "GO" for us. As believers, we have been called, equipped and prepped for our mission. There is nothing more we need, or He can provide other than opportunity. Constant and consistent utilization of prayer, the Word, mutual exhortation and encouragement from a true believer's fellowship, and His love compels us.

My favorite television show of all time is "The Andy Griffith Show."[271] I recall one episode where Barney and Andy, along with a stranded guest from out of town, were sitting on the front porch on a hot Sunday afternoon. Andy appears to be passing the time rocking while Barney is in a semi-Sunday afternoon stupor – somewhere between sleep and reality. Barney mumbles his desire to call his girlfriend Thelma Lou and walk downtown to the drugstore for an ice cream cone. He repeats himself several times without moving, when finally, the guest turns and confronts him abruptly – "Go man! Call Thelma Lou and for Pete's sake, get up and move!"

The one who is genuinely saved – both mind and heart – has no reason to ever need "revival." He needs encouragement and exhortation from his peers–"for Pete's sake, get off your knees and rise to your feet! You have been assigned a duty – a Great Commission! Get up and go!" Nothing will revive spiritual apathy more than a lost soul being led to a saving knowledge of Jesus Christ as a result of our testimony! *"Those who go out weeping, carrying seed to sow, will return with songs of joy, carrying sheaves with them"* – *Psalms 126:6;* "*For this reason, I remind you to fan into flame the gift of God, which is in you through the laying on of my hands. For the Spirit God gave us does not make us timid, but give us power, love and self-discipline"* – *2 Timothy 1:6-7.* Apathy is not of God; nor is "revival" in the sense we understand it today. "Revival" came from God through His Son – His life, death and resurrection – but it will not come in this manner again. The best advice for one in the depths of spiritual lethargy – *"Be sure of your salvation!"*

Chapter 17

"WHY RELIGION?"

"The difference between religion and true discipleship is, religion is fonder of committees, programs, and house-work; it is more concerned about quiet times than in human service. It prides itself on serving in the church, but in God's eyes, has got things the wrong way around. There is a cowardice of thought, a lethargy of mind and of sleep of the soul which are terrible things. To Jesus the most important thing was not the correct performance of a ritual or formal worship liturgy, but the spontaneous answer to the cry of human need."[272] (William Barclay)

According to Pastor and blog writer Rob Wilkerson, "we as human beings deeply crave conformity. It is part of the sin nature we are all born with. We naturally gravitate toward others who share our likes and dislikes. In order to gain regular access to a group, we must constantly monitor the moods and views of everyone else in the group and monitor their reaction to our mood and view. Meanwhile, everyone in the group is constantly reforming their behavior, attempting to conform to the group. And it never stops. And if it does, you will find yourself on the outs with that group. Then you will be off to find another group. Plug this model into religion and it is really no different. If you are a Christian, just add whatever flavor or brand of Jesus you like, and the pattern is the same. You find a group, denomination, or movement that shares your theological or religious likes and dislikes. The moment you begin to think or feel differently, you suddenly perceive a strange distance and coldness forming which eventually means your departure. And off you go to start all over again with another group or movement. Human beings crave leadership in our lives and secondly, we crave performance. The Bible warns these cravings are unavoidable fruits of our fallen nature."[273]

Based on "Ramsey Theology," "religion" is man's feeble attempt to systematically substitute his intuitive doctrine, tenets and dogmas as replacement for the message of truth proclaimed through Jesus Christ. Officially, "religion" is defined as, "a belief binding the spiritual nature of man to a supernatural being, as involving a feeling of dependence and responsibility, together with the feelings and practices which naturally flow from a belief."[274] According to Google, "there are 4,300 world religions."[275]

Religion consists of "denominations"—defined as "a distinct religious body within Christianity identified by traits such as a name, organization, leadership and doctrine."[276] As noted earlier, "there are over 40,000 Christian denominations in the world, with over 1,500 in the United States alone." [277] Within denominations are "sects," defined as "a group of people with somewhat different religious beliefs (typically regarded as heretical) from those of a larger group to which they belong."[278] Since "sects" can be somewhat covert and similar in doctrine to denominations, it is almost impossible to estimate their numbers. In addition are "cults," defined as "systems of religious veneration and devotion directed toward particular figures or objects; a misplaced or excessive admiration for a particular person or thing."[279] As with "sects," many "cults" are so obscure and attract limited attention to the point estimating their numbers is also near impossible. "Cults" that practice polygamy—marriage between more than one person—have long been followed, and although they are considered a minority, it is estimated there are around 50,000 members of polygamist cults in North America alone.[280] There are also certain secretive fraternal organizations arguably considered "cults" whose estimates of worldwide membership in the early 21st century ranged from approximately two million to more than six million.[281] All are considered part of religion's umbrella, their development predominantly resulting from doctrinal disputes among those seeking teaching that best applies to their individual personal beliefs and lifestyles.

The questions that are posed in this book all relate to one ultimate point of concern – "how did Christianity reach this point; how did those who are supposedly called by His name succumb to the deception of Satan and not only allow, but participate in the "form of godliness" we see today, all in the name of religion?" Summarizing in "layman's" terms, religion" is a system – a network of denominations, sects, and cults – driven by man-made theology based on human tradition and doctrine – resulting in an inner sense of nirvana for adherence to its rules, regula-tions and tradition – all espoused by men in paid, titled, self-appointed positions – established by men for men – all in the name of serving a god – themselves. Jesus came into the world over 2000 years ago to confront "religion" and pronounce judgment upon it. The "religion" of the Pharisees was all about tradition, rules, regulations, man-made laws, and adherence to all. How are we so different?

In 2008, a Christian charity, the Joseph Rowntree Foundation, commis-sioned a poll to discover what are now regarded as social evils and were surprised to find that the "dominant opinion" was that religion was a social evil. People regarded religion as intolerant and used to justify persecution.[282] Without question, "religion" is a powerful motivator – it motivates discussion, debate, argument, disruption, contention, divi-sion – to the point some people fight over it – from individuals and families to churches and governments. According to David B. Barrett, editor of the "World Christian Encyclopedia," "of the 1763 known, recorded conflicts in world history, 123, or 6.98%, had religion as the primary cause."[283] With over 40,000 denominations in the world, each claiming their "god" is the "God," one can readily see *why*. From the "U.S Handbook of Denominations," there are over thirty-one subgroups of the "Baptist" denomination alone in the United States.[284] What has happened since the church at Antioch where, as described by Luke in *Acts 11:26 – "The disciples were called Christians first at Antioch"*?

As mentioned earlier, I actively served in a Christian, business-men's association – the Gideons – that received the bulk of its financial sup-port from the local Protestant church. One hundred percent of church donations go to purchase a copy of God's Word which are distributed to lost men and women around the world. When allowed by the pastor, annual reports are presented orally to supporting churches, updating them on the results of their investment in the ministry. These updates are shared in five-minute to full-service reports, as deemed appropriate by the pastor. I remember receiving a call from a frantic pastor of a church where a report was scheduled, and I was assigned to conduct. It was not a church of my denomination, so the various formalities of the "worship" service were foreign to me. The pastor noted he and the music director were to be away for an off-site convention on that Sunday and asked if I would conduct the entire service – including the music. Let us be clear – perfectly clear – when the Lord handed out talents, the gift of music was not one I was blessed to possess – far from it. This was an unusual request – one I had never experienced in all my years of serving in this ministry. I reluctantly complied out of obligation and since this was a sizable fellowship, I selfishly (in the Spirit) knew a significant supporting offering would likely be forthcoming.

Wanting to concentrate on the report itself, I contacted our State President and asked if he had any insight as to the formalities of service for this denomination and he confirmed my worst fears – he was clueless. Nevertheless, he agreed to assist and assured me the order of service would be listed in the bulletin, along with the music (he was a gifted musician), so off we went. What could go wrong? Remarkably, all went well – at least so I thought. At the close of the service as we were standing at the exiting door greeting the attendees, a "seasoned" lady of the fellowship shook my hand and took me to task – "during the Gloria Patri, we stand; you allowed us to sit. This was not good and very irreligious."

I appreciated her concern for religious formality and my lack thereof, and was politely receptive of the criticism, but her lack of attention to the message of how God was working in 175 countries (the number being reached at that time) around the world, and the millions of people receiving a copy of the Word of God (soldiers, college students, nurses, hospital, hotels, individuals, doctor's offices, business lobbies, prisons, etc.), along with a personal witness for Jesus Christ, and the resulting testimonies shared of those finding salvation through His written Word, was lost in a mistake of formality. I could not help but ask myself, are we so different from the temple worship of the Pharisees with their rites and rituals, that Jesus so vehemently hated and eventually destroyed? We are more concerned about the formality of our services than the sincerity of our proclamation. William Barclay notes: *"It is like the man who believes religion consist of going to church, reading the Bible, passively sitting through a boring sermon, tithing out of requirement, saying grace at meals, having family worship, and carrying out all the external acts which are looked on as religious, and yet never puts himself out to do anything for anyone – no desire to sacrifice himself or his time – blinded by a system to the needs of the world."*

Scripture implies the emotion of anger from Jesus on two occasions: *Matthew 21:12-13 and John 2:15-17 ("Jesus entered the temple courts and drove out all who were buying and selling there. He overturned the tables of the money changers and the benches of those selling doves. 'It is written,' He said to them, 'My house will be called a house of prayer, but you are making it a den of robbers'." "So, He made a whip out of cords, and drove all from the temple courts, both sheep and cattle; He scattered the coins of the money changers and overturned their tables. To those who sold doves He said, 'Get these out of here! Stop turning my Father's house into a market!' His disciples remembered that it is written: 'Zeal for your house will consume me'.")* – both referencing the abuse of money in the temple courts. However, *Mark 3:1-5*, specifically notes His emotion of anger upon His healing of a man with a withered hand on the Sabbath and being challenged by the religious elite – the Pharisees – regarding His disregard of their rules, regulations, and traditions. Scripture says He, *"looked around at them in anger and, deeply distressed at their stubborn hearts..."* A people more concerned about the formality of their religion than the needs of a lost and dying world, brought the wrath of Jesus. Would His attitude be any different today?

A similar confrontation arose in *Mark 7:1-23*, when we once again find His disciples being accused of not washing their hands before a meal – *"the Pharisees and all the Jews do not eat unless they give their hands a ceremonial washing, holding to the tradition of the elders."* The key word here is *"tradition." Leviticus 22:6-7*, provides laws for priests and the washing of hands for sacrifices, but no Scripture exists for others to wash before eating. It may have been the healthy thing to do, but it was a religious regulation not mandated in Scripture. The stern reply from Jesus should be a wake-up call to modern-day religious elitists – *"He replied, 'Isaiah was right when He prophesied about you hypocrites'* ("hupokrites" – fakes, actors, impostors); *as it is written: 'These people honor Me with their lips, but their hearts are far away from Me. They worship Me in vain; their teachings are merely human rules.' You have let go of the commands of God and are holding on to human traditions'"–Mark 7:6-8*. In his blog, "Nine Reasons Jesus Hates Religion,"

Frank Powell's "ninth" reason really sums up Jesus' hatred of what religion represents – "Religion says come to church and serve me; Jesus says go into the world and serve them through *ME*."[285]

Timothy was a native of Lystra in modern Turkey – the son of a Greek father and Jewish mother. As a young boy, he was invited by the Apostle Paul on his Second Missionary journey and subsequent visit to Lystra, to accompany him. He proved himself to be a worthy asset. Paul later left Timothy in charge of the *"ekklesia"* and fragmented house churches in Ephesus while he traveled on to Macedonia. He wrote him two Letters, the first of which, to charge and advise him on his new responsibilities. The second, written some two years later, was written to express his concern over the welfare of the *"ekklesia"* in view of increased persecution from without and deception from within. There are numerous warnings and charges to the young Timothy, and believers in general, from the lips of the Apostle Paul in his second Letter, regarding the Gospel versus religion (*2 Timothy*):

a. Religion fosters passivity. The Holy Spirit empowers. *1:6-7 – "fan into flame the gift of God, which is in you. For the Spirit God gave us does not make us timid."* The warning of *"timidity"* implies its existence within the body.

b. Religion fosters service to each other. *1:8a – "...do not be ashamed of the testimony about our Lord."*

c. Religion fosters comfort within its walls. *1:8b – "join with me in suffering for the Gospel."*

d. Religion fosters neglect of the Holy Spirit and His true purpose. *1:14 – "Guard the good deposit that was entrusted to you – guard it with the help of the Holy Spirit who lives in us." "Always be prepared to give an answer to everyone who asks you to give the reason for the hope that you have" (1 Peter 3:15).*

e. Religion fosters formality. *2:4 – "No one serving as a soldier gets entangled in civilian affairs."*

f. Religion fosters inactivity on the Gospel's behalf. *2:5 – "...anyone who competes as an athlete does not receive the victors crown except by competing according to the rules."*

g. Religion fosters minutia. *2:14 – "warn them before God about quarreling about words."*

h. Religion fosters spiritual laziness without retribution. *2:15a – "...present yourself to God as one approved, a worker..."*

i. Religion fosters being a hearer of the Word, but not a doer. *2:15b* – *"who correctly handle the word of truth."*

j. Religion fosters being dependent on man's intuition. *2:16-17a* – *"Avoid godless chatter, because those who indulge in it will become more and more ungodly."*

k. Religion fosters pettiness – diversion from the mission. *2:23-24* – *"Don't have anything to do with foolish and stupid arguments."*

l. Religion fosters maintaining the "peace" rather than "rocking the boat." *3:12-13* – *"everyone who wants to live a godly life in Christ Jesus will be persecuted, while evildoers and impostors will go from bad to worse, deceiving and being deceived."*

m. Religion fosters man's wisdom over God's truth. *3:16-17* – *"All Scripture is God breathed, and is useful for teaching, rebuking, correcting and training in righteousness so that the servant of God may be thoroughly equipped for every good work."*

n. Religion fosters convenience and comfort over discipleship. *4:2* – *"Preach* (proclaim) *the word* (Jesus Christ*); be prepared in season and out of season."*

o. Religion fosters hypocrisy. *(4:3) "people will not put up with sound doctrine. Instead, to suit their own desires, they will gather around them a great number of teachers* (well compensated at that) *to say what their itching ears want to hear* (a *"feel-good religion"*)."*

p. "Religion fosters a "do nothing" salvation," believing all the while its participants are in good standing with the Master. *4:4-5* – *"They will turn their ears away from the truth and turn aside to myths. But you do the work of an evangelist, discharge all the duties of your ministry."*

Perhaps the severest warning from Paul to Timothy regarding the hypocrisy of religion, is found in Chapter 3 of his second Letter – *"There will be terrible* (perilous) *times in the last days"* (time between His resurrection and His second coming) *3:1.* The "church of man" – the church of the Laodicean Age – the church of the 21st century – will be:

1. *"Lovers of themselves"* (*"philautoi"* – placing oneself on a pedestal; worshipping oneself); *Revelation 3:14-15* – *"I know your deeds, that you are neither cold nor hot. I wish you were one or the other. So, because you are lukewarm – neither hot nor cold–I am about to spit you out of My mouth."* Per Dennis

McCallum, "When enough believers conclude that evangelism doesn't matter much, the entire church grinds to a halt in its mission."[286] In the church made by human hands, Paul warns Timothy – they will love and serve themselves, being oblivious to the needs of the world.

2. *"Lovers of money" – Revelation 3:17 – "You say, ' I am rich; I have acquired wealth and do not need a thing. But you do not realize you are wretched, pitiful, poor, blind and naked."* When today's "church" spends on average, 85-95% of its annual budget on itself, then we can readily surmise where its heart lies. Religion worships itself because it is forced to do so to meet its financial obligations.

3. *"Boastful"* (*"alazones"* – bragadocious) – *Revelation 3:17 – "...I am rich; I have acquired wealth and do not need a thing."* "Lord, we know where you are; we'll call You when we need you."

4. *"Proud"* (*"hyperephanoi"* – arrogant); Reverend David Platt notes, "Consider the cost when Christians ignore Jesus' com-mands. Consider the cost when Christians gather in churches and choose to spend millions of dollars on nice buildings to drive up to, cushioned chairs to sit in, and endless programs to enjoy for themselves. Consider the cost for starving multi-tudes – physically and spiritually – who sit outside the realm of Christian affluence."[287] *Luke 18:11 – "God, I thank you that I am not like other people – robbers, evildoers, adulterers – or even like this tax collector."*

5. *"Abusive"* (*"blasphemoi"* – blasphemers); blasphemers by their denial of the power of Jesus Christ through the Holy Spirit. We blaspheme His name when we refuse to allow His Holy Spirit to be manifested through us, thereby becoming "abusive" to the Gospel and to those that need to hear it.

6. *"Disobedient to their parents"* (*"apeitheis"*- lack of truth); this can also be translated as "disobedience of parental spiritual responsibility." *Deuteronomy 11:18-21 – "Fix these words of mine in your hearts and minds; tie them as symbols on your hands and bind them on your foreheads. Teach them to your children, talking about them when you sit at home and when you walk along the road, when you lie down and when you get up."*

Paul's emphasis appears to be on parental responsibility for the child's spiritual growth; the lack thereof resulting in disrespect and ultimately disobedience to authority in general. He implies in later days parents will ignore the spiritual growth of their children. It is not the Sunday School teacher or the Christian Daycare leader's responsibility for the spiritual growth of our children. Per Dennis McCallum, "Parents in America are pushing their kids toward worldly accomplishments with rapidly increasing zeal. "ABC News" quoted 'The American Academy of Pediatrics,' saying that children spend 30% more hours at organized activities than children 15 years ago."[288] Two authoritarians, Alvin Rosenfield and Nicole Wise, refer to the child-pushing fad gripping our country today as, "hyper-parenting" – the growing belief that kids will be happier if they get top grades, enter top universities, get top careers and are the best at multiple sports; it is not surprising when it comes from non-Christians. The problem is that Christians apparently agree. When Christian parents compromise with the world, their affections are diverted to the world and in essence they and their children will become ineffective in God's service."[289] The parent is ultimately responsible for their child's salvation.

7. *"Ungrateful"* (*"archaristoi"* – unrecognizing; oblivious from whence something received originated); Reminiscent of the swine being slopped; they never raise their head to see from whence cometh their sustenance. Once again–*"You say, ' I am rich; I have acquired wealth and do not need a thing'"* – *Revelation 3:17*. It is all about "us."

8. *"Unholy"* (*"anosioi"* – lawless, profane); no regard for what is sacred. To be "holy" is to be set apart for God's use and viewed as righteous and acceptable in His sight; to be "unholy" is to be the opposite – to be no different from the world around us. Per George Barna–"As the nation's culture changes in diverse ways, one of the most significant shifts is in the declining reputation of Christianity, especially among young Americans. In just a decade, many measures of the Christian image have shifted downward. Currently just 16% of non-Christians in their late teens and early twenties, say they have a positive impression of Christianity."[290] Paul warns in the "church of man," there will

be no difference between those claiming to be of the body and those outside – they are one and the same.

9. *"Without love"* (*"astorgoi"* – without natural affection); the natural desire of a believer is to grow the kingdom of God through the sharing of the Gospel. One "without love" has no desire to bear spiritual fruit of any kind and is therefore "useless or worthless – fit only for burning" (*Matthew 7:19*). How many who fill our pews have convinced themselves they are safe in His hands, yet have not led a single person to Christ in years and literally have no desire to do so? This is "unnatural affection" for a believer.

10. *"Unforgiving"* (*"aspondus"* – without truce, truce breaker, without libation; unbound) – Paul is describing those who are bound by no promise or oath; those who made a commitment but did not live up to it. In this case, people who professed belief in the Gospel, but were not genuinely committed, or broke their commitment (depending on your religious viewpoint). Sadly, these "truce breakers" are convinced they are in His will by their service within the body, all the while ignoring the needs of those on the outside to whom they are obligated. "When the evil one convinces us to expend efforts in directions that do not contribute to our true mission, we can work our hearts out and never pose a threat to Satan's kingdom. This is diversion."[291] One who succumbs to this deception is a "truce breaker."

11. *"Slanderous"* (*"diaboloi"* – false accusers; gossips); Fellow believers are to be encouragers. The Apostle James, as leader of the Jewish believers in Jerusalem, in an attempt to offer words of encouragement and warning from Satan's destruction from within the body, warned–*"Those who consider themselves religious and yet do not keep a tight rein on their tongues, deceives themselves and their religion is worthless"* (*James 1:26*).

12. *"Without self-control"* (*"akrateis"* – inability to restrain oneself; impotent; incontinent); lest we forget – this is war. True believers are called to service. God has given us a mission of carrying the Gospel to a lost world. Every believer is to heed the call – *Philippians 1:27; 2:2* – *"Whatever happens, conduct yourselves in a manner worthy of the Gospel of Christ. Then, whether I come and see you or only hear about you in my absence, I will know that you stand firm in the one Spirit,*

striving together as one for the faith of the gospel without being frightened in any way by those who oppose you. ...make my joy complete by being like-minded, having the same love, being one in spirit and of one mind." Lacking the motivation – being incontinent or impotent – reveals intellectual knowledge of Jesus Christ, but no heart commitment.

13. "*Brutal*" ("*anemeroi*" – wild; anything contrary to gentleness); literally a non-compassionate heart. One of the foremost adjectives describing Jesus Christ was His compassion for the lost – seeing them as sheep without a shepherd – no spiritual food, no spiritual protector, no spiritual leadership (*Matthew 9:36 – "When He saw the crowds, He had compassion on them, because they were harassed and helpless, like sheep without a shepherd;" Matthew 14:14 – "When Jesus landed and saw a large crowd, He had compassion on them and healed their sick;" Matthew 15:32 – "Jesus called His disciples to Him and said, 'I have compassion for these people';" Matthew 20:34 – "Jesus had compassion on them and touched their eyes. Immediately they received their sight and followed Him;" Luke 15:20 – "But while he was still a long way off, his father saw him and was filled with compassion for him; he ran to his son, threw his arms around him and kissed him"*). Sharing the Gospel requires a compassionate heart – without it we see the lost simply as people we do not want to be or do not want period. Paul is referencing those who say with their lips they care, but their actions show otherwise. This type attitude, per the Apostle Paul, is "*brutal*" and prevalent among those worshipping religion.

14. "*Not lovers of the good*" ("*aphilagathoi*" – despiser of all that is good); placing our needs and desires over those of the Lord; despising His directives. *Galatians 5:26 – "Let us not become conceited, provoking and envying each other."* If they do not love the message then they don't love the One who authored the message. They are fake – professed, but not committed to the good. These are those Jesus warned us in *Matthew 7:15-16 – "Watch out for false prophets. They come to you in sheep's clothing, but inwardly they are ferocious wolves."* These individuals will not only warm our pews but will stand in the pulpits of the church in the last days.

15. "*Treacherous*" ("*prodotai*" – traitor) – those who deliver up to an enemy the person who has put their trust in them. It

describes a person who is more interested in his own good, while giving the impression he is concerned about the good of others. They are pretenders; pretending outwardly they have compassion for the lost but inwardly, could care less. Fortunately, they are easily recognized – *"By their fruit you will recognize them" (Matthew 7:16)*.

16. *"Rash"* (*"propeteis"* – reckless) – Relying on one's own intuition rather than seeking and awaiting the will and guidance of God. Recklessness in a spiritual setting is destructive since it is eternal in scope. Numerous examples are found throughout Scripture where men relied on their own intuition rather than seeking the will of God and it resulted in eternal adverse ramifications. Perhaps none so true than Abraham, Sarai, Hagar and Ishmael (*Genesis 16*) – a reckless, rash decision we are still reaping the consequences today. Paul is warning Timothy, beware leaders and their followers who rely on their own intuition and exclude Him altogether.

17. *"Conceited"* (*"tetyphomenoi"* – high minded) – There are two ways to view religious "conceit:" first, "conceit of riches," which has already been discussed; secondly, "conceit of spirituality" – *"For there is no difference between Jew and Gentile – the same Lord is Lord of all and richly blesses all who call on Him, for, 'Everyone who calls on the name of the Lord will be saved'"* – *Romans 10:12-13*.

Being presently involved in a Hispanic fellowship that has evolved into an outreach to young kids of differing ethnic backgrounds, I am completely in awe of the impoverished neighborhoods my bus takes me to retrieve them. My awe comes from the fact that every single one of these neighborhoods are within walking distance of churches of my own denomination that have less than twenty cars in the lot on Sunday evening, yet none of these neighborhoods are being ministered with the Gospel.

In a recent associational meeting I attended, the speaker noted in the county which our associational office is headquartered, there were over 1,000 homeless children. She also noted this number is likely low since most are too embarrassed or ashamed to admit being homeless. Searching on-line, I noticed

our county – Anderson County, South Carolina–has a population of 198,759.[292] According to sources, there are 230 coun-
ty-wide churches[293] – 125 of my own denomination.[294] There is
a "church" for every 864 people; there is a "church" for every
4.35 homeless child. How can this be? Granted these folks are
takers – not givers–and from a dollars and cents standpoint
are not eligible for membership privileges in today's "church,"
their souls considered expendable. *"Live in harmony with
one another. Do not be proud but be willing to associate with
people of low position. Do not be conceited" (Romans 12:16).*
Church be warned! *"The Lord Almighty has a day in store for
all the proud and lofty, for all that is exalted (and they will be
humbled)." (Isaiah 2:12).*

18. *"Lovers of pleasure rather than lovers of God"* ("*philedonoi*" –
lovers of worldly things and comforts) – focusing on the "wants"
of the "ninety-nine" and ignoring the needs of the "one." When
we choose to focus on our $5 million buildings, coffee kiosks,
padded pews, gymnasiums, elaborate sound systems and video
boards, and all the comforts, bells and whistles we choose to
invest, our attention is diverted, and the mission becomes all
about "us." Paul admonishes Timothy to, *"Flee from all this"*
(*1 Timothy 6:11*). Jesus Christ Himself warns us, *"No one can
serve two masters. Either you will hate the one and love the
other, or you will be devoted to the one and despise the other.
You cannot serve both God and money" (Matthew 6:24).*

"When Christians compromise with the world, they may continue to attend church, tithe, pray and even read the Bible. The
things of God may occupy a section of their lives, but the main
thrust of their devotion is to the world."[295] To keep peace with
the world and peace within the "church," one must compromise with both, since appeasing both will keep the cash flowing.
So long as preachers preach, *"what their itching ears want to
hear," (2 Timothy 4:3)*, people will come and bring their wallets.
Preach truth and you are in trouble – too discriminatory, too
scary and too judgmental. Preach what condones their lifestyle
and they are happy. However, be warned – God is not! *"Do
not be deceived: God cannot be mocked. A man reaps what he
sows" (Galatians 6:7).*

19. *"Having a form of Godliness but denying its power"* – For those who do not believe Paul's warnings to Timothy in *Verses 1-5* of *2 Timothy 3* are a reference to "religion's" majority in today's church, this statement clearly debunks their contention. According to David Guzik, pastor of Calvary Chapel Santa Barbara, California, and noted commentary writer, Paul is warning of a "salad bar" religion. "They feel free to be "spiritual," but sense no obligation to be Biblical."[296] Paul warns, *"Have nothing to do with them."* He is describing "hypocrites" (*"hupokrites"* – fakes, actors, pretenders) – a trait prevalent in "religion" and its followers.

"What is so scary is that we can pretend we are the people of God. We can comfortably turn a blind eye to the Bible and go on with our affluent model of Christianity and church, and even be successful in our church culture for doing so. It will be seen as a sign of success and growth when we spend millions on ourselves and believe what we are doing is Biblical. So did His disciples. That is one of the reasons they were so shocked when Jesus walked away from His conversation with a rich young man saying, *'How hard it is for the rich to enter the kingdom of God!' (Mark 10:23-24).* The disciples were amazed. Why were they so surprised?"[297] Religion and those who believe in its rites, rituals, traditions, rules, regulations, and leadership to save them, are the very ones Jesus references – *"Depart from Me. I never knew you" (Matthew 7:14).* "Religion is one of the most powerful tools for keeping people away from the true God."[298]

AFTERWORD

"Theology" is defined as, "the systematic study of the nature of the divine, and more broadly, of religious belief; it is taught as an academic discipline, typically in universities and seminaries." "Theologian" is defined as, "a person who is an expert in theology."[299] I personally question if a true "theologian" exists, but if we were to confront twenty "theologians" with the question – "What is "God's will?" – we would likely receive twenty different answers – from the "experts." I do not qualify myself as a "theologian," but through the leadership of the Holy Spirit, allow me to submit the twenty-first explanation – God has a "will" and God has a "plan." There is a difference.

Numerous times in Scripture, we find references to – *"God's will;" "the Lord's will;"* or *"His will."* We hear sermons, prayers from professed believers and others imploring God to, "Let His will be done in our lives." In the "Model Prayer," Jesus Himself prayed, *"Your kingdom come, Your will be done" (Matthew 6:10).* Both Jesus and Paul issued stern warnings against those who refuse to do "God's will" – *"Not everyone who says to Me, 'Lord, Lord,' will enter the kingdom of Heaven, but only he who does the WILL of My Father who is in Heaven" (Matthew 7:21); "Therefore, do not be foolish, but understand what the Lord's WILL is" (Ephesians 5:17).* What *is* God's will and how does His will apply to my life?

Based on "Ramsey Theology," "God's will" is universal. Arguably, the two most enlightening verses rendering the most precise Biblical definition on "God's will" are, *2 Peter 3:9 – "The Lord is not slow in keeping His promise, as some understand slowness. He is patient with you, not wanting anyone to perish, but everyone to come to repentance";* and *1*

Timothy 2:3-4 – *"This is good, and pleases God our Savior, who wants all men to be saved and to come to a knowledge of the truth."* "God's will" is for all to be saved! He wants everyone to find salvation through His Son, Jesus Christ! He is holding back the curtain of judgment for one more soul. Will all find salvation and be saved? No, they will not.

As earlier noted in His "Parable of the Sower" (or "Recipient"), as found in *Mark 4*, Jesus revealed how the Gospel will or will not be received. He notes many will hear the message, but flat-out refuse it – *"Some people are like seed along the path, where the word is sown. As soon as they hear it, Satan comes and takes away the word that was sown in them" (Verse 15)*. Then, there are those who pretend to receive it, but their belief is only of the mind – not of the heart – *"Others, like seed sown on rocky places, hear the word and at once receive it with joy. But since they have no root, they last only a short time. When trouble or persecution comes because of the word, they quickly fall away" (Verses 16-17)*. Then there are those who hear and accept it, but are lured away by the things of the world – *"Still others, like seed sown among thorns, hear the word; but the worries of this life, the deceitfulness of wealth and the desires for other things, come in and choke the word, making it unfruitful" (Verses 18-19)*. The above recipients of the Gospel hear it but are lost for rejecting it. Although most hearers will refuse the message (*"But small is the gate and narrow the road that leads to life, and only a few find it"* – Matthew 7:14), it is God's "will" for all to hear it and be saved. He has no desire for anyone to go to hell – *"Say to them, 'As surely as I live,' declares the Sovereign Lord, 'I take no pleasure in the death of the wicked, but rather that they turn from their ways and live'"* – Ezekiel 33:11. Unfortunately, most will.

Whereas "God's will" is universal, His "plan" is "individual." His "plan" is designed for the accomplishment of His "will." As a believer, God has a "plan" – a blue-print – for each of our lives, designed specifically for us and the accomplishment of His "will" – *"Before I formed you in the womb, I knew you, before you were born, I set you apart; I appointed you as a prophet to the nations" (Jeremiah 1:5)*; *"Surely I was sinful at birth, sinful from the time my mother conceived me. Yet you desired faithfulness even in the womb; you taught me wisdom in that secret place" (Psalm 51:5)*; *"For you created my inmost being; you knit me together in my mother's womb. I praise you because I am fearfully and wonderfully made; your works, are wonderful, I know that full well. My frame was not hidden from you when I was made in the secret place, when I was woven together in the depths of the earth. Your eyes saw my unformed body; all the days ordained for me were written in your book before one of them came to be" (Psalm 139:13-16); "This is what the Lord says – your Redeemer, who formed you in the womb: 'I am the Lord, the Maker of all things, who stretches out the heavens, who spreads out the earth by myself'" (Isaiah 44:24); "But when God, who set me apart from my mother's womb and called me by His grace, was pleased to reveal His Son in me so that I might preach Him among the Gentiles, my immediate response was not to consult any human being"* (Galatians 1:15).

His "will" is for all to hear the Gospel message and be saved; His "plan" is designed so believers have a customized blueprint for the accomplishment of His "will." Our first responsibility as a believer is to seek His guidance in understanding and realizing His plan for our life. We do this through prayer – on our knees – just us and God – seeking His face – to reveal that "plan" to us in His time and once revealed, to make sure we live that "plan." To do otherwise, risks divine judgment – *"But everyone who hears these words of Mine and does not put them into practice is like a foolish man who built his house on sand" (Matthew 7:26).*

The message of this book should not be deemed as advising anyone against being a part of a believer's fellowship! In fact, quite the opposite, since it is a Biblical mandate – *"Do not give up meeting together, as some are in the habit of doing, but encouraging one another – and all the more as you see the Day approaching" (Hebrews 10:25).* A "believer's fellowship" is just that – a group of mind and heart believers – not "pretenders" going through the motions – who understand "God's will" and either know or are earnestly seeking His "plan" for their lives, thereby positioning themselves for the accomplishment of His will through the Gospel. Be warned! Participation in a "fellowship" is not the same as a "believer's fellowship." "Believer's fellowships" are not perfect, as nothing involving man is, but a "believer's fellowship" is a spiritual "orchard" full of "fruit-bearing trees;" "fellowships," on the other hand, are orchards full of trees but typically bearing no fruit – *"Thus, by their fruit, you will recognize them" (Matthew 7:20).* Or to put it another way, by their numbers (salvations and baptisms) you will recognize the fruits of their labor – or lack thereof.

A "believer's fellowship" is based on God's Word, both living and written and one where its members are discipled and trained for the mission their Lord has called them to fulfill. *"Fields white for harvest"* do not grow under the roof of a building, but rather outside in the pastures of life. *"Don't you have a saying, 'It's still four months until harvest?' I tell you, open your eyes and look at the fields! They are ripe for harvest"* – *John 4:35*. Those who are content with cultivating under a roof are outside His "will" and in no way will assist you in realizing and building upon His "plan" for your life. How can they when they have no clue themselves? From such, steer clear!

CLOSING THOUGHTS

Matthew 12:34 – "For the mouth speaks what the heart is full of." Matthew 15:18 – "But the things that come out of a person's mouth come from the heart, and these defile them." Jeremiah 17:9 – "The heart is deceitful above all things, and beyond cure. Who can understand it?"

This compilation is a result of a lifetime of prayer, study, research and collection of questions regarding the "religion" I fear I have served, in place of the Savior's mission I fear I have rejected. Although it does not necessarily afford me peace of mind, it has at least provided me an open analytical forum. My desire is the reader has been challenged to consider for one moment – is what I believe, and basing my eternity – established on truth, or is it based on man's teaching, word of mouth, inheritance, tradition or religious inuendo? Once again, my prayer is you have been challenged to not think like me, but to think along with me, so together we will not be afraid to ask *"why"* before it becomes eternally too late.

Upon reading this book, if it seems indicting in any way, understand it is an indictment against its author and no one else. For me to say this book was written from the "heart" would be dangerous. I do believe, due to the free flowing of my thoughts and the indescribable peace that has come as a result, the Father's hand has been evident in guiding me through His Holy Spirit. I pray it is truly not a product of my heart. It is in no way to be construed as vindictive or destructive to those who support organized "religion." After all, I am a product of the same system. The issue I wrestle is perhaps the same as yours – is it remotely possible we have been "subtlety" deceived into believing service to a system is the same as service to Jesus Christ? This is my greatest fear.

Matthew 7:13-26 has been referenced frequently throughout this book. It is a message to arguably the most religious people in the world – the Jews. They were deceived by their religion and its leaders, who themselves had been duped by the greatest deceiver of all – Satan (*Revelation 12:9*). His message of deception is religion and service to it, guarantees us proper standing before God and eternal life with the Father. It worked then – why should it not work now? Eight points regarding this passage:

1. *"But small is the gate and narrow the road that leads to life, and only a few find it" (7:14).* Only a few (*"oligoi"* – rarity) will be saved. So, how many is a 'few'? 10, 100, 1000, 10,000, 100,000, 1 million, 1 billion? We do not know, but if indeed this message is addressed to religious peoples, what does this tell us? It confirms, just as with His Jewish audience – most filling today's synagogues and churches believe they are saved but are not.

2. *"Watch out for false prophets ("pseudoprophetron"* – claiming to be of God but are not; fake; almost approaching; having the appearance of) – *(7:15a). "It is much less disturbing to proclaim about the niceties of theological belief, doctrines and programs offered by the church, than it is to preach about the needs of men, the abuses of life, and the judgmental wrath of God. It is a notable thing that it was not what Jesus said about God that got Him into trouble; it was what He said about man and about the needs of man that disturbed the, "religious," of His day"*–William Barclay.

3. *"They come to you in sheep's clothing, but inwardly they are ferocious wolves" – (7:15b).* "Lost" people are blind. Professed believers are deceived. Satan has succeeded when the message from the pulpit to professed believers convinces them they can profess salvation and not lift a finger on behalf of God's kingdom and feel perfectly at ease that they are delivered to the Master – all for a price.

4. *"By their fruit* (or lack) *you will recognize them" (7:16).*

5. *"Every tree that does not bear good fruit is cut down and thrown into the fire" (7:19).* There are three kinds of spiritual

fruit – good, bad and none. "Bad fruit" bearers would be considered the "lost;" "no fruit bearers" would be considered the "pretenders" – their spiritual plight the same as the lost; "good fruit bearers" are those mind and heart committed, fully grasping both His will and His plan for their lives.

6. *"Not everyone who says to Me, 'Lord, Lord,' will enter the kingdom of heaven, but only the one who does the will of my Father who is in heaven. Many will say to Me on that day, 'Lord, Lord, did we not prophesy in your name and in your name drive out demons and in Your name perform many miracles?' Then I will tell them plainly, 'I never knew you. Away from Me you evildoers'" (7:21-23).* These could be classified as the "eternally surprised;" those who based their salvation on religion and its service to one another.

7. *"Therefore, everyone who hears these words of mine and puts them into practice is like a wise man who built his house on the rock" (7:24).* Two key words – *"hears"* and *"practices." "Do not merely listen to the word, and so deceive yourselves. Do what it says" – James 1:22.* The *"house on the rock"* is constructed by one who is both a *"hearer"* and a *"doer."*

8. *"But everyone who hears these words of mine and does not put them into practice is like a foolish man who built his house on the sand" (7:26). "Foolish"* literally translates *"worthless."* These are those who are content to be *"hearers"* but not *"doers."* The implication is they are *"useless"* in service to Him. They are apostate. *"The Son of Man will go just as it is written about Him. But woe to that man who betrays the Son of Man! It would be better for him if he had not been born" – Matthew 26:24.*

This is our salvation; our gift; our eternal decision. We should not be deceived into believing service to each other suffices for our lack of outreach to others. We "go" because He commanded it! Nowhere did He command us to stay where it is comfortable, throw those doors open, establish those programs and I will send them to you! A "select" few will indeed come – but again, the "unselect majority" will not.

The Gospel outreach of the New Testament *"ekklesia"* was Christ centered under the direction of the Holy Spirit and responded to His Great Commission. Consider the results:

a. *"Those who accepted his message were baptized, and about three thousand were added to their number that day"* – Acts 2:41.

b. *"And the Lord added to their number daily those who were being saved"* – Acts 2:47.

c. *"But many who heard the message believed; so the number of men who believed grew to about five thousand"* – Acts 4:4.

d. *"Nevertheless, more and more men and women believed in the Lord and were added to their number"* – Acts 5:14.

e. *"Day after day, in the temple courts and from house to house, they never stopped teaching and proclaiming the good news that Jesus is the Messiah"* – Acts 5:42.

f. *"Then the church throughout Judea, Galilee and Samaria enjoyed a time of peace and was strengthened. Living in the fear of the Lord and encouraged by the Holy Spirit, it increased in numbers"* – Acts 9:31.

g. *"The Lord's hand was with them, and a great number of people believed and turned to the Lord"* – Acts 11:21.

h. *"But the word of God continued to spread and flourish"* – Acts 12:24.

i. *"So, the churches were strengthened in the faith and grew daily in numbers"* – Acts 16:5.

During one of my Small Group Bible Study sessions discussing the Gospel efforts of the New Testament Church, one of my attendees made the statement, "this is the 21st century; in no way would their style and template be feasible today." In other words, "our way is better; their ways are old and outdated." Lest we be reminded – *"Jesus Christ is the same yesterday, today, and forever"* – Hebrews 13:8. Are we seeing His evangelistic hand moving in like manner today? I think not!

ENDNOTES

The Author

1   All Scripture quotation are taken from the *New International Version* unless otherwise noted, Biblica; 1973,1978,1984,2011.

2   Thayer & Smith Greek Lexicon

Foreword

3   Oxford English Dictionary

4   Wikipedia; en.m.wikipedia.org

Preface

5   "Pagan Christianity", Frank Viola, PP. 77, 136, 142, 181, 267

Chapter 1

6   WYFF Television; Greenville, SC, December 10, 2019

7   Wikipedia; en.m.wikipedia.org

8   Barna Group; "Shocking Statistics about Church Decline;" April 9, 2015

9   Statistics & Reasons for Church Decline", by Dr. Richard Krejcir

10   South Carolina Baptist Convention, Columbia, S.C

11   FullInsite Report; missioninsite at misupport@missioninsite.com

12   "FullInsite Report;" 2015; Five Mile Radius of 206 Washington Church Road; Pelzer, SC; Short term projections – 5 year–2020; 10 year – 2025

13   Andrew Strom; "Out of Church Christians"

14 The Vietnam Conflict Extract Data File of the Defense Casualty
    Analysis System
15 Encyclopedia Britannica Dictionary
16 Coleman; 2006
17 Streett, "Effective Invitation," pp.97,193-194,197
18 Pagan Christianity," Frank Viola, George Barna, p.70
19 "Satan & His Kingdom"; Dennis McCallum; pp.76,79
20 "Satan & His Kingdom"; Dennis McCallum; p.79
21 "A Call to Spiritual Reformation;" D.A. Carson
22 "Why We Crave Religious Systems & Why I'm Not Leading
    Churches for a While Longer," robwilerrson.net; September
    21, 2015
23 Pastor Eli James; April 27, 2008
24 Radical;" Reverend David Platt – PP 2-3; 48-49
25 Webster's New World Dictionary

Chapter 2

26 "Why We Crave Religious Systems;" Rev. Rod Wilkerson;
    September 21, 2015, robwilkerson.net
27 Wikipedia; "Business"; en.m.wikipedia.org
28 The Gideons International; gideons.org
29 "The Unarguable Facts;" Doug Perry; "Kansas City Businessman"
30 "Scary Statistics;" Doug Perry
31 "Scary Statistics;" Doug Perry
32 "Median Households;" Gallup Poll Survey – 2006-2012
33 "Holy Soup"; Thom Schultz, Aug. 6, 2013
34 US Federal Government Statistics; "Federal Budget 101";
    'National Priorities Project'
35 "Washington Post"; August 22, 2013
36 "The Economist"; Earthly Concerns; 2010
37 "Radical"; Reverend David Platt;p.118
38 "Humans Are Free"; 10-28-15
39 "Scary Statistics"; Doug Perry
40 Gene Veith; http://www.worldmag.com/articles/11176
41 "Gleanings"; Morgan Lee; 9-12-14
42 "Why Most Churches Are Businesses;" Darren Shearer; theolo-
    gyofbusiness.com
43 "Would Jesus Want Your Church to Be Run Like A Business?";
    Tony Morgan; tonymorganlive.com

44   "Should Your Church Start A Business?"; Outreach Magazine; Christine Bove; July 7, 2019;outreachmagazine.com

Chapter 3

45   "Position Yourself for a Blessing;" blog posted by Victoria Osteen; June 13, 2014
46   "Online Magazine;" "Top 15 Richest Pastors in the World;" August 23, 2019
47   Wikipedia; "Joel Osteen"; en.m.wikipedia.org
48   Rev. Ike; Google
49   "Herod the Great;" Jewish Encyclopedia
50   "What Is the Temple Tax?", gotquestions.org.
51   "Opentheword.org;" Dean Smith
52   biblical stewardship.net
53   "Holy Soup"; Thom Schultz, Aug. 6, 2013
54   "Question of the Day;" Ken Copeland Ministries ; November 13, 2019
55   "Twenty-One Fascinating Tithing Statistics;" healthresearch-funding.org
56   Churchgoers Views-Tithing; August 22-30,2017; Lifeway Research
57   "New Study Shows Trends in tithing & Donating;" Barna Research; April 14, 2008
58   "Baptist Courier;" October 2, 2019; Rudy Gray
59   "Church Giving Statistics, 2019 Edition;" Jayson D. Bradley; July 18, 2019
60   "Why the Giving in Your Church is Decreasing;" Thom S. Ranier; March 5, 2018
61   "The MacArthur New Testament Commentary;" John MacArthur, Mark 9-16
62   "Pagan Christianity;" Frank Viola & George Barna; pp.172-173
63   "Pagan Christianity;" Frank Viola & George Barna; p.178
64   "Pagan Christianity", Frank Viola, George Barna; p.41

Chapter 4

65   "Five Groups that Don't Pay Taxes;" Investopedia; Mark P. Cussen; June 25, 2019
66   "Churches Defined;" Publication 1828, Tax Guide for Churches & Religious Organizations; irs.gov

67   religionnews.com; October 26,2018

68   New York Times; April 26,2018

69   "Are Church Employees Eligible for Unemployment Benefits?";
      "Content & Business Development; Matthew Branaugh;
      April 7, 2020

70   "The Conversion of Constantine"; ReligionFacts.com; 2017

71   "Indestructible Book"; Connolly; pp. 39-40

72   "Worshipping Like Pagans"; Hinson; p.20

73   "History of Church & Taxes;" Procon.org

74   "Pagan Christianity"; Frank Viola, George Barna; p.271

75   "History of Church & Taxes"; Procon.org

76   "Should Churches Pay Taxes;" debate.org; 2020

77   "You Give Religions More Than $82.5 Billion A Year;" The
      Washington Post; Dylan Matthews; August 22, 2013

78   "The Ten Warning Signs of an Inwardly Obsessed Church;" Thom
      S. Ranier; May 2, 2012

79   "Why Dying Churches Die;" Thom S Ranier; August 9, 2017; The
      Christian Post; christianpost.com; Thom S Ranier – Christian Post
      contributor; August 13, 2017

80   Rev. Brandon Ware; Life Path; lifepath.org

81   "Scary Statistics;" Doug Perry

82   "Holy Soup;" Thom Schultz; Aug. 6, 2013

83   "Ethics & Religious Liberty Commission;" Southern Baptist
      Convention; erlc.com

84   "Cooperative Program;" Southern Baptist Convention; sbc.net

85   "Ethics & Religious Liberty Commission;" Southern Baptist
      Convention; erlc.com

86   "Southern Baptist Church Voices;" blog March. 26, 2010;
      Matt Svoboda

87   "Understanding the Hidden $1.1 Trillion Welfare System";
      Heritage Foundation; heritage.org; April 5, 2018

88   "Annual Church Profile;" Palmetto Baptist Association; sbc.net

Chapter 5

89   Palmetto Baptist Association; Williamston, SC; palmettobap-
      tistsc.org

90   Palmetto Baptist Association; Williamston, SC; Annual Church
      Profile 2017-2018; sbc.net

91   "Why Are So Many Christians Quitting Church," Matthew Green;
      Charisma Magazine

92 "Church 3.0: Upgrades for the Future of the Church;" Neil Cole
93 "World Net Daily;" Jim Rutz; jimrutz.wordpress.com; "Ten Massive Changes Will Soon Transform Your Life;" June, 2007
94 "House Church Involvement is Growing;" George Barna; June 19, 2006
95 "A Historical Approach to Evangelical Worship"; Jones; p.103
96 "History of the Christian Church", Schaff'
97 "To Preach or Not"; David C. Norrington; p. 29
98 "Church Buildings or House-Churches?;" "Truth According to Scripture blog;" Darryl Erkel
99 "Toward A House-Church Theology"; New Testament Restoration Newsletter – October-1991, Vol,1/No.6: p,2
100 "House Church Movement;" "A Study of Denominations;" study-ofdenominations.com
101 "How Many People Really Attend a House Church;" George Barna; August 31, 2009
102 Rev. Mike Baker; Director of Missions; Palmetto Baptist Association; Williamston, SC
103 WSPA Television; Spartanburg, SC; Kimberely Brown; May 27, 2020
104 WYFF Television; Greenville, SC; Taggart Houck; March 29, 2020

Chapter 6

105 "Hallucinogenic Drugs;" myDr.com.au
106 "Hallucinogenic Drugs;" National Institute On-Drug-Abuse," Revised April 2019
107 "The Invitation System;" Iain Murray; 1967
108 "The Big Beat- A Rock Blast;_" Frank Garlock
109 "God's Answers to Man's Questions;" "Rock Music-A Symptom or a Cause; Alban Douglas; p.XXIII
110 "What Is Worship? A Survey of Scripture;" Michael Morrison; Grace Communion International; https://www.gci.org/GodWorship

Chapter 7

111 "Pagan Christianity;" Frank Viola & George Barna; pp.42-43
112 "Webster's New World Dictionary"
113 "ROI-Return on Investment;" Wikipedia
114 "Britannica World Language Dictionary"

115 "Satan & His Kingdom;" Dennis McCallum; p.61

116 "A Call-To Spiritual Reformation"; D.A. Carson; Grand Rapids: Baker Academic, 1992

117 "Stealing Sheep: The Church's Hidden Problems with Transfer Growth;" William Chadwick; 2001

118 "Eleven Observations about Church Transfer Growth;" Thom Ranier; August 9, 2014; Church Answers; thomranier.com

119 "Satan & His Kingdom;" Dennis McCallum; p.278

120 "Stealing Sheep: The Church's Hidden Problems with Transfer Growth;" William Chadwick; 2001

121 "Financial Peace University Website;" Dave Ramsey; February, 2011)

122 "Cities Need Housing; Churches Have Property. Can They Work Something Out?"; The Washington Post; November 5, 2019; Patton Dodd

123 "America's Epidemic of Empty Churches;" The Atlantic Monthly Group; Jonathan Merritt; November 25, 2018

124 "Praying for Empty Churches in Europe to Be Filled"; Carrie Borden; February 11, 2019; imb.org

Chapter 8

125 "The NAS New Testament Greek Lexicon"

126 "Defining the Mission of the Church;" March 19, 2012; Trevin Wax; thegospelcoalition.org

127 "The American Church in Crisis: Groundbreaking Research on a National Database of Over 200,000 Churches;" David Olson

128 "Quitting Church: Why the Faithful Are Fleeing, & What to Do About It;" Julia Duin

129 "D Day;" Baptist Courier:" Lee Clamp;_October, 2017

130 "U.S. Church Membership Down Sharply in Past Two Decades;" Gallup News; Jeffrey M. Jones; April 18, 2019

131 "Hope for Dying Churches blog;" Thom Ranier; factsandtrends. net; January 16, 2018

132 "Five Reasons Why Most Southern Baptist Churches Baptize Almost No Millennials;" "Christianity Today;" Kate Tracy; May 29, 2014

133 "Growing True Disciples;" George Barna; Issachar Resources; Chapters 6-7

134 "Scary Statistics;" Doug Perry

135 www.xenos.org/satan

Chapter 9

136 "Ordinary Radicals: A Return to Christ-Centered Discipleship;" Jonathan Hayashi

137 "Are Sermons Biblical;" Matthew Pierce; matthewepierce.com

138 Oxford Language Dictionary

139 "The Bible Never Mentions Sermons!"; Lon Martin; www. everlastingkingdom

140 Webster's New World Dictionary

141 "The Bible Never Mentions Sermons!"; Lon Martin; www. everlastingkingdom

142 King James Version

143 Thayer & Smith Greek Lexicon

144 Thayer & Smith Greek Lexicon; Interlinear Bible Hub

145 "The Bible Never Mentions Sermons!"; Lon Martin; www. everlastingkingdom

146 "The Bible Never Mentions Sermons!"; Lon Martin; www. everlastingkingdom

147 "The Empty Pulpit;" Clyde H. Reid; 1967

148 "Tyndale Biblical Theology Lecture;" Klaas Runia; 1976

149 "The Apostolic Preaching & Its Developments;" C.H. Dodd

150 "Evangelism in The Early church;" Michael Green

151 "Pagan Christianity;" Frank Viola & George Barna, p.100

Chapter 10

152 "Tyndale Biblical Theology Lecture;" Klaas Runia; 1976

153 "No Biblical Defense for Paid Pastors;" Lew Ayotte

154 "No Biblical Defense for Paid Pastors;" Lew Ayotte

155 Thayer & Smith Greek Lexicon

156 "Like the Master Ministries;" "Never Thirsty;" neverthirsty.org

157 "Like the Master Ministries;" "Never Thirsty;" neverthirsty.org

158 "The Origin of the Clergy Salary;" Sharon Balloch; February 19, 2009

159 "History of the Church of God;" C B Hassell; 374-392,472

160 "Pagan Christianity;" Viola, Barna; p.178

161 "Selling Forgiveness: How Money Sparked the Protestant Reformation;" Randy Petersen

162 "Infamous Indulgence Led to Reformation;" Christianity.com

163 "Ministry in Historical Perspectives;" Nieuhr, Williams; p.111

164 "Ministry in Historic Perspectives;" Nieuhr, Williams; pp.114-115; "Theology of Martin Luther;" Althaus; p. 326; "Pagan Christianity;" George Barna, Frank Viola; p.133
165 "A History of the Cure of Souls;" McNeil
166 Thayer & Smith Greek Lexicon
167 Ray Konig; azbible.com
168 "Radical;" Reverend David Platt; p.13
169 "Pagan Christianity;" Frank Viola & George Barna; p.139
170 "James Jones;" Wikipedia
171 "David Koresh;" Wikipedia
172 "Five Considerable Challenges for Today's Missionary;" Paul Akin; International Mission Board; August 16, 2018
173 "Radical;" David Platt; pp. 19-20
174 "Joshua Project"
175 Winter et al.,3
176 Baxter 2007, 12
177 Baxter 2007,12
178 Baxter 2007,12
179 Barrett & Johnson; 2001; 656
180 The Traveling Team; 1999
181 World Evangelization Research Center
182 "Revolution in World Missions;" Yohannan; pp.142, 143
183 "Scary Statistics;" Doug Perry
184 "Scary Statistics;" Doug Perry
185 "Scary Statistics;" Doug Perry
186 "Scary Statistics;" Doug Perry
187 The Traveling Team; 1999
188 "Come Let's Reach the World;" Yohannan; p.45
189 "World Magazine;" Gene Veith
190 "Salary.com" – US & Canadian salaries by job
191 "Missionary Income: How Much Money Do They Make?'; Bethany Global University; Madeline Pena; February 3, 2020; bethanygu.edu
192 "Demand Media;" Houston Chronicle; Dana Stevenson
193 "National Congregation Study;" Mark Chaves; Duke Divinity School
194 Mike & Debbie Baker; Director of Missions; Palmetto Baptist Association; Williamston, South Carolina
195 "Church Budgets: Shame on American Evangelicals;" The Reformed Mind

Chapter 11

196 "The Demon Haunted World;" Carl Sagan
197 Oxford English Dictionary
198 Strong's Concordance
199 Webster's New World Dictionary
200 "Hebrews; Chapter 8-13"; J Vernon McGee; p. 133
201 "Breakout Churches;" Thom Ranier
202 "Christian Education" Web Site
203 "Growing True Disciples;" George Barna, pp 98-99
204 "The World Christian Encyclopedia;" Barrett, Kurian, & Johnson; Oxford University Press; Vol 1, p.16
205 "The National Catholic Register;" Scot Eric Alt, post February 19, 2011
206 "What Do Methodists Believe About Heaven;" First United Methodist Church, Sioux City, Iowa
207 "What Do Presbyterians Believe About Salvation?"; Highland Presbyterian Church, Fayetteville, NC
208 "Episcopal Church Doctrines & Beliefs;" www.netbiblestudy.net/episcopal
209 "The Religious, Political & Cultural Journalism of George Conger;" posted by the "Church of England Newspaper, Syncretum, The Episcopal Church; April 17, 2009
210 "How to Go to Heaven"; Jimmy Akin, May 12, 2015
211 "'How-To Become a Christian;" Southern Baptist Convention Web Site
212 "Personal Prayer Book;" Martin Luther, 1522
213 "What do Lutherans Believe About Jesus?"; www.Lutheranresources.com
214 "Pentecostal Beliefs – Where Do We Go When We Die?'; "Opposing Views"
215 The Torah; Wikipedia
216 "How Does a Jew Attain Salvation;" Anti Missionary Gateway
217 "Understanding Kufr;" Islamiccity.org – Hesham A. Hassaballa
218 "Opposing Views;" people.opposingviews.com
219 "Muslim Heaven or Paradise;" truthand grace.com
220 "Watchtower;" December 15, 1989, p.30; February 15, 1983, p.12, 15; January 15, 1994, p.16; January 15, 1995, p.28; "Keep Watch Over Yourselves;" pp.98-99, p.92,95,96, 135

Chapter 12

221 Baptist Hymnal; 1991; p.322
222 Nelson's Illustrated Bible Dictionary; pp.830-831
223 David Ring Ministries; davidring.org
224 "Radical;" Reverend David Platt; pp.36-38
225 Dailyverses.net
226 "Hebrews Chapters 8-13;" J. Vernon McGee; p.68
227 "If We Confess Our Sins;" John MacArthur; oneplace.com
228 "Alcoholics Anonymous;" http://aa.org
229 Thayer & Smith Greek Lexicon
230 "The MacArthur New Testament Commentary, Hebrews;" Dr. John MacArthur; Introduction
231 "Radical;" Reverend David Platt; p.38
232 Thayer & Smith Greek Lexicon
233 BibleHub.com
234 Strong's Concordance
235 Oxford English Dictionary
236 Webster's New World Dictionary
237 E W Bullinger, Arndt & Gingrich, Grimm & Thayer, Abbot, Smith, Liddell & Scott, W E Vine, Cremer, Perschbacher, Sopocles, Lawrence O. Richards, Paul McReynolds, Geoffrey Brommiley, Robert H. Mounce

Chapter 13

238 "Am I Really A Christian?"; Mike McKinley; Crossway Books; June 7, 2011
239 Webster's New World Dictionary

Chapter 14

240 "Experiencing the Spirit: The Power of Pentecost Every Day;" Henry Blackaby; Multnomah Books; February 17, 2009
241 "The Andy Griffith Show;" CBS Television; Desilu Productions; 1960-68
242 "Hebrews – Chapter 8-13;" J Vernon McGee; P. 149
243 "Radical", Reverend David Platt; pp.8-9,38
244 "Radical;" Reverend David Platt; p. 54
245 "Magnum Force;" 1973; written by John Milius & Michael Cimino; directed by Ted Post

Chapter 15

246 "Radical;" Reverend David Platt; p. 51
247 " "Eternal Security – Can You Be Sure?"; Doctor Charles Stanley; p. 80
248 "Do a Christian's Sins Damn His Soul?"; Doctor Sam Morris; First Baptist Church, Stamford, Texas
249 "Grace Evangelical Society;" 1986; Corinth, Tx.
250 "The Purifying Power of Living by Faith in Future Grace;" John Piper
251 Anonymous High School Student Question to Ordained Pastor
252 "Wycliffe's Gold Rule of Interpretation; John Wycliffe; 1324-1380
253 "The MacArthur NT Commentary-Hebrews", Dr. John MacArthur; pp xi-xiv
254 "The MacArthur NT Commentary-Hebrews; Dr. John MacArthur; p.144
255 Webster's New World Dictionary
256 "The McArthur New Testament Commentary – Hebrews;" Dr. John MacArthur; p.272
257 "BibleHub.com Interlinear;" Thayer & Smith Greek Lexicon
258 "Hebrews Chapters 8-13;" J. Vernon McGee; p. 42; "The MacArthur New Testament Commentary – Hebrews;" Dr. John MacArthur; p. 235
259 "Through the Bible Commentary Series-Romans;" J. Vernon McGee, p.104
260 Commentaries referenced – "The MacArthur NT Commentary-Hebrews;" Dr. John MacArthur; "Hebrews Chapters 1-7;" Hebrews Chapters 8-13; J. Vernon McGee; "The MacArthur NT Commentary-Mark;" Dr. John MacArthur; "The Letter to the Hebrews;" William Barclay

Chapter 16

261 "BibleHub.com Interlinear;" Thayer & Smith Greek Lexicon
262 "What Does It Mean That God Is Our Abba Father?"; gotquestions.org; "Got Questions Ministries"; Colorado Springs, Co.
263 "You've Lost That Loving Feeling;" The Righteous Brothers – Bill Medley, Bobby Hatfield; 1964; Phil Spector, Barry Mann, Cynthia Weil; Philles Records
264 Oxford English Dictionary
265 "Revival;" Dictionary.com

266 "BibleHub.com Interlinear;" Thayer & Smith Greek Lexicon
267 "Revive Us Again;" Dr. William P. Mackay; 1839-1885
268 "The Gospel of Mark;" William Barclay, p.123
269 "Jesus Alive;" Steve Shirley
270 Strong's Greek Concordance
271 "The Andy Griffith Show;" CBS Television; Desilu Productions; 1960-68

Chapter 17

272 William Barclay
273 "Why We Crave Religious Systems," Rob Wilkerson, September 21, 2015, robwilkerson.net
274 Encyclopedia Britannica Dictionary
275 "Number of Religions in the World;" Google; Adherents; October 6, 2006
276 Encyclopedia Britannica Dictionary
277 "thefollowersofChrist.org;" 2015
278 Oxford English Dictionary
279 Oxford English Dictionary
280 "Cult"; Wikipedia; en.m.wikipedia.org
281 "Freemasonry-Secret Organization"; Britannica.com
282 "Moral Dangers of Religion;" newsaboutchristianity.com
283 "World Christian Encyclopedia;" David B. Barrett, Todd M. Johnson Editors
284 "Handbook of Denominations;" Roger E. Olson; 14th Edition
285 "9 Reasons Jesus Hates Religion (And You Should Too);" Frank Powell; faithit.com
286 "Satan & His Kingdom;" Dennis McCallum; p.164
287 "Radical;" Reverend David Platt; p.15
288 "Satan & His Kingdom;" Dennis McCallum; p. 276
289 "The Over Scheduled Child: Avoiding the Trap of Hyper-Parenting;" Alvin Rosenfield, Nicole Wise
290 "The Barna Update", Barna Group; September 24, 2007
291 "Satan & His Kingdom;" Dennis McCallum; p.160
292 2017 US Census: Anderson County, SC
293 "South Carolina Gazetteer"
294 South Carolina Baptist Convention; Columbia, SC
295 "Satan & His Kingdom;" Dennis McCallum; p. 167
296 "Perilous Times & Precious Truth;" David Guzik; Enduring Word; December 7, 2015

297 "Radical;" Reverend David Platt; pp. 115-116
298 "Satan & His Kingdom;" David McCallum; p.52

Afterword

299 Oxford English Dictionary

CPSIA information can be obtained
at www.ICGtesting.com
Printed in the USA
LVHW040828051020
667943LV00019B/422